Biography of a Family
Catherine de Medici and her Children

BOOKS BY MILTON WALDMAN

ENGLAND'S ELIZABETH
BIOGRAPHY OF A FAMILY

BY MILTON WALDMAN

Biography of a Family

*Catherine de Medici
and her Children*

WITH ILLUSTRATIONS

HOUGHTON MIFFLIN COMPANY · BOSTON

The Riverside Press Cambridge

1936

COPYRIGHT, 1936, BY MILTON WALDMAN

ALL RIGHTS RESERVED INCLUDING THE RIGHT TO REPRODUCE
THIS BOOK OR PARTS THEREOF IN ANY FORM

The Riverside Press
CAMBRIDGE · MASSACHUSETTS
PRINTED IN THE U.S.A.

TO
MY WIFE
WHOSE
CAPRICE IT IS
THAT THE IMPORTANT FACT
ABOUT HISTORY IS THAT THE PEOPLE
IN IT ONCE ACTUALLY
LIVED

'... for I the Lord thy God am a jealous God, visiting the iniquity of the fathers upon the children unto the third and fourth generation...'

Contents

INTRODUCTION	xi
LIST OF CHARACTERS	xix

BOOK I: FRANCIS

I. THE FAMILY	3
II. SOME RELATIVES	17
III. THE RESULT OF PATIENCE	26

BOOK II: THE MATRIARCH

IV. MY SON'S ESTATE	41
V. INTERLUDE ON THE WAY	54
VI. THE GREAT MATRIARCHY	64

BOOK III: CHARLES

VII. THE CHILDREN	77
VIII. MOTHER AND SON	92
IX. MARGOT IS MARRIED	104
X. THE EVE OF SAINT BARTHOLOMEW'S	116
XI. A SLIP OF THE IMAGINATION	129

BOOK IV: HENRY

XII. INTERREGNUM	143
XIII. TWO CROWNS AND A RIDE	159
XIV. THE ELEGANT MISFIT	174
XV. ONE BROTHER TOO MANY	197
XVI. DÉBÂCLE	217
XVII. PASSING OF THE FAMILY	238
BIBLIOGRAPHY	259
INDEX	263

Illustrations

CATHERINE DE MEDICI *Frontispiece*
    From a portrait in the Louvre

FRANÇOIS II 20
    From a portrait by François Clouet, 1560, in the Bibliothèque Nationale

MARGUERITE DE VALOIS 50
    From a portrait by François Clouet, about 1557, in the Bibliothèque Nationale

CHARLES IX 80
    From a portrait attributed to François Clouet, in the Louvre

HENRI IV 110
    From a portrait attributed to François Quesnel, about 1582, in the Bibliothèque Nationale

HENRI III 168
    From a portrait in the Musée de Versailles

THE DUKE OF ALENÇON, IN 1570 198
    From a portrait by François Clouet, in the Bibliothèque Nationale

HENRI DE LORRAINE, DUKE OF GUISE 230

Introduction

(containing a menu of historical facts precedent which the biography proper was unable to digest, but which may yet assist the understanding or refresh the memory of those readers who, like Doctor Johnson, quite rightly insist on liking the biographical part of history best)

THE France of 1559, when our story begins, had in many ways, in most of the essential ones, attained its present form. Its boundaries, as fixed by the general European peace of Câteau-Cambrésis signed in that year, were virtually what they are now except for a few provinces in the northeast and southeast — Artois, Lorraine, Franche-Comté, Savoy, and several smaller tracts. An average of estimates would place its population, very much the largest in Europe, at not much less than fifteen million. Exactly as today the great majority of the people cultivated and lived off their own land: free peasant proprietors except for the ancient feudal rents and fines they owed to the local lords of the manor or the great provincial magnates. Even the townsmen, the artisans and shopkeepers, cultivated their little freehold acre or so behind their tiny thatched and gabled houses.

Fundamentally it was a rich country, in its own resources the richest in the West. Its neighbours relied upon it for a large part of their corn, oil, fruit and vegetables, and animal fodder. Bordeaux, Burgundy, and the Touraine did a brisk international trade in their respective wines, Vichy and Pougues in mineral waters. French cheeses had already grown into a staple at home and a delicacy abroad. Coal mines were being worked in Languedoc in the south, marble quarries in Anjou in the west. A thrifty, energetic, gravely hopeful community and — until the time of Catherine de Medici and her children — on the whole a united and happy one.

At the head of it stood the King, an absolute monarch with an unimpeachable title derived from God. He was the supreme lawgiver and sole fount of justice, the head of all administration, whether civil, military, or fiscal, the arbiter of peace or war. No written constitution limited him, no institution existed save as an offshoot of his will. 'We have no thought, Sire,' said the spokesman for the Parlement of Paris, the highest bench of magistrates in the kingdom, to Francis I in 1527, 'of revoking or casting doubt on your powers, for that would be a species of sacrilege, and we recognize that you are above the laws and that laws and ordinances cannot constrain you.'

The King took advice on matters of state from his Council; nominally an assembly of the Princes of the Blood, dukes, cardinals, high officers of the Crown, etc., actually his select cabinet from amongst them consisting of his trained servants — such as the Chancellor and the Secretaries of State — together with a few nobles in his intimate confidence. He administered the law through various officials and official bodies ranging downward from the eight Courts of Parlement distributed through the realm (originally courts of justice which had widely extended their activities into other fields, especially finance). In times of emergency he might summon the three Orders, nobility, clergy, and the middle class, to elect delegates to an Estates-General for the consideration of public grievances and the means of replenishing his treasury. But he could, if he chose, ignore the Council, overrule the Parlements,[1] dismiss the Estates if they became frac-

---

[1] His edicts did not formally become law until registered by the Parlement of the district affected by them, but by going in person to hold a *lit de justice* he could suspend the formality.

tious or compel them to remain in attendance till they had concluded the business for which he had convoked them. The weakness of his character or a judicious regard for old custom or public opinion might persuade him to defer to these auxiliaries of government, but nothing on earth short of force could compel him to.

That was the theory, and during the first part of the sixteenth century very nearly the practice. Louis XI (1461–83) had put down the lawless 'great' and tidied up the mess after the Hundred Years' War; his successors, Charles VIII and Louis XII, had brought the country to an extraordinary height of prosperity; Francis I (1515–47) had entranced it as the gifted showman of his imported Renaissance: for most of that time the reverence for the monarchy fell little short of idolatry. The great feudal Houses, still unreconciled to the new trend toward centralization but helpless for the time being to reverse it, vied with one another for the King's favour instead of combining, as in the Middle Ages, to put him in his place.

The generations of quiescence had not weakened them; in some ways it had even strengthened them. They still lived in their great stone castles which no known artillery could demolish, held fortified towns which scarcely any army could hope to storm or surprise. They still drew vast revenues from their fiefs, although they no longer exercised direct suzerainty over the inhabitants. Some of them kept up establishments costing a hundred thousand pounds a year in an age when a hundred was a substantial income. The governorships of provinces fell to them as hereditary rights: a Bourbon always ruled in Gascony and Picardy, a Guise in Champagne, a Montmorency in Languedoc, a Châtillon in Normandy. It was quite possible for them to levy an urbane blackmail on the sovereign for mustering their followers with the necessary expedition in time of war; it was practically impossible for anyone in quest of office or promotion to gain the royal notice without their paid intervention. They could and did see to it that the richest sinecures fell to their dependents. Meantime they made prudent marriages, intrigued against one another, took turns as chief beneficiaries and instruments of whatever happened to be the current royal policy — and waited for the occasion that would enable one of them to assert a conclusive supremacy over the rest and claim the old quasi-equality with the throne itself.

Their chance came, in three stages. From 1494 to 1559 the country was engaged in an almost continuous series of foreign wars, for the possession of Italy, against the encroachments of the Spanish Empire and its German allies. Individually the wars were popular, collectively they nibbled away the foundations of the dynasty's popularity. Although Italy was several times overrun, she was not annexed, and of the enormous tribute expected from her little crossed the Alps except wagon-loads of paintings and manuscripts for the embellishment of the royal palaces. Spain closed one market after another, including Flanders, the most valuable of all. The people suffered, the revenues fell. To meet the deficit the King — who was still vaguely expected, as immeasurably the largest proprietor in France, 'to live of his own' — had first to pawn his lands, then to impose new taxes, finally to create new offices for sale. The interest on the mortgages fell into arrears, the taxes assumed unpleasantly ingenious forms, the public services exhibited symptoms of growing demoralization. Men began to look about for champions of their discontents.

And simultaneously there arose the new threat to the unity of every state in Christendom. Already in the fifteen-twenties Martin Luther's doctrines had begun to pervade France; by the end of the fifteen-thirties his most redoubtable disciple, a Frenchman named John Calvin, had impressed them in their extremer forms upon thousands of the middle and lower-middle classes — the very section of the community most harmfully affected by the Crown's desperate financial expedients. For a long time the members of the new sect were very little molested. King Francis himself gave warmly receptive attention to their ideas, as he did to all fresh investigations of the mind; his sister Marguerite, authoress of the *Heptameron* and most famous blue-stocking of her time, openly espoused their cause. The Church opposed them, but not to the extent of ejecting them officially from its bosom. Their numbers grew, especially amongst the business and professional folk and the skilled artisans in the more populous towns — the most suitable soil everywhere for the hopes and discontents of the new age, whether secular or religious.

Parties formed. The Bourbons, the clan nearest in blood to the reigning House and therefore by all historical precedent the natural focus of opposition, assumed the leadership of the dissenters (or Huguenots, as they soon came to be called). The Princess Marguerite married Henry d'Albret, King of Navarre, a minute vassal state in the Pyrenees; her only daughter and her husband's heir, Jeanne, married Antoine, Duke of Vendôme, chief of the Bourbons, to whom the throne of France would lapse by virtue of his descent from Saint Louis (1226-70) if ever the Valois gave out: and so a corner of the kingdom and a branch of the royal family became definitely and overtly Protestant.

The other great Houses aligned themselves according to inclination and policy. The Guises, mighty soldiers and astute politicians, but out-and-out adventurers, juniors of the family which ruled the Duchy of Lorraine as a nominal fief of the Holy Roman Empire who had not long since immigrated into France to seek wider opportunities there, adopted the creed of extreme reaction, religious and political, and so established an unshakeable sway over the fiercely conservative, traditionally anti-monarchical Paris proletariat. The Montmorencys, allied by marriage to both Bourbons and Guises, hit upon the middle course as the one most likely to win the Crown and country in the end. The cleavages grew sharp, feelings hot: the Huguenot Châtillons threw in their lot with their distant kin the Bourbons, the Bourbon but Catholic Duke of Montpensier his with the Guises. By the end of the reign of Henry II, who succeeded his father in 1547, nothing but the royal authority held them and their followers from flying at one another's throats.

But that authority was still overriding. Particularly with the King fighting the nation's battles with Spain. The people hoped and believed that when the struggle was over Henry would settle down to internal reform of his realm and healing of the religious breach. They knew him to be an earnest young man who shared the Catholic sentiments of the considerable majority of his subjects. And he had solidly behind him the most stable element in the country: the small gentry with a few hundred or thousand acres radiating from a homely manor house sprawled round three sides of a dung-heaped courtyard — a hard-headed squirearchy that rode and read, loved order though trained to arms, and lived on terms of democratic neighbourliness with tenant and peasant, on whom they exercised a strong moral suasion. So long as the King's prestige remained intact with such sturdy subjects, so long as he knew his strength and dared to use it, there seemed little probability that the leaders of faction would be able to usurp his functions or disturb the repose of his kingdom.

Henry's sudden death threw the field open to them. A feeble boy of fifteen ruled by ordinance of God: but no earthly ordinance prescribed who should rule the boy. The post awaited whoever was strong enough to seize and hold it. That, I think, is the secret of the age's fascination: it had outgrown one system of society, the ecclesiastic and feudal, and had not yet grown into the other, the lay and bureaucratic, which was to follow. No seasoned institutions hampered the ambitions of the individual, nothing but the limitations of his own strength and that of his adversaries. Never were pride, greed, and appetite for power given more magnificent scope, never did Fate contrive more slily that they should destroy themselves to make way for the oncoming order which they sought to destroy before it could be born.

But this is running ahead of the story — the story of how Henry's Italian widow sought amidst these gathering forces to preserve for her young and his 'the reverence wherewith a king is girt about from God.'

Cast of Characters

THE VALOIS: THE HOUSE OF FRANCE

Henry II, King of France (1547–1559), son of Francis I (1515–1547)
Catherine de Medici, his wife, daughter of Lorenzo Duke of Urbino, great granddaughter of Lorenzo the Magnificent

  Their children:
    Francis II, born 1543, died 1560
    Elizabeth, Queen of Spain, born 1545, died 1568
    Claude, Duchess of Lorraine, born 1547, died 1575
    Charles IX, born 1550, died 1574
    Henry III (also King of Poland), born 1551, died 1589
    Marguerite, called Margot, Queen of Navarre, later Queen of France, born 1552, died 1615
    Hercules (later rechristened Francis), Duke of Alençon, born 1554, died 1584
    Three dead in infancy

THE BOURBONS

Antoine, King of Navarre, died 1562
Louis, Prince of Condé, his brother, died 1569
Charles, Cardinal of Bourbon, his brother, 'The Red Ass' and Pretender to the throne after 1585, died 1590
Jeanne d'Albret, Queen of Navarre in her own right, Antoine's wife, first cousin of Henry II, died 1572
Henry, King of Navarre, son of Antoine and Jeanne d'Albret, born 1553, died 1610
Henry, Prince of Condé, son of Louis, died 1588. Married Marie de Clèves

Cast of Characters

THE GUISES

Francis, Duke of Guise, died 1563
Charles, Cardinal of Lorraine, his brother, died 1574
Anne d'Este, wife to Francis
Henry, Duke of Guise, their son, 1551–1588
Two Dukes of Aumale who enter briefly, one, the brother of Duke Francis, in 1572, the other, brother of Duke Henry, in 1589
Louis, Cardinal of Guise, brother to Henry, died 1588
Mary Stuart, Queen of France and Scotland, wife to Francis II of France, niece to Francis, Duke of Guise, and Charles, the Cardinal, 1542–1587

THE MONTMORENCYS

Anne, Duke of Montmorency, Constable of France, 1491–1567
Francis, Duke of Montmorency, his son, died 1578
Henry, Duke of Damville (after his brother Francis's death Duke of Montmorency)
Two younger sons who appear very briefly

THE CHÂTILLONS

Gaspard, Lord of Coligny, Admiral of France, 1517–1572
Francis, Lord of Andelot, died 1569, his brother
[A third brother, the Cardinal of Châtillon, though politically important as Huguenot Ambassador to Elizabeth of England, does not appear in the story]

> This generation of Châtillons were nephews of the Constable Montmorency, their mother being his sister. Coligny stood in the same relation to Louis of Bourbon, Prince of Condé.

HENRY III'S MIGNONS

Bernard de Nogaret, Lord of La Valette, Duke of Épernon
Anne d'Arques, Duke of Joyeuse

> These were the chief ones. The others are briefly indicated as they enter the story.

THE HOUSE OF LORRAINE

The *Guises* were a junior branch of this house. The three members of it who enter the story at a late stage are:

Louise de Vaudemont, married Henry III in 1575

The Marquis of Pont-à-Mousson, son to Claude of Valois, Duchess of Lorraine

Christine, Claude's daughter, married in 1588 to the Grand Duke of Tuscany

BOOK I

FRANCIS

Chapter I

THE FAMILY

The family was the fruit of a transaction between two middle-aged gentlemen ambitious to better themselves. The one, very highborn, desired to increase his estates; the other, of an important commercial strain, aspired to augment its dignity. A bargain was struck, with the result that the son of the first gentleman and the niece of the second were produced at the altar, formally presented to one another, and straightway married.

It would no doubt have been better if — but just as lands, bank balances, and herds of cattle demand owners, so kingdoms and duchies must be provided with rulers; and though millions of people might have found their earthly lot more tolerable if Francis I and Clement VII had not designated that particular family for existence, it is certainly no less true that the family would have been far happier if it had not been created for so high and unescapable an inheritance. Very likely the King of France and the Sovereign Pontiff hoped that the unborn children for whom they were making such rich provision would somehow possess the necessary goodness, wisdom, and health to enjoy it usefully. What more could they do?

So it came to pass that the union of Henry of Valois and

Catherine de Medici, each aged fourteen years, was blessed by the Pope at Marseilles in the autumn of 1533. The marriage was consummated the same night, in accordance with a proviso expressly inserted in the contract by the Pope: for he had an exceedingly troublesome annulment suit on his hands at the moment, that of the King of England, Henry VIII, against his wife, Catherine of Aragon, and thought it best to take every possible precaution to avoid another. Nevertheless, ten years mysteriously elapsed before the new family sustained any addition, twelve more before it reached its full profusion. On the last day of June, 1559, in the twenty-sixth year of his marriage and the thirteenth of his reign, King Henry II received, in the course of a tourney in celebration of his eldest daughter's marriage, a lance-thrust in the eye and died after ten days of agony, leaving Catherine a widow with seven children — the family of this biography.

By the high altar of Notre-Dame, amidst ranks of tall candles and a phalanx of praying monks, lies Henry II, twenty-fifth in the dynasty founded by Hugh Capet and tenth in that branch of it styled the House of Valois, waiting to be carried to the tombs of his fathers in Saint-Denis. The leaden coffin is open, and the face of the King, dexterously composed by the surgeons, is as grave and tranquil in death as it was in life. It is a pleasant face, with all the principal family characteristics — dark skin, brown hair and beard, high nose, and small, well-cut mouth.
'I pray God you may be more fortunate than I have been,' had been his parting wish to his eldest son. It might have been his own epitaph, for he had been, all things considered, an unlucky man. For himself he had asked little of life: the love of his children, plenty of hard and dangerous exercise to satisfy the needs of his powerful body, the company of his friends, a good practical joke now and then, evenings of music... Through many troubled years he had looked for-

ward to enjoying these things at leisure; and now, at the beginning of leisure, in the full vigour of his age, to have them snatched away by a cruel and improbable accident in the midst of his rejoicings...

He was unlucky to have been the unpretentious son of a brilliant father. To have been saddled with the consequences of that father's infatuated ambition to own Italy, about which he did not care a fig. To have been bound all his manhood to the long quarrel with Spain (and half Europe as well), and then to have lost it. And to have died just as he had concluded peace.

He was lucky in only one thing, perhaps, to have been spared the terrible years that were on the way. In that respect it was France that was unlucky: her last chance to be saved from herself vanished when the crown passed from the head of a strong man to that of the weak boy his successor. And France, knowing it, trembled.

About a mile to the east of the Cathedral, on the outskirts of Paris, the mellow little palace of the Tournelles stands enclosed between the smiling river on the one side and the frowning walls of the Bastille on the other. At one end of its gardens two rows of wooden stands, now undraped of their gay colours, indicate the tilt-yard where the late king received his death-wound twelve days ago. On the ground floor of the palace sits, propped up in the bed in which he died, a painted effigy dressed in his clothes who presides noon and evening during the forty days of mourning over a table spread and served exactly as in his lifetime, except that the guests are the poor and old of his capital. In a similar room on the next floor his successor, Francis II, lies weeping brokenly without regard to the many discreet glances bent upon him.

The new king is fifteen years old, but looks even younger. His pallid tear-stained cheeks have the roundness, and his lips, when he can control their quivering, the drooping petulance, of a child's. His body is so thin it looks emaciated, and its twitching betrays the disorder of his nerves. The shock of his father's death has accentuated these weaknesses, but they have been rooted in him since birth.

Sitting beside him and trying to comfort him with soothing words is his wife, an enchanting fair-haired girl of sixteen, Mary Stuart, Queen of Scotland. They have been married a little over a year, were engaged for ten years before that, ever since she fled out of her kingdom before an invading English army, and it is plain that they adore each other. On the other side of the bed stands a grim old man, Anne de Montmorency, Constable of France and Grand Master of the Household, veteran of every war since the time of Francis's great-grandfather Louis XII. The old soldier suggests, with all the gentleness he can put into his gruff voice, that it is not seemly for kings to weep. The boy mutters something, but his voice is almost inaudible at the best of times owing to an adenoidal obstruction, and the answer is lost. He does not repeat, but turns on his pillow and shuts his eyes.

He realizes only too well the justice of the Constable's words, but he cannot help himself. The last thing he ever wanted was to be a king. During his father's final conscious moments, unable any longer to keep down the fear and despair in his heart, he burst out, 'Oh God, how can I live if my father dies!' His sick imagination is ceaselessly tormented with the knowledge that he is neither clever enough nor strong enough in body or character to rule. He would gladly *be* ruled; by the wife he loves, by the mother he holds in deep respect, by almost anyone he can trust who will take the trouble. If he could have one prayer granted, he would eagerly choose the privilege of being as other boys, able to ride and hunt as much as he liked without paying for it afterward in days and weeks of prostration.

A few miles farther to the east, in its clearing of forest,

The Family

stands the palace of Vincennes, a grey old fortress built round a series of courtyards. In one of them at the front, three small boys and a small girl are playing under the supervision of a cluster of tutors and governesses. There is something very staid in their manner of going about their play. It cannot be out of respect to the violet and black they wear in token of their mourning, for they are all too young to feel their father's loss very deeply. Perhaps the presence of so many critical watchers and the stiff formality of the garden dampen their spirits; certainly it would not be easy for them to let themselves go in the elaborate paraphernalia of doublet, cloak, and hose, or trailing voluminous skirts which the young people of their time wear from the moment they leave off swaddling clothes. Even the games they attempt are modelled on the more weighty amongst their elders' occupations — Frenchmen gravely fighting Spaniards varied by Catholics soberly burning Huguenots.

The director of the sport is the eldest, Charles, a boy of nine, broad-shouldered but spindly-legged, with a hoarse voice and eyes full of a troubled melancholy. It is obvious that he enjoys the bloodthirsty make-believe and that the others are somewhat put off by the quiet violence with which he throws himself into it; he does not mind hurting. The girl, christened Marguerite but called Margot, a saucy, round-faced minx of six with gleaming coppery hair that refuses to stay in order under her demure little cap, can more than hold her own against him with her tongue, but prefers to keep out of range of his fists. She is by far the most high-spirited of the lot and exerts her craving for authority on her smallest brother, who obediently, even gladly, fetches and carries at her command. He is a minute, extraordinarily hideous urchin of five, with bandy legs, the skin of a Moor, and the promising beginnings of a bulbous nose; a caricature, as Charles is in many ways a replica, of their father. Through a failure of foresight on somebody's part he was christened

Hercules, but the solecism is somewhat mitigated through the etiquette which requires him to be addressed by his title of Duke of Alençon.

Of the intermediate brother it is at once plain that he holds a special position with regard to the rest. Big Charles never ventures to bully him, little Alençon shrinks from him without apparent provocation, spitfire Margot becomes positively maidenly at a glance from his sombre dark eyes. He joins wholly in their game, yet remains subtly not of it, just as he is equally a part of the family without resembling any other member of it. Indeed, he gives the impression of not quite belonging to any family of flesh and blood. One fancies that Lucifer at eight might have been very much like this boy — the same proud, graceful carriage and dusky perfection of feature, the same thoughtful sobriety without and disturbing radiance within. The few who have had the chance to observe the young Duke of Anjou expect more of him than of any other prince of his generation.[1]

At the opposite end of Paris thick black curtains shut out the daylight from a long row of windows on the first floor of the Louvre. The room is the royal bedchamber, where the late king's widow must by ancient law pass her forty days of mourning secluded 'from the light of the sun and the moon.' Every surface, of walls and furniture alike, is shrouded in black. Two candles burn on an altar in one corner and near-by, on a low stool, sits Catherine, noisily sobbing out her misery.

People pass in and out softly, ambassadors to pay their condolences, her ladies to see if there is anything she wishes. She whispers her thanks and resumes her sobbing. Over and over she moans to herself that she wants only to die, and has no doubt that she means it. But already weariness and grief

---

[1] To avoid confusion Anjou and Alençon are here given the titles which they will presently bear. Even their baptismal names, Alexander Edward and Hercules, will be changed at their confirmation to Henry and Francis, by which names they will thenceforth be known.

are engaged in a losing battle with her vast gusto for the business of life... the many absorbing employments that will thrust themselves into her thoughts... the old scores that can at last be paid off... plans for her children and the dangers that beset her and them....

Two girls stand before her at the sight of whom her face momentarily lights up. She embraces them tenderly, the taller first, and bids them sit on the floor on either side of her, the shorter doing so awkwardly and with obvious discomfort. It is with the other that Catherine principally converses, the cripple looking dully before her. She resembles her mother more than does the elder sister, though her face is pale and square while Catherine's is plump and pink. All three have prominent eyes and large mouths, but those of the younger daughter lack the animation and expressiveness of the others'. Poor Claude has limped the earth most of her twelve years in one type of steel truss after another without appreciable benefit to her tubercular hip and twisted back, the least prepossessing mentally and physically of Henry and Catherine's children. Since three months she has been Duchess of Lorraine — a minor marriage of convenience for a daughter of France — and will play an important part in her family's story only after she is dead.

Of Elizabeth, her father's darling, grander things have always been expected. Once asked why he allowed his younger daughter to be married before the elder, in defiance of all convention, he replied, 'My Elizabeth is not one to marry to a duchy — a kingdom is the least that is worthy of her and not a little one either, but the greatest.... She can afford to wait.' He lived to see that he was right: a fortnight ago he gave her in marriage by proxy to Philip II of Spain, who seven months earlier had lost his second wife, the unfortunate Queen of England known as 'Bloody Mary.' Elizabeth begins her married life with a fairer title, that of 'Princess of the Peace,' but under clouds of sadness and uncertainty; for it was in the course of celebrating her nuptials that her father met his end and she must shortly set out for a strange country to begin a new life with a husband she has never seen.

She is a dark-eyed brunette of fourteen, very serious, intensely devout, with an air of filial submissiveness that would be cloying if the firm structure of mouth and chin did not proclaim it a result of training rather than of fundamental character. All men agree that she is lovely: Philip II, debating whether to have her for himself or his son Carlos, received her portrait and after careful study decided as he did.... Men who had travelled in Italy gazed upon her for the first time with startled recognition, recalling masterpieces: Botticelli's painting of her great-great-grandfather Lorenzo the Magnificent, or Michelangelo's chiselled likeness of her grandfather, the younger Lorenzo, brooding forever with chin on hand upon Dawn and Twilight in the Medici chapel at Florence....

Catherine, too, broods when her daughters have left her. Upon the past that she mourns, however shabbily it had treated her; upon the future that she is impatient to encounter, though every aspect of it seems so ominous. Of the husband who was never anything but kind or ever anything but unfaithful. Of the children who are now — at least so she sincerely believes — the whole meaning of her existence. Of the people who tried to come between her and her husband for their own selfish purposes and would now for greater cause and with better chance of success try to separate her from her children.

The main purpose of her life is gone; she must quickly adjust herself to another and a harder. For twenty-six years it has been her business and pleasure to ascertain and carry out Henry's wishes, not only because he was her husband and, later, her lord and king, but because she loved him. Something in the tall, shy, awkward boy with whom she was brought together at Marseilles aroused almost immediately in her a tenderness that went on with little change as they grew up together, evenly, dutifully, untroubled by imagination or his failure to love her in return. One could not have everything. Girls in her station were born not to be loved but to be married, and in that respect she has done surpassingly well; better than Pope Clement's fondest expectation, for in his time Henry was only a younger son. Even yet Catherine often finds it hard to believe that she, the daughter of merchants, was privileged to mate with the son of twenty anointed kings. The chief ingredient of her love for Henry was and always will be gratitude for his condescension in marrying her and his courtesy in forbearing ever to remind her of it.

Others were not so forbearing. She had much to put up with, and a great deal to learn during her first years in France. Coming almost directly from the convent in which she had spent her childhood into her father-in-law's brilliant court, a pudgy little Italian without graces or experience of the world, she became the instant target for the wit of the lovely ladies who resented her position as wife of the King's son; luckily she was blessed with a thick skin from which mere malice, if otherwise harmless, rebounded painlessly. But there was always danger that her husband would begin to find her contemptible... and even greater danger in the satirical references of the lords to 'the gems beyond price' missing from her dowry — the rich Italian cities which Pope Clement had used to tempt Francis into accepting her and then failed to deliver. For in those allusions were already the kernel of repudiation, divorce....

And then her husband's mistress. To this day Catherine does not know whether Diane de Poitiers was her friend or enemy during that critical time. Whether she supported the divorce or opposed it lest a more attractive wife should be dangerous to her own ascendancy. There had been no use ever in trying to learn what she felt from observing her — her impenetrable serenity was as much part of her as of the remote silver goddess, her namesake, whom she acknowledged as patron. It was her own secret, like the devil's art with which she kept her body beautiful and held Henry's love, though all the world knew she would not see sixty again. Catherine does not particularly care any longer. She does not hate the woman — she does not really hate anybody — but she sees no reason why she should go on pretending to love her. It had been necessary, perhaps even right to do so for Henry's sake, and for the sake of appearances, upon which she had learned from Diane to set a high value, as she had learned from the same instructress to conceal her feelings. But the lessons were learned and paid for, in Catherine's meek submission to her rival, in the humiliation of having had only such share in her husband as his mistress's policy or good-nature allowed her. She has her own reckoning drawn up in her mind for those twenty-three years, ready to be presented as soon as she may venture forth....

It was not the sexual aspect of the relationship that troubled Catherine. She was not jealous of Henry's other women, the Italian who bore him a daughter, or of Mary Stuart's pretty little governess, Lady Fleming, who had given him a son. In fact, she is devoted to these children and bringing them up almost as her own. And nobody laughed more heartily than she when Henry was caught out visiting Fleming by night dressed in a sheet like a ghost. What made the Diane affair different was that it threatened her security ... for at Francis I's court even an ignorant girl quickly learned the difference between sex as amorous and sex as political intrigue....

It was in the fourth year of her marriage and the first of Diane's ascendancy that the peril came to a head. Her brother-in-law the Dauphin Francis died, Henry became heir to the throne — and she was still childless. Her enemies went to the King and told him plainly that the new dauphin could do better if he were to put away his unaccomplished, disappointingly dowered, and — worst of all — unfertile wife, naming certain unmarried princesses to replace her. They even whispered that she had brought about her brother-in-law's death to promote herself and her husband, though the autopsy had revealed pneumonia and a man had already been torn by horses on suspicion of having administered poison on behalf of the King of Spain. But one had to expect suspicion when things turned out to one's advantage, especially if one was an Italian and there was talk of poison about.

For months she walked about with dread uncertainty, staring into every face out of her short-sighted pop eyes in search of comfort or at least confirmation of the worst, tormented by nightmares of being returned to the cold hospitality of her relatives in Florence. At last, unable to bear it any longer, she went to the man on whom her fate depended, Francis I, and on her knees begged him not to send her away, to let her at least remain to serve the worthier princess whom he should choose as her successor. It was the right move, whatever instinct prompted it. The kindly King raised her up and dried her tears, saying, 'Have no fear, my daughter. Since God has willed that you should be wife to the Dauphin' (the bargain with the Pope was so old he may have forgotten it), 'perhaps it will please Him in this matter to grant you and me the gift we so long for.'

And God had, after seven more years of waiting, thus establishing in Catherine the comfortable belief that He kept a particular eye on the welfare of the Valois family. Ungenerous people, of course, cited the weakness of her children, especially of the first-born, as proof that the Deity had not acted alone in the matter. But what else was there to do? The women of her family bore children either late or never. And how was she to decide between the comparative virtues of pilgrimages barefoot to the shrines of Our Lady of the Conception, the weird incantations and gruesome mixtures of the thaumaturgists, the prescriptions and pills of the doctors? She tried them all, paying staggering sums in fees to every class of practitioner, swallowing tons of drugs and prevailing on the doubtful Henry to swallow them with her. Prayers, midnight sacrifices, intercourse at forbidden periods of the month, aphrodisiacs...

She feels no guilt or regret. It was all in God's hands, Who decreed equally that she should bear ten children, that five of them should be sickly, that three should die in infancy. She would be glad if she could trust the Almighty as implicitly with the future as with the past...

All things considered she can find marvellously little to regret. Especially in the latter years, with Henry coming in to spend the hour after dinner with her each day before going on to his business or sport; consulting with her about the children, confiding great matters of state, relaxing more and more into the middle-aged intimacy of marriage. That is her sorrow, to have waited so long for a happiness that the splintering of a lance destroyed in an instant. Though even the early years now have their compensation in retrospect. The rides in the forest that she grew to love... his admiration for her pluck when she resumed after a painful fall that nearly killed her... even today she would ride any horse against any woman in the court — this very minute, if she were not chained here for another month and more. The struggle with Greek to please the royal humanist her father-in-law... she has forgotten every word, but he repaid her effort a thousand-fold.... Many were the useful lessons she learned in that hard decade, and none more useful to the timid convent-bred stranger in France than to laugh, to laugh most heartily when she felt least like it... an armour better than tears to a woman never very pretty and now no longer young....

But that painfully acquired armour of defence will not longer suffice now that her rôle is not simply to obey, but to command, attack if necessary, or go under. All the power for which men are ready to kill, or die, is vested in her eldest son; whoever controls his young will is master of France. To preserve him and his estate from such men, she must be mistress of France; if she tries and fails, not only he but her younger sons, his heirs so long as he remains childless, may be taken from her forever. She has no thought of not trying.

She knows that while she sits there, bound hand and foot by the ancient ineluctable custom, the Guises, Mary Stuart's powerful uncles, will be using every artifice to obtain from the new king the seals of government in her absence, probably stuffing his poor head with tales to her hurt. Meantime in the south, the Bourbons, the nearest Princes of the Blood, are of a certainty mustering their clan for a dash on Paris and a bid for the supreme power. For though Francis is technically of age, having passed his fourteenth year, ancient tradition gives his nearest male kin the right to precedence over other guides until he reaches maturity, and it is scarcely likely that they will permit the Guises to deprive them of that right without a struggle. Whoever prevails, her children's inheritance will be torn to destruction.... Unless someone steps forth to assert the authority of the Crown over all subjects, even the greatest.

And there is no one but herself. A great exaltation surges up within her, an overwhelming urgency of unknown powers clamouring to be used. It was for this that she was born: to lead Henry's children on to their great destiny, as trustee of his estate and high priestess of his spirit; to preserve them in their youth and weakness against their enemies out of her own abundant strength — scheme, lie, kill if necessary.

A dim sense of her body's mysterious significance touches her, the fleshy entity which the old transaction between the Pope and King Francis made into one of the most important things in the world. In it are concentrated all the splendid greeds of the Medici, the semi-divinity extorted from time by the Valois. In it alone. She is the last of all the Medici who rose and fell with Florence in the Renaissance;[1] her children

---

[1] Except for Catherine the senior branch of the Medici founded by Cosimo the Elder in the 1430's was extinct; since 1537 a junior line had been installed in Florence of which Duke Cosimo I was the present head.

are the sole heirs of the Valois who carried France from the Middle Ages to the threshold of a new world. From her will stem not only the unborn kings of France but of Spain and the Indies, and of many other realms besides whose names are still veiled by the future. The stars themselves, through Michael Nostradamus, greatest of the astrologers, have proclaimed that all her sons shall be kings. The stars cannot lie: though it sometimes happens that common mortals misread their meanings.

A man in a robe, one of her secretaries, bows before her and awaits permission to speak. The King has left for Saint-Germain with the Queen and her uncles; no one else. He bows himself out.

So soon! Catherine meditates for a moment. Her son alone with the Guises thirty miles away and she fettered here.... Abruptly rising to her feet and flinging the veil from her tear-swollen face, she summons her ladies from the adjacent room and commands them to make ready to go to Saint-Germain.

Chapter II

SOME RELATIVES

THE news that the Queen Mother's carriage is mounting the avenue quickly brings the Guises — seven brothers backed by four wives and numerous clients — to the lofty presence chamber, where they stand waiting to receive her. Surprised and uneasy, they discuss in low tones the possible reasons for her coming and what is to be done about her; for though they do not exactly fear Catherine, they recognize that she may be able, through her moral influence over the King, to stir up trouble for them.

The seven together make a striking group. All are of imposing stature, all but one distinctly handsome, none of them is over forty. Their predominantly fair colouring, though much admired by other people, is not an unmixed blessing to themselves, since it calls attention to a fact that they would prefer to be forgotten, namely, their foreign origin. Their native soil is Lorraine, the ancient duchy erected by Charlemagne at his death between the French and Germanic portions of his empire; the elder branch of their family still rules there (in direct line, they maintain, from the eponymous founder, Charlemagne's own son Lothair), but the duchy proving too cramped for their energies, the cadets emigrated a generation ago and took service with the kings of France. They flourished beyond all anticipation — their own perhaps excepted — in wealth, influence, and numbers, until at the end of Francis I's reign they wrung from that monarch the dismal prediction that 'the Guises will strip my children to their waistcoats and my poor people to their shirts.' But Henry II, in need of their abilities, had been compelled to disregard the warning until it was too late to help himself. They had had the forethought to ally themselves with his mistress, Diane de Poitiers, who in return for favours helped them to obtain a daughter of France for the young Duke of Lorraine and the Dauphin himself, the future Francis II, for their niece. By now even France is scarcely too big for their ambitions.

Most conspicuous of the seven, both by reason of his dark ugliness and his air of acknowledged leadership, is the eldest, Francis, Duke of Guise. His shaggy brows overhang deepset eyes, a scar gained in battle seams one weatherbeaten cheek, mouth and chin thrust aggressively forward through a sparse beard. He affects the gruff speech of a soldier, partly out of taste, partly from a desire that people shall not forget who defended Metz successfully against Spain and wrested Calais from the English — the only French victories of note in the late war. He owns the reputation of being merciless to his enemies until they admit themselves beaten, when he can be magnanimous, and of fearing nothing that walks on legs.

Next in age and importance comes the man with the flowing golden beard, dressed in a light grey and crimson robe, Charles, Cardinal of Lorraine, in whose fine intelligent-looking head are hatched most of the schemes for his own and his brother's profit. He is Archbishop of Rheims, hence Primate of France — an office virtually hereditary, as it were, from Guise uncle to nephew — and one of the ablest diplomats and most eloquent preachers in Christendom. But if his talents are written on his face, so is his character in his eyes: he is a coward, a snob, unbearably haughty in success, unashamed to cringe when things are going against him, a priest without faith and a politician without principle. As his brother's grand vizier he is formidable; as a leader on his own he would be contemptible.

The others are loyal and able collaborators in what the two eldest devise for the common good; three of them are soldiers and two churchmen, including — perhaps because it was desired to keep as fair a balance as possible between the two professions — the family bastard. Of the wives (who have a way on marrying of becoming more Guise than the Guises) the chief is the Duke's consort, Anne d'Este, a ripe brunette of thirty, who joins freely in the men's conversation and is listened to with obvious respect. She has lineage — a King of France, Louis XII, on her mother's side, on her father's a pope's daughter, Lucrezia Borgia — and brains: to her is entrusted the upbringing of the eight-year-old son who will one day inherit whatever his father and uncles shall succeed in accumulating. A legacy that may yet comprise that which it would be treason to name aloud....

Catherine enters, a ponderous ghost in her billowing crêpe, her tread slow and firm on the stone floor. The Guises, kneeling, allege their delight at seeing her and their profound devotion to her person. She thanks them, bids them rise, embraces the Duchess, her very dear friend and gossip. The Cardinal then proceeds, as spokesman for his brothers, to crave assurance that she has not been incommoded by her journey: assuring her in return that the King's affairs are being so well looked after that she need not give herself a moment's anxiety on that score.

Catherine requires no interpreter. She has received fair notice that the Guises are in charge and prepared to resist any intruders. Behind them is the influence of the Queen their niece, and Catherine realizes the unwisdom of forcing her son to choose between his love for his wife and his love for his mother; realizes also that he will cling to whatever he has done with the peculiar stubbornness of the weak. Behind a barrage of tears she composes her response, the Guises watching her expression in the hope of detecting the effect of their words and the intention behind hers. She has come, she imparts brokenly, to bring comfort to her son and derive what comfort she can from him; in all things she is prepared to place herself at his disposal and that of his chosen ministers. Wrapping her veils about her, as if retiring physically into her bereavement, she withdraws with her ladies into her own apartment, leaving the Guises divided between hope and perplexity.

It does not take her long to re-orient herself. Patience is what matters. All men make mistakes, have their ups and downs. The Guises have been lucky in the moment of Henry's death, but the luck may be on her side next time. The important thing is to be allowed to stay. If she provokes the Guises to get rid of her, their first thought will be to separate her from the three small sons who stand next in line to the throne; that would be mere practical politics. So long as they are in power she must co-operate with them, even save them if necessary from their enemies, the Bourbons, the Montmorencys: for if either party succeeds in destroying the other, there will be nothing to prevent its doing what it likes with her and her children.

A compact is concluded in the King's presence. To show the world that their arrangement has the fullest possible colour of her son's authority, the Guises offer and Catherine accepts a place in the inner council of state. Everything else, army, treasury, domestic and foreign affairs, is divided amongst the brothers. They agree to their old friend Diane's banishment from court (after restoring the jewels Henry gave her and a castle, Chenonceaux, that his widow covets) in return for Catherine getting rid of her old friend Montmorency. The King, overjoyed at the amiability between his mother and his wife's uncles, declares that all laws shall be published in her name, under the impression that the arrangement leaves her in control of the kingdom. No one enlightens him.

FRANÇOIS II

Catherine, as if indifferent to everything but what she said she came for, gives herself devotedly to restoring his health. Illness and its cure is one of her hobbies, and she has always on hand a stock of carefully selected medicines for her friends' complaints. But for her children's ailments she has evolved a different and novel sort of therapeutics. She orders the windows of the sick-room flung wide open and the invalid's diet reduced to thin broth and bread crumbs in place of the customary meats and wines, having convinced herself by long experiment that her young thrive best on simple food in small quantities. It is a treatment she is always meaning to try for her own excess of weight, but can never bring herself to undergo because the open-air exercise she is so fond of leaves her too hungry.

Three days later she has her interview with the Constable: a painful scene. Their friendship began on the day she stepped off the galley at Marseilles, when he came to greet her on behalf of King Francis; she is godmother of his eldest son and he the agent that induced hers into the world, to judge by her letter in the second month of her pregnancy joyfully thanking him for having sent her what turned out to be the effective remedy for sterility. But he is Grand Master of the Household, an office that carries with it the keys of the royal castles, hence the King's custody in an emergency, and the Guises naturally want those keys. Catherine finally contrives to have her son pronounce the sentence of dismissal in the presence of his new ministers, so that the Constable may see for himself who is prompting his young master. Altogether she does not come out of it badly, she reflects, as she gives the angry old man a warm embrace on parting: she has shifted the burden of his wrath onto other shoulders, and with the Bourbons on the way, the Guises would have done better not to offend the greatest feudal landlord in France.

For the Bourbons are not like other rivals whose greatness depends on the temporary favour of the King, since not even the King can depose them from their place in the hierarchy of his realm. He may give them his confidence or withhold it, but so long as the Valois sit on the throne the Bourbons stand next to it by right of the blood in their veins; the blood of Hugh Capet which they, and they alone, share with the royal house.[1] Men may dispose of power, but only God can create lawful dynasties: and nothing can alter the fact that He long ago marked the Bourbons to rule France if ever the Valois gave out. Therefore the Guises, in daring their enmity, are committing themselves to a colossal gamble with the future which may compel them to challenge the divine will itself....

The newcomers arrive tired, dusty, and in a huff. No one had ridden out to bring them the welcome due to their rank — 'Was ever Prince of the Blood so treated?' grumbles their leader, the King of Navarre, with justice. It was not Catherine's fault: in the hope of starting with a good atmosphere she had pled with the Guises to ride out the previous day, but they haughtily declined to make any gesture which might be construed as an admission of inferiority. Anxious to cover their disrespect, Catherine then urged the King to meet his relatives as if by chance while out hunting, but the Guises had already filled the nervous lad with tales of hair-raising Bourbon plots to lay an ambush for him and stab him in the back. There was not even proper accommodation in the palace for any of them but the King of Navarre, and at the last moment the Queen Mother herself might be seen scurrying about the village in search of lodgings. In the end the King

---

[1] The so-called Third Dynasty, founded by Hugh Capet in 987, went on from father to son until 1328, when the direct male line failed and the throne passed to Philip of Valois, grandson of the eldest son of Saint Louis (Louis IX), 1226–70. The Bourbons were descended from Saint Louis's sixth son, Robert of Clermont, the intervening two hundred and thirty years having by the mid-sixteenth century eliminated all other direct descendants of Hugh Capet except through females, who under the Salic Law did not count. It was the effort of Edward III of England, descended from Louis IX on the distaff side, to dispute the Salic Law that caused the Hundred Years' War.

elected to absent himself as a sign of his displeasure at his relatives' murderous intentions toward him, leaving his mother to act as a reception committee of one.

They troop in: Antoine, King of Navarre, with his brothers Charles, Cardinal of Bourbon, and Louis, Prince of Condé, the three together constituting the senior branch of the clan; two Bourbon cousins of a junior line; and various kin bearing other names, notably the three dignified brothers Châtillon (nephews also of the Constable Montmorency) headed by the eldest, Gaspard, Lord of Coligny and Admiral of France. With them the *dramatis personae* is complete. The family's drama falls into two acts of a generation each, and the chief players of the first are now all assembled at Saint-Germain. In the second act the personages will change, but names, features, even characters will remain the same as new Valois, Bourbons, Guises, Condés, Colignys, etc., grow up to take their elders' places. Only Catherine will hold the stage from first curtain almost to last.

Presently she is closeted alone with the King of Navarre, the rest having separated to their lodgings. She sees them go with relief: this man she feels able to manage; impetuous fellows like his brother the Prince of Condé cramp her style and men of principle like Coligny make her uneasy. She has before her a tall deep-chested man of forty-five, whose fine eyes and forehead surmount without dominating a scanty, prematurely grey beard and the mobile mouth of a buffoon. Both ends of his head tell the truth. Antoine of Bourbon is full of great schemes that never come to anything because he can always think of greater ones; so free with his money that he never has any; so unaffectedly affable to everybody regardless of rank that great and small adore him and rejoice in fitting the syllables of his name into the latest unprintable doggerel. A speaker whom everybody praises and nobody pays much attention to, a gallant soldier in battles lost from the start by his own inconsequential strategy.

He talks. It is all wrong, it is a scandal.... The King's nearest male relatives have *always* directed affairs during the King's youth.... Who ever heard of Princes of the Blood giving way to a pack of upstarts from the suburbs of the kingdom? He does not hold Catherine altogether blameless — she should never have consented to the Constable being jettisoned.... He and his friends will not endure it.... To see their places usurped, their honour insulted, their very lives put in jeopardy. Not to speak of the welfare of the State.... By way of summing up he rises, the more effectively to let his hand fall on the hilt of his sword.

Catherine draws her own weapon, the lace handkerchief in her sleeve, and holds it ready for use. She admits everything, though not in words that he can later use against her. But what could she do, one helpless woman, with five babes to look after and ruthless men all round? Yes, even the King is a babe, for all that he is legally of age.... All the more reason why the nearest of his blood, the most illustrious of his kinsmen, the natural protector designated for him and his poor brothers and sisters by God, should not turn against him. Antoine opens his mouth to dispute this construction, but she rushes on, the handkerchief in vigorous use.

She delicately alludes to his wife, Jeanne d'Albret, the actual sovereign of the tiny vassal state in the Pyrenees from which he derives his title. Everybody knows that Antoine is henpecked by that indomitable lady and would like to be a king on his own. Catherine refers to the fond intimacy between herself and her son-in-law the King of Spain... outlines the possibility of his agreeing to restore to its rightful *lord* the portion of Navarre held by Spain since the last war... hints that Sardinia, a land flowing (she has been assured) with milk and honey, is to be erected into a separate monarchy... or the Barbary Coast, when conquered from the Moors.... It is not worthy of a king (Antoine loves to hear the title) with so much greatness before him to dispute with lesser men over trifling causes. If he will but forbear now to bring trouble upon her, and assist her in patience with his wisdom and strength, he may be assured that he will have all her, all France's gratitude, when his day comes.

Antoine sits down. His hand stops playing with his sword hilt and begins twirling his moustaches. By nature he is so much a lover of women that their tears can move him when they themselves are past doing so. He has much to think about: a kingdom of his own has always been a greater temptation than a career in France and he is a little tired of the doleful, psalm-singing Huguenotry that his wife enforces with an iron hand in her little kingdom. It is not his idea of a royal good time. He mentions his colleagues. With a laugh of flattering scepticism Catherine affirms her belief that he can manage them if he chooses to. He hems, agrees — particularly as they were acutely divided before coming on whether to take a strong line or not, Condé being for, Coligny against. Finally he says he will think it over.

It is all that Catherine asks. She has gained time without losing either the Montmorencys or the Bourbons — they will be on hand when she needs them. To have patience, to gain time, to balance adversaries against one another... the instinct is in her blood, the lesson graven on her mind from close study of the classic textbook for princes dedicated to her father by its author, Niccolo Machiavelli. Only time can show whether she has the mind to understand and the character to apply the sage's teachings....

Chapter III

THE RESULT OF PATIENCE

NEXT day the court left for Paris to assist at the final week of Henry's obsequies, and shortly thereafter moved on to Rheims for Francis II's coronation. In the course of both solemnities the Guises and the Bourbons fell into a violent squabble over the privilege of carrying the King's robe, a grave matter of precedence which was miraculously resolved without bloodshed. Antoine was still thinking and hence still incapacitated for action: the Queen Mother had every reason to congratulate herself on not having sat out the whole forty days in the Louvre. To avoid the risk of further incidents, Condé was induced to accept a commission abroad and Navarre appointed to escort the Queen of Spain to her husband's frontier. Meantime, Catherine paid a useful visit with the King to the Constable at Chantilly. Early in November, after a slow progress with frequent pauses for hunting, the court reached Blois, favourite of all the royal castles on the Loire, where it was proposed to pass the winter.

The intention was not fulfilled. That winter saw the first blast of the storm that was not to blow over till the family had disappeared and nearly every man then at Blois had perished in it. Neither Francis I nor Henry II had ever adopted a definite line about the new religion rapidly spreading through

France. Both had at one period taken an interest in it, as part of the modern trend in ideas, at another burned a few Huguenots [1] to appease the more bigoted amongst the Catholic majority. The Guises, however, who appreciated perfectly that the best rôle for the adventurer in politics was that of champion of the most conservative tradition and had assumed in consequence the leadership of the ultra-orthodox, issued a proclamation five days after Henry's death ordering the strict enforcement of the old penal laws against dissenters. It was a partisan manoeuvre pure and simple: though the Bourbons were by no means all Huguenots, Antoine of Navarre had taken them under his benevolent protection, while his brother Condé was their recognized leader and Coligny first in character and ability of their converts.

Incidents followed, culminating in December in the unexpected execution of a high officer of justice who had been awaiting trial since the previous spring on a charge of Protestant sympathies. The outraged Huguenots promptly assassinated one of his fellow judges and accusers. In revenge the Paris mob, rabidly fanatical and pro-Guise, erected images at the street-corners of the Madonna and saints and trampled upon whoever refused to salute them. The Huguenots attempted to rescue their friends and pitched battles took place in the streets; in the parts of France, especially the south and west, where they were strong, they retaliated with direct violence upon the Catholics. The Guises, instead of taking steps to keep the peace, added to the tumult by burning more Huguenots.

In February the court suddenly packed up and fled to the fortified stronghold of Amboise down the river. Rumours had begun to drift in from Spain, Paris, Geneva, of a vast conspiracy against the government. No one yet knew who was in it, whence it would burst, whom it meant to destroy.

[1] This French term for Protestants was derived from the German *Eidgenossen*, meaning 'bound together' or 'confederated.'

Every day brought fresh alarms: the whole Huguenot population was on the move, hundreds of thousands of them... the figure of a Silent Leader began to emerge, a Prince of the Blood, who was preparing to make a bid for the throne. The guards round the castle were doubled and doubled again, all the gates locked by night and all but one by day. Men arrived and departed on mysterious errands. Coligny was sent for and detained, Condé kept under strict surveillance. The Cardinal of Lorraine's nerve broke; recalling a prophecy that was made to him long before in Rome by a Jew that he would die in the year 1560, he offered an amnesty to the Huguenots in the hope of averting the impending catastrophe.

This was on March the eighth and for a week there was a lull in the tension. On the fifteenth some boatmen caught sight of fifty or sixty armed men coming down a hill on the opposite side of the river. They were arrested without trouble and explained, on being questioned, that they were demobilized soldiers whom some gentlemen of their acquaintance had hired to make a demonstration of protest to the King, giving them a small sum as earnest money. The King, on his own initiative, ordered them to be released with a few francs apiece to take them home. Next day the royal huntsmen picked up a few more in the woods. By then the troops had been brought in from the near-by garrisons and sent out to scour the neighbourhood. Numerous straggling bands were encountered and dispersed after a skirmish, in one of which the organizer of the plot, one La Renaudie, was killed, and a large number of prisoners taken, including several of those released on the first day.

It then appeared that this was the great conspiracy itself and that it was over; over, that is, but for the poor devils caught in it. The hopes and grievances of a million people seeking expression in a few thousand workless men, picked up at random in the streets of the big cities for an employment they did not understand, and sent off by their leaders in unorganized groups with the vague hope that something might come of it. The Tumult of Amboise was a strange sequel to the panic it aroused, an even stranger prelude to the most terrible religious wars in Christian history.

The Guises took charge of the prisoners' examination. The results were unsatisfactory. What they wanted was to uncover treason against the King himself: to convict Condé as the Silent Leader, outlaw the Bourbons, keep Francis permanently cowering for safety in their protection. Instead, they discovered that the plot arose from hatred of themselves and that its sole end was their elimination. Not one of the prisoners would name the Silent Leader, not one but who proudly proclaimed himself 'a soldier and minister of the Word of God' ready to die to rid the King of the usurpers who were ruining him.[1] This was not treason; not yet, at least.... Baffled and terrified, the Guises inaugurated a carnival of massacre. Prisoners hung in batches from the battlements of the castle, floated in the river attached by sixes and eights to long poles; while the quality daily mounted the scaffold before the main gate to offer their heads as a spectacle for the inmates of the castle. The Guises made a special point of securing the fullest possible attendance.

It went on for a week until even their friends sickened and advised them to call a halt. The Duchess Anne herself fainted with horror. The King wandered up and down like a young madman, clasping his hands to his eyes or ears, crying to know what it was that made his people hate him so, imploring the Guises to go away for a little while so that he might see if it was they or he who was really hated. In soothing terms they explained to him that this was all for his sake.

Imperturbably, as imperturbably as she was to look upon a more terrible scene of her own setting, Catherine went her

[1] The Guises had made themselves widely unpopular by involving the country in a losing war against the Scottish Reformers on behalf of their sister, Mary Stuart's mother, the Regent of Scotland. Elizabeth of England had come in decisively on the rebels' side.

way. To the unhappy wretches outside she gave not a thought except as items in her calculations regarding herself and her children. She deplored that Francis — and, indeed, all her children — were prone to suffer from too much imagination, unaware that she was not altogether blessed in having too little. The letters she wrote during the month before the Tumult and in the week of butchery that followed it breathe a cheerful content with a very slight alloy of anxiety as to how it would all come out.

She had a certain sentiment for Amboise, for it was there that the father and the little French mother that she had never seen had been married in another springtime forty-three years before. And she had her younger children around her, the castle being their habitual residence at this season, as well as of their playmates, the little Prince Henry of Navarre and his sister Catherine, the Duke of Guise's eldest son, her husband's bastard the Duke of Angoulême. She gave herself wholeheartedly to their lessons, correcting their exercises in Latin and Italian, history and geography, mathematics and elementary astrology, watching the little girls at their painting, music, and domestic arts, the little boys practising with the bow, the lance, and the sword. It does not appear in her words or letters that she gave any thought to the effect upon their education of the Guises' schooling to rebels outside the windows.

She learned one lesson herself, however. Her sense of responsibility for her children's estate was as strong as her sensitiveness to the miseries of the people in it was weak, and she shrewdly perceived the inexpediency of being too closely implicated with men who could arouse the feelings that exploded at Amboise. A few more Tumults, and particularly a successful one, and there might be no estate left.... During the height of the excitement the royal chancellor died, the highest permanent official in the State, and she procured the appointment of Michel L'Hôpital in his place. Benign of countenance and a lover of the classics, the Guises saw no harm in him, especially as he was a former dependent of theirs; they failed to see, as Catherine saw, that he was a just man and a great administrator who 'carried the lilies of France in his heart.' In July he published, with the Queen Mother's encouragement, the most tolerant edict of religion that had ever become law in a Catholic country; and in August an Assembly of Notables, convoked at Fontainebleau ' to find the remedy for the present evils [the words are Catherine's] and appease the troubles which we see in the realm,' decided that the Estates-General,[1] the historic representative body for remedy and reform which had not met in seventy-six years, should be summoned to meet at Orleans on December tenth.

And the Guises swallowed everything down to the Estates-General, which might (it was more than conceivable) demand of the King their dismissal, even their exile, as the price of pacification. The world asked in wonder whether the leopard could have changed his spots, or rather the Devouring Tiger (the name by which the Cardinal individually and the brothers collectively were called by their enemies) his stripes? Not at all. They merely did not want another Amboise; even if it failed, the King might sicken of them, and if it succeeded, they were all dead men. But bending, they gathered themselves for another spring, a final one.... From the Hôtel de

---

[1] The Estates-General were not a legislative body, there being no such thing in France, where absolute authority resided in the Crown. They were specially elected delegates from the lords, clergy, and commons to advise the King of his people's grievances and of ways to redress them, including suggestions for the least painful ways of raising subsidies for him. The three Estates first met separately to determine their line of policy at the Estates-General, where there was debate but no vote, the King taking the opinion of the majority's sentiment or not as he pleased. At Orleans there were about 107 delegates to each of the first two Estates, about 224 to the Third.

In ordinary times (since the Estates-General were convoked but rarely) there met at irregular intervals provincial Estates, but the Crown usually dealt with the people through the permanent *Parlements*, of which there were eight in the country; these bodies, originally and primarily courts of justice, assisted the King to raise money in their districts, though again he was not compelled to avail himself of their intermediation; if he did so it was a matter of policy based on old custom, not on law.

Lorraine agents with full purses and strong arms sifted into the provinces to prepare for the elections to the Estates-General; discreet negotiators departed for Madrid with seductive offers to Philip for an invasion of Navarre simultaneously with a Catholic *coup d'état* at Orleans; in the same mansion cipher experts and lawyers worked over the correspondence of the Prince of Condé and his friends as it was ferreted out by other agents, in order to have the evidence complete before December tenth.

The Prince was not the man to be caught asleep nor to wait tamely to be attacked. Materializing suddenly before the King, he demanded an immediate hearing. It was a right no one dared refuse him and the Council was assembled. He rose in his place, a dapper little man of thirty, lithe and brown, with pointed beard and sparkling eyes — an engaging anachronism in his century, a figure out of the pages of chivalry slightly parodied. Angry as only a man can be who knows himself justly suspected, he declared that anyone who accused him of mixing in sedition was a liar, and flinging his glove on the floor offered to prove his assertion at the point of the sword. Everyone looked at the Guises; and the Guises, disconcerted, looked at one another. It was a dangerous business accusing a Prince of the Blood and they were not yet ready with their proofs. The Duke finally stood up, glanced at the waiting glove, and offered to act as his friend Condé's second if any slanderer ventured to take up the challenge. Thereby the Guises, champions of bygone days, proved themselves considerably more advanced in the spirit of the new age than the man of the Reformation.

At the end of October the court moved to Orleans to prepare for the meeting of the Estates. The Constable, shaken by a pointed hint of danger from the Guises, debated with himself at Chantilly whether to go or to fall ill; finally compromising by starting and falling ill on the way. The Bourbons, impressed by the warnings of their friends and the pleas of their families, wavered a long time; it was Catherine who, anxious to balance the Guises' influence at the Estates, brought them to Orleans on the thirty-first with a solemn promise that they would be safe. The same day, in the King's presence, Condé was arrested on a charge of high treason.

Antoine turned upon Catherine and overwhelmed her with reproaches, accusing her of having lured his brother to his death, his family to its downfall. She swore that it was not so, 'that the King has done everything of his own will.' It must have been true because there was every reason why it should have been. She knew what was brewing, as everyone did, but she could not believe — no one could — that when it came to the pinch the Guises would dare attack openly a Prince of the Blood. If Condé died, it would be all over with her. Antoine had not the character to keep the Bourbons together, the Montmorencies would be easily crushed, her turn would come next. The Guises, left alone, could then at their leisure reduce her son to a *roi fainéant*, a puppet king, with themselves as Mayors of the Palace, after the example of their vaunted ancestors. Just so had Pepin the Short, Charlemagne's father, ended the Merovingian dynasty and substituted his own.

Desperately Catherine fought for a compromise. Not daring to give herself away too plainly, she depicted the danger at home and the scandal abroad if a prince of Condé's influence were put to death. Screening herself behind L'Hôpital's resource and acumen, she exploited every twist of the law to put off the trial. It was all of no use. With skill and patience the Guises had constructed their case — out of the confessions of kidnapped and tortured witnesses, of a relative of the Bourbons caught redhanded and imprisoned, of Condé's own trunk of papers forced in a pretended burglary — to prove him the Silent Leader. With even greater skill and cunning they worked upon the King's terrors to convince him that the evidence pointed only incidentally to a plot against themselves, primarily to a design upon his life and crown. Condé, a gallant knight and a hot-headed fool, played into their hands: when called upon to plead, he haughtily took his stand upon his honour and his rank, and refused even to give his enemies the satisfaction of an answer.

As a sign that everything was over, the King planned to go hunting from the middle of November until the convocation of the Estates, but his departure was delayed by a feverish cold. Meantime, the Guises filled Orleans with troops to prevent any effort at rescue and as an object lesson to the assembling deputies. On the most redoubtable of the Prince's supporters, Coligny, they put a close watch and dared even to arrest his sister, Condé's mother-in-law, a lady of great spirit, to prevent her from making trouble. To Navarre, who was moving heaven (through its vicar the Pope) [1] and earth for his brother, they intimated that he would meet with an accident unless he made prompt arrangements to go home. The King's cold improved; the Privy Council, constituting itself a court especially for the purpose, pronounced Condé guilty of the charges against him. Catherine made one last effort to avert or at least postpone the death sentence — and failed.

The King suddenly took a turn for the worse. He complained of severe pains in the head, and a large lump began to form behind his right ear. The doctors were still hopeful, but their faces grew longer as the lump refused to yield to treatment and the King fell into fits of delirium. Through the court and the city the whisper began to circulate that he would not recover... a ten-year-old boy would succeed him ... and then? Navarre as Regent, Condé released, the end of the Guises — or civil war?

But another figure loomed larger and larger as the King sank, the corpulent, black-robed figure of the Queen Mother.

---

[1] This is not so improbable as it sounds. The Vatican was ready to go a long way in placating great nobles with Protestant leanings.

The Result of Patience

What would she do? Which side would she take? She alone professed no party, to her France largely owed the unexpected tranquillity after Henry's death. The law on the subject of a regency had never been clearly defined — there was an illustrious precedent even for a woman holding it, in Blanche of Castile, mother of Saint Louis. A regent disagreeable to the new king would sooner or later invite trouble... whereas her influence over him, as over all her children, was absolute, notorious....

Catherine herself, an inscrutable lump of misery, sat day and night by her son's bedside, peering with her short-sighted eyes into the doctors' faces for signs of hope, rocking herself to and fro and wailing that she could not live if her firstborn died. The baby so long waited for, the tiny shield against all she had dreaded, the precious bond with all that she had loved. She prayed the God Who gave him to her that he might live — knowing even as she prayed that if he did, his brothers and sisters, he himself, were irretrievably lost; knowing also that if he died, she must without loss of time prepare herself for what would come after. The doctors still gave him more than an even chance, but in her heart she doubted... the great Nostradamus had said long ago that Francis would not see his eighteenth year — now barely seven weeks away. The same Nostradamus who predicted Henry's death in a 'duel' ten years before Montgomery's lance pierced his eye in the fatal tourney... the Nostradamus who told her that all her sons would be kings. Nostradamus, the infallible decipherer of the stars, was near-by at Chaumont. She would go to him and find out the worst — whatever the worst was....

She goes by night to his laboratory, high up in a tower, and composes herself in an anteroom to wait until he can see her: for he is engaged with a blond young man, the angel Anael, whom he has just succeeded in invoking after forty days and nights of tireless incantation and ritual. His heavenly visitor gone, the great seer traces a magic circle on the ground in the Queen Mother's presence and invites her to take her place inside it. Before her on a table is a disc of polished steel on whose corners are inscribed in pigeon's blood JEHOVAH, MITTATRON, ELOHIM, ADONAI — the four Hebrew names of God. The two faces, one plump and smooth under the widow's coif, the other haggard and bearded, bend over it.

Across the glittering surface cloudy forms float and form into shapes. Catherine sees her eldest son walk round the depth of the mirror as upon a stage and disappear. Charles follows him, making fourteen turns before giving way to Anjou, the son she loves above all other creatures on earth, almost beyond sanity.... Her breath locked in her bosom, she counts: one, two ... fifteen.... And before she can ask what it means he vanishes, to be replaced by a stocky lad with the noble brow and buffoon's mouth of Antoine of Navarre — his graceless son Henry. Her eyes start from her head.

'What! Will he reign too?' she gasps.

Without answering, the mage blows upon the mirror and its bright surface stares back at her as blank as the mystery of life and death. And pondering what she has seen as she rides home in the dawn, she has a glimmering that the human destinies written in the stars may be fulfilled in many ways. That though her sons are to be kings, the same kingdom may be allotted to all of them one after the other ... until of her seed and Henry's all shall have disappeared into darkness.

The doctors tell her that Francis is better, almost out of danger. She knows not what to think, and in her chapel says Mass and burns candles in an equal torment for his recovery and the repose of his soul. But between whiles she takes Navarre aside and walks with him under the eyes of the court, preparing him. Warning him that she means to claim the Regency for herself and will tolerate no interference if it so happens that God means to call her son to Him. Offering to make him her second-in-command if he agrees to support her against any opposition from the Estates, otherwise to throw her influence to the Guises .. who would not linger (she has scarcely to hint) in preferring a charge of high treason against him and finishing off Condé....

It is a battle of character entirely. If it were Condé, he would stand upon his rights, but the easy-going Navarre, fearful for his brother as well as for himself, hesitates to issue the irrevocable challenge. Meantime the Guises look at them together, not knowing what to believe or do.... And while they hang in doubt Catherine sends a messenger to the Constable, her one sure ally, bidding him hurry; for his sake and hers, to hurry as fast as horses can bring him.

On the third of December the doctors confess that all hope is gone; the diseased mastoid has burst, the King has sunk into a final coma. The Guises, terrified of Navarre, seeing in Catherine their only saviour, kneel to her, vowing to be her good and true servants forevermore. Navarre, his nerve gone, kneels too.... Montmorency rides in and takes military control of Orleans in the name of the new King Charles IX and the Regent his mother. On the fifth at midnight Francis dies, and the new mistress of France retires to the solitude of her own room to order the plans in her head and relieve the burden upon her heart.

Some of it she poured out to her daughter Elizabeth, the Queen of Spain.

Orleans
Undated [early December, 1560]

To My Daughter, The Queen Catholic:
Madame My Daughter,
   I am charging the present bearer with many messages for you, which will spare me from writing you too long a letter, only to beg you not to let yourself be troubled for me and to assure you that I shall not fail to govern myself in such a manner

that God and the world will have reason to be satisfied with me, for it is always my chief aim to have God's honour before my eyes in everything and to uphold my authority, not for myself, but to preserve this realm for the good of your brothers, whom I love, as I love you all who are your father's children.

And therefore, my daughter, my darling, commend yourself well to God, for you have seen me as happy as you are now, thinking of no other tribulation except to be loved as much as I could wish by the King your father, who honoured me more than I deserved; but I loved him so that I was always afraid, as you well know; and God took him from me, and not content with that, took your brother also whom I loved, as you know, and left me with three small sons, and in a realm altogether divided, having no one in whom I can trust, there being no one who is disinterested.

And therefore, my darling, think of me and let me be an example to you not to depend wholly on your husband's love, on the honour and contentment you now have, but commend yourself to Him Who alone can protect your good fortune and also, when it please Him, place you in the state in which I now am, which I would rather die than see you in, for fear that you would not be able to bear all the evils I have had and now have, which I assure you I should not be able to bear without His aid.

Your affectionate mother

CATERINE

BOOK II

THE MATRIARCH

We take cunning for a sinister, a crooked, wisdom... there be [those] that can pack the cards and yet cannot play well....

BACON

Chapter IV

MY SON'S ESTATE

To HAVE been born of a dwindling stock of merchant politicians, an unwanted orphan, a *duchessina* without a duchy: to have been narrowly saved at eleven from exposure to gunfire on the walls of Florence or internment in a brothel while her exiled relatives, aided by a Spanish army, were hammering at the gates; to have been palmed off on a second son, nearly discarded for sterility, left a widow, a supernumerary with the most dismal prospects... and in a bare seventeen months to have become virtual sovereign of the greatest state in Europe, a place no woman had held since Blanche of Castile, mother of Saint Louis, three hundred years before: one stroke of luck after another; or, as Catherine put it to her sister-in-law the Duchess of Savoy in gratified amazement, 'God has never neglected me, even when it looked darkest.'

She would have been less jubilant had she not fondly anticipated that the same mysterious agency which operated to place her children's patrimony in the hands of their rightful guardian would feel bound to assist her in looking after it. For the condition of the 'estate' was appalling. The long war with Spain and the extravagance of her predecessors had pawned the King's lands for years in advance, and piled up a debt on which even the interest (as high as sixteen per cent now, owing to the country's bad credit) could not be met. The taxes were heavy and unjustly distributed, yet yielded little, the officials universally corrupt and practically irremovable. In the urgency of their need, Louis XII, Francis I, and Henry II had created and sold fifty thousand offices in fifty years, the purchasers reimbursing themselves, of course, at the public expense. The King sold offices, the officers sold justice; or, if the law was not in their line, took such firm charge of his finances that his debts remained unpaid and less than ten per cent of the money extracted from the people reached the treasury. Rogues were in clover, honest men in despair, while the unruly lords (who paid no taxes whatever) shared the profits of the one lot and built up their factions out of the griefs of the other.

Nor was that the worst of it. Men were arming to battle for salvation. To the Catholic the Real Presence of God's flesh and blood, the repetition of His body's sacrifice in the miracle of the Mass, constituted the promise of immortality, the sustaining comfort of man through the dangers, disappointments, and miseries of his life here below; to the Protestant it was an impious fraud inspired by the Devil and carried out by the priests to justify their privileged and corrupt existences. Each had been taught that to tolerate error in his neighbour was to forfeit his own soul — better for a few to suffer now than for all to be damned forever. In addition the Catholics detested the Huguenots for their irritating righteousness, their dismal psalm-singing in the highways, the general gloom cast by their dress and deportment, while the Huguenots with equal fervour despised the Catholics for sensual, superstitious, priest-ridden image-worshippers.[1]

[1] Complicating these feelings were the elements of a fierce class hatred. The Reformers, though small in number, were almost solidly from the middle class of small landowners, professional men, merchants, and skilled artisans; the class upon which the greater part of the financial burden fell, since they could claim neither the exemption of poverty nor power. They were the strong nucleus of the Bourbons' party, as the ultra-Catholics, and particularly the Paris mob, were of the Guises'.

My Son's Estate 43

The Estates-General, meeting a week after Francis's death, showed exactly how things stood. The Crown asked for an urgent subsidy to pay the army and civil services. Make the clergy disgorge some of their ill-gotten hoard, shouted the Third Estate, or, better yet, confiscate it altogether as the English had done. Not a sou, bellowed the bishops, unless the Crown showed its good faith by sending the heretics to burn in hell where they belonged. A warning, clear as it was ugly, that the only terms on which the new regent could hope for the loyalty of one section of her subjects was by the despoilment or death of another. The story of the next thirty years in a nutshell.

Catherine cheerfully refused to take too desperate a view of the situation. To her the dispute that was rending Christendom was simply an exaggerated fuss over trifles — vestments and images and whether prayers should be recited in Latin or French: nothing that well-intentioned people could not settle by getting round a table and talking things over. Had not the well-bred folk at Francis I's court, herself amongst them, joined in the fashionable discussion of the new doctrine and the collective singing of Clement Marot's 'sweet and soothing' hymns without forswearing the Mass or a yearning to cut one another's throats? Merely let her keep her power — which, thank God, she still had, an incipient revolt in the Estates having fizzled out — and the rest could be managed. After all, what did it really matter whether France was Catholic or Protestant so long as it was her children's?

From this homely premise the new regent set out with brisk self-confidence to do a very great thing. Nothing less than to find a way for each of her son's subjects to worship God without molesting or being molested by his neighbours. She did not of herself expect to reach a permanent solution; the problem was too complicated and far-reaching for that. All she hoped for was some compromise that would enable Frenchmen to live side by side without killing each other until the Church itself had time to work out a new order or unity for Christendom.¹ She abolished the right of the State to search out and punish private beliefs by bribes, threats, force, cajolery; laboured to put down — with indifferent success — local persecution. In August of 1561 she assembled the leaders of both sects at Poissy to help her devise some formula that would rejoin Catholic and Protestant in a temporary common creed, but when the venerable doctors fell to assaulting one another over the nature of the Eucharist, she was compelled, with regretful surprise, to dismiss them. Without giving up her ambition to merge the religions through some happy inspiration of dialectic, she instructed her chancellor L'Hôpital to draw up an edict giving the Huguenots broad freedom of worship and practically complete civil rights. Not until the Edict of Nantes, whereby Henry IV established the basis of peace for the most brilliant century in her history, did France again receive a religious law so generous as Catherine de Medici's Edict of January, 1562.

Across the English Channel another queen was trying to pacify a turbulent kingdom through a common form of worship. Difficult as was Elizabeth's position, it was incomparably easier than Catherine's. Elizabeth was sovereign in her own right, the one certain bulwark against anarchy, trusted by the majority of her people because she was one of them ('mere English' in her own proud words), necessary to the very existence of the dominant faction, the Protestant. Catherine had no claim on her subjects' loyalty save as one of the possible vicars for an infant king, suffered the usual distrust of foreigners in high place (she had never even learned to speak French well), could command the allegiance of no party, since by their very nature they were as much against her as against one another. She had to fight for herself if she

---

¹ The Council of Trent, which had adjourned a decade earlier after its failure to heal the schism, was due to resume its labours in 1562, with a fairly general expectation of success.

was to continue working for her son's subjects, Elizabeth worked for her subjects *by* fighting for herself — in that distinction lay the tragic difference between what the younger woman was to do for England and what the elder was to do to France.

It was of the very essence of Elizabeth's task that she hold her power till she died, of Catherine's that she surrender hers gracefully when her son was old enough to take it over. Would she? She herself did not know. She did not even think about it in the first freshness of delight at wielding her new authority. Particularly since she could not doubt that she was doing it extraordinarily well, for was she not by maintaining the peace contributing, as no one else could have done, to the preservation of her children's estate? What other regent had the same motive as she to put the interest of the Crown, and therefore of all France, before that of any party? She was quite right, as things stood: though it did not strike her that the fact of the best for herself happening to be also the best for her son and his realm was merely a happy coincidence, not an immutable law of nature. And there already lay the seeds of a dangerous delusion for anyone with an overdeveloped liking for power. . . .

How hugely she enjoyed the business of ruling, the very mechanics of it even! The hard work, the long talks with ambassadors and public officials while strolling back and forth in a crowded room or, preferably, a garden, the endless letter-writing (as many as forty a day in her own hand alone) to her dear sisters and brothers the crowned heads of Europe. Above all the cunning intrigues, that blessed art which allowed her woman's wit and highly schooled self-control such a pleasant sense of mastery over the obtuser brains and more unruly tempers of the men with whom she had principally to deal. Often she grumbled that she was overworked, that everybody was making it all too difficult for her, but she loved it: an acute fellow Italian, after listening respectfully to her lamentations, wrote dryly to his employers in Venice, '*ha un affetto potentissimo... di signoreggiare*' — her keenest pleasure is in running things. Especially the great lords who had so recently been in a position to snub her, and whose simple weaknesses it was so much easier to understand than the complicated wants of the anonymous millions. 'If the great are in accord the small will dwell in peace.' It was a comfortable maxim for her peculiar talents, and she had endless fun in pursuing it through all its stages of intrigue and private feud — straight on to its senseless and terrible conclusion.

Naturally the Guises could not tolerate what Catherine was trying to do; if she succeeded in combining all the factions into a single faction — her own or the King's, whatever one chose to call it — they might as well go back to their native Lorraine and stay there. Too weak to oppose her unaided since Francis's death, they brought to their side the Constable, who as a Catholic was grieved at the Queen Mother's lenience to the Huguenots and as a beneficiary of Henry II sore at L' Hôpital's proposal to assist the national finances by compelling the favourites of that overgenerous monarch to restore some of his gifts. With him and the Duke of Guise joined the Marshal Saint-André, a rich and popular soldier also afflicted by the Chancellor's notions of financial reform, to form a Triumvirate (as they called themselves) which then waited upon the King of Navarre with the offer of their support if he would challenge Catherine's right to the Regency when the Estates reassembled in August. They engaged, in addition, if he would turn Catholic, to procure him a papal divorce and the hand of the young, lovely, and sorrowing widow Mary Stuart... with the throne of England to follow when the Catholic powers should have deposed Mary's bastard cousin Elizabeth.

There was more to the scheme, but that was all that they thought fit to divulge to Antoine at the moment. They planned to tell him the rest of it after they had completely estranged him from his followers and used him to turn out Catherine: that the Guises were at the moment negotiating a marriage for their niece with Don Carlos, the King of Spain's heir, on the basis of Philip II maintaining the Triumvirate in the government of France, placing Mary on the throne of England, and recompensing himself for his trouble with the subsequent friendship of both countries and the remaining shred of the kingdom of Navarre. What was to be done with Antoine after that had not yet been ripely considered; perhaps it was intended that he should join Catherine in some Italian retreat.

It was no impossible fantasy, no domestic day-dream, that the Guises had spun, but the beginnings of the Great Design (as it came to be styled) whose attempted execution was to dominate the history of Europe for the next thirty years. To assume the government of France and ultimately replace the Valois by themselves as an out-and-out Catholic dynasty holding the divine sanction through Rome, to achieve a similar revolution in England in their niece's behalf — from these two simple and related purposes followed directly the revolt against Elizabeth in 1569 and her formal excommunication, the imprisonment and death of Mary Stuart, the sailing of the Armada and the last and worst of the French civil wars which ended only when Henry IV agreed to say a Mass for Paris. Of the Church's support there was never a doubt nor, ultimately, of Spain's, the most mightily armed power in the world: for if the Huguenots were allowed to flourish in France, it would only be a matter of time, a very short time, before they stimulated a rebellion amongst their co-religionists in Spain's richest province just over the border in the Netherlands. Beyond any personal inclination to bigotry, Philip II was bound to make his basic rule of self-defence, 'Put out the fire in thy neighbour's house before it start a conflagration in thine own.'

Navarre summoned his kin to march on Paris for the assertion of his rights. The Provincial Estates of the Ile de

France, the most important in the kingdom, passed a resolution demanding that the Queen Mother resign in the King of Navarre's favour — a bad omen for the meeting of the Estates-General. Sympathetic riots against her usurpation broke out in other places. The King of Spain threatened her with an invasion unless she withdrew her protection from the Reformers. Before she had a fair chance to enjoy her power or show what she could do with it, Catherine was presented with the choice of abdicating or risking for it what she most wished to avoid, a civil war of religion.

Or so at least the Triumvirate and Navarre thought. And it would be immediately true when they confronted her united and ready-armed. That was why Catherine preferred peace to war for herself (as distinct from the needs of France), realizing that force was not a business at which a woman might reasonably expect to show at her best. But so long as they left her room for the employment of her own particular style of fighting, she felt able to take on the lot of them.

Calling Antoine to her she spread before him a sheaf of letters addressed to her son and daughter of Spain, to her cousin Duke Cosimo I of Florence and her other cousin Gian Angelo de Medici, Pope Pius IV,[1] all strongly bespeaking their favour for her brother of Navarre ... adding verbal comment on Sardinia's gold-bearing sands ... and / or the Barbary Coast's silks and perfumes and Circassian dancing-girls. Strong letters, strong words: but Antoine had heard all this before and remained non-committal. Catherine thereupon revealed to him those parts of the Triumvirate's design which his new friends had omitted to mention. Could she prove it, demurred Navarre, recovering from his start. Easily — and handed him a letter that had somehow disappeared from under the frock of a monk to whom the Guises had entrusted it for delivery into Spain. These lucky accidents were always happening to her. Her enemies said that she kept spies in their

[1] The two latter were of a junior branch of the Medici now ruling in Florence.

My Son's Estate 49

houses and retained highwaymen with specialized scents for diplomatic pouches; slanders she loudly denied.

Antoine was shaken. Talking very fast, Catherine promised to see to his divorce herself — a mere family matter between herself and the Pope — being who he was — reviewed the princesses of Europe, amongst whom he would have the widest choice — what could he ever be to Mary Stuart but another Queen's husband? And that the interval till all this could be arranged should not prove too tedious, she produced a charming companion to share it with him, Mademoiselle de Rouet, one of her ladies of honour from amongst her own seminary of beauties later to be known as the 'flying squadron' and already celebrated for their proficiency in the arts of love and boudoir diplomacy.

Leaving the gallant Antoine to his honeymoon and the gentle vigilance of Mademoiselle de Rouet, Catherine turned briskly to deal with the Guises' other and far more redoubtable ally, Philip of Spain. One resource her adversaries had forgotten which she never forgot — her children. How could she forget them when their images were ever with her, in exquisite miniatures bound in a little sacred volume that hung by a chain from her belt during all her waking hours? There they all were, down to the twins who had died at birth, wrapped in their swaddling clothes like tiny mummies, and up to 'the most dutiful and loving daughter in all the world,' Her Most Catholic Majesty, Elizabeth the Queen of Spain. ... Catherine tried hard not to play favourites amongst her children, but to combat her idolatry of Elizabeth and Anjou with stern self-reminders to be impartially just. It was no use: if she purchased jewels and velvets for Elizabeth, conscience compelled her to spend immediately an equivalent amount on gifts for Claude — only she neglected to take the endless time and trouble to find exactly the right adornment for the plain Duchess as for the exquisite Queen her sister: the circlet of diamonds that would set off so well her long slender throat, the deep red brocade that would sort so perfectly with the dusky shadows thrown upon her transparent skin from her dark eyes and hair. Any returned traveller was sure of the Queen Mother's undivided attention as he repeated the oft-told tales of how the Spanish lords could not take their eyes off their young mistress, yet dared not stare for fear of Philip's alert jealousy; of how ordinary men, catching a glimpse of her in street or garden, would tell their families on returning home in the evening, 'I have seen the Queen today,' with the same rapt wonder as if they had seen an angel.

In return for the love and care she lavished on them, Catherine exacted an implicit obedience, above all where the interest of the family was involved. What were children for if not to help the mother, who was giving up her whole life to them (as she completely believed), when it was in their power? Why else did one struggle and scheme to provide such good marriages for them? The result of her training was a hold over her young that was the marvel of Europe, so far did it go beyond the normal measure of filial respect and affection. Her Catholic Majesty's hand shook so on receiving a letter from her mother for fear it contained one of her rare reproofs that she scarcely dared open it, while the young King himself, even the unruly Margot, trembled with awe on entering her presence. Though it would no doubt have been much more marvellous had the too sensitive failed to pay its usual tribute to the insensitive — especially when the latter had to offer an almost animal devotion and a comforting certainty of what was in all circumstances right.

But — of all ill-timed misfortunes — Elizabeth fell ill of smallpox at the very moment Catherine needed her help against the Guises. Prayer and the medicines sent by special courier from Paris to Madrid got the upper hand of the disease: the patient was recovering. Yet the good news abated only half of the maternal anxiety. If she should be disfigured for life, ruminated Catherine in anguish, if Philip should turn

MARGUERITE DE VALOIS

from her in disgust...? The harassed woman resorted again to her physicians, her wizards, her own long and diverse experience of therapeutics. From the combined wisdom of these oracles issued a lotion of cream and pigeon's blood, which Catherine despatched by express to her ambassador at the Escorial, the Bishop of Limoges, together with hints as to diet and after-care — and a request for the quickest possible report on the results achieved, direct and indirect. To Elizabeth followed a letter enjoining strict attention to the régime prescribed, 'that you may be pleasing in your husband's sight, which you should desire not only for your own sake but for the good and repose of all Christianity.' In other words, take care of such attractions as God has given you for God's sake. The precautions were successful: nothing remained but a few slight pock-marks on the nose. The good Bishop concluded his report with the satisfactory announcement that 'The King and Queen Catholic began to renew their marriage five or six days ago.'

Then to business. Catherine commanded her daughter to put a spoke at once into the Mary Stuart-Don Carlos marriage for reasons given, and if possible substitute as bride her sister Margot, which 'you are not to lose one hour or a single occasion... to bring about.' For Catherine was looking forward already to the time when Europe should be one vast matriarchy, every throne tenanted by a grandson who would turn to her for advice on the upbringing, health, and marriages of his children and the proper management of his kingdom. Try also, added Catherine, to do something for Navarre to keep him in order. 'Urge these things upon your husband by every persuasion you can think of...': and lest Elizabeth should not be able to think up the right ones when the occasion arose, Catherine wrote out a speech for her to commit to memory.

There was still the matter of religion, however, on which the Guises had her. No use blowing full-throated commands on this theme, for the devout Elizabeth would merely shut her ears, or be refused permission to listen. Catherine, versatile performer, laid aside her trombone and put to her lips the dulcet flute of evasion. Do not, my child, ran her wistful piping, believe what you hear of my paltering with the heretics... these are but inventions of my enemies, your brother, the King's disloyal servants... by all the piety in which I brought you up and which you have always seen in me, believe your mother and trust not those who slander her. Having made herself champion of religious peace without the slightest motive of principle, there was no reason why Catherine should not pursue that great cause with a robust contempt for scruple.

Again the Estates-General met, at Pontoise in the very Ile de France that had recently demanded Catherine's dismissal. Amongst those present were the King of Navarre, the new Lieutenant-General of the Realm, whose face was all smiles for the lady president of the assembly, whose back, one large scowl (so to speak) for his late friends of the Triumvirate. Those gentlemen took their places with a somewhat hangdog look. In their pockets reposed letters, consigned by Philip in blank to the Queen Mother and by her selectively distributed, stressing the displeasure His Majesty of Spain would feel toward anyone who might attempt to deprive his mother-in-law of the authority she was so worthily exercising. The Guises also possessed a further document from the same source declining the honour of their niece's hand for Don Carlos. The Estates confirmed Catherine's Regency without a dissenting voice and received a holiday for fifteen years, at the same time that Mary Stuart, on her uncles' advice, took ship for Scotland and the future that there awaited her. What a useful thing is an obedient and credulous child in high place! No wonder Catherine yearned to see more of them there. The Bourbons went home, then the Montmorencys, finally the Guises, all sulkily resigned to playing second fiddles to the Queen Mother. Rosy with delight Catherine wrote to Madrid,

'I cannot see that the King my son has anything to fear so long as I hold both ends of the rope, as I do.' How could anything go wrong so long as a well-meaning mother, blessed with such dutiful offspring and such skill at outwitting her adversaries, maintained her power over her children's estate?

Apparently something could. Passing through Champagne the Duke of Guise's men stopped (it was a Sunday in March, 1562) to investigate a Huguenot service in the village of Vassy, a murderous riot followed, and in a twinkling all France rose to arms.... As Guise rode in triumph into Paris by one gate, Catherine and her children fled in terror by another: and force reigned till a self-tortured people discovered that it brought them no nearer a cure for their differences than banished cunning.

Chapter V

INTERLUDE ON THE WAY

On Monday afternoon, the thirteenth of March, 1564, an expeditionary force leaves Fontainebleau for the peaceful conquest of Europe by matrimony. To a gravely martial air from the Swiss Guard's drums and fifes, the hundred Gentlemen of the Household lead the way through the castle gates, their plumes and embroidered cloaks waving in the breeze. Behind them trot the sixty Grooms of the Stable and the Pages of Honour, twelve youngsters in their middle teens, trying not to show their excitement and their pride in their new finery. Next come in order the archers, mounted or on foot, in close-fitting caps and leather jerkins, the Swiss and Scottish Guards brightly cuirassed and helmeted. Then the Provost of the Household and his staff, who will see to the billeting of the royal party and mark in each village with chalk upon the doors of the houses to be occupied; and after them the sober ranks of physicians and surgeons, of butlers and carvers, the falconers with their birds on their wrists and the huntsmen leading their dogs.

In the next section come the households of the various princes of the blood; the marshals of France with their suites; plain carriages containing the councillors and secretaries, headed by the Chancellor, to carry on the business of state at each stop on the way; the diplomatic corps in carriages painted with the arms of every nation in Europe; and presently the great royal coach, blazoned inside and out with the fleur-de-lys, through the window of which may be seen the pink face and broad bosom of the expedition's commander-in-chief.

She has been through desperate times, but not a sign of them shows in an additional wrinkle or grey hair; she is plumper and healthier than ever, more cheerfully optimistic, fuller of dazzling schemes like the one on which she is now embarked. Just two years ago she fled in terror through these very gates of Fontainebleau while Paris hysterically welcomed the Duke of Guise as his country's saviour. The Triumvirate followed her, carried off Charles and Anjou to give their quarrel the colour of the royal authority, bare minutes before Condé, to whom she had in her panic appealed for protection, came galloping into the courtyard at the head of his Huguenots. By then she, too, was on the road back to the capital with her sons and their captors, the little King weeping bitterly in the belief that he was being taken to prison. (Poor lad, he had not had much fun out of being king so far: at his coronation the previous May he had cried from misery at the length of the ceremony and the weight of his crown and robes... helplessly bullied and his kingdom torn in two, he had every reason to cry again.) As the price of being allowed to remain with her children, Catherine was compelled to denounce Condé publicly as a rebel; he retaliated by publishing the letters in which she had summoned him to her assistance; and so, bound hand and foot to one side, the false friend who had betrayed the other, she was plainly doomed whichever side won. Yet here she rides undisputed mistress of the kingdom she is about to survey.

All in all this is the happiest day of her life. Not only Charles, but Margot and Henry (for she has renamed her favourite after his father), are with her, the two younger for good and not, as in their childhood, on a fleeting visit. Soon she will have sight of her first grandchild, Claude's new son, and presently of her darling Elizabeth, soon also to be a mother, whom she has not seen for over four years. Her bulging eyes sparkle as they peer ahead to the column winding for miles to the east, since she adores a brave show and even she has never arranged a braver....

Certain familiar figures are missing from that column as a result of the recent war. While she ran around vainly striving for peace to save herself, they went on eliminating one another for her sole benefit... Navarre, Saint-André, Guise: her astonishing luck, craftier than she, stronger than they, had again seen her through.

She still misses Antoine; he had been a friendly, even useful, sort of enemy. During the siege of Rouen when he commanded the royal forces (for he had gone over to the Triumvirate, after all), he was wounded in the shoulder. To be on the safe side he called in a Catholic and a Huguenot doctor, who nevertheless managed to arrive at a common diagnosis that the wound was not serious. On this assurance the patient, though in great pain, collected his cronies and prepared to make one long party of his convalescence. Fever set in and the doctors ordered intervals of quiet. He whiled them away discoursing to Mademoiselle de Rouet of the high state they would keep in Sardinia or possibly the Barbary Coast. Gangrene developed and he learned that he was going to die. At this news he sent for a Catholic priest and a Huguenot minister, unable even in this ultimate emergency quite to make up his mind. And then he died, with Mademoiselle de Rouet on one side of him to appreciate his final joke, and on the other, to receive some excellent parental advice, the little Henry who looked so absurdly like him and would one day do all that he had ever talked of doing and far greater things besides.

Two only of the great lords are left to serve the Queen Mother as adjutants in her campaign, Condé and the old Constable, riding in that order with their retainers at the head of the second section. They owe their survival to the fortunes of a strange battle where they commanded the opposing armies and got themselves captured in rapid exchange. In the same battle Saint-André was killed, leaving Guise as sole chieftain of the Catholic cause.... He went forth to exterminate the Huguenots in their last stronghold, Orleans, and so make himself absolute dictator of France. It came very near: Orleans was tottering, deserters coming over to him in a steady stream; among them a young man named Poltrot de Méré, a relative of La Renaudie, the dead leader of the Tumult of Amboise — who at the first opportunity avenged his kinsman and the Protestant cause with a fatal shot in the Duke's back from behind a hedge. So with nearly every leader on both sides dead or a prisoner, the Queen Mother entered upon her powers again: and as a first step to guard them had Charles proclaimed of age at thirteen, by virtue of a forgotten precedent; whereat Charles begged her, in a moving speech of her own composition, to administer his realm as his other self.

No Guise adorns the brilliant column. The clan has sworn a blood-feud upon Coligny and his family in the conviction that the Admiral secretly instigated the Duke's murder;[1] and though Catherine, by the exercise of her now overwhelming prestige, has managed to bind both parties to keep the peace for a term of years, she sensibly decided not to expose them to temptation by throwing them into one another's company. Who would have dreamed that the amiable and determined peacemaker would herself deliberately unloose that blood-feud a few years hence as a prelude to unnameable horrors?

Yet, if one ignores the beaming content that the lucky issue of her troubles has stamped with seeming permanence on

---

[1] Poltrot had accused the Admiral under torture, recanted, retracted, and died exculpating him. The trial and execution having been hurried on in the midst of the civil war owing to the revengeful ferocity of the Paris mob against their idol's murderer, it had not been possible to confront accuser and accused, as Coligny requested. He admitted with characteristic candour that the assassin had approached him, that he had dismissed the proposal as the vapourings of an imbecile, but that he considered the Duke's death 'the greatest of blessings to my family and to France.'

Catherine's exterior and looks deep, very deep into the change that time has made in her character, one will be less unprepared for anything she may do given the circumstances. She remembers with too vivid anguish how near she came to losing her power, has found its recovery too sweet, to conceive life again possible without it: 'I had rather die,' she frankly admits. She has quite lost the humble wonder, expressed in her letter to Elizabeth at Francis's death, that God had thought fit to vest her with authority for her children's sake. In its place rules the unshakeable conviction, reinforced by her astounding luck, that He means her to hold on to that authority whatever happens and by whatever means; and against anybody... including her children.

Often she glances behind at the carriages immediately following and her heart leaps at the contrast between herself pleading to be admitted into the ranks of her father-in-law's ladies and herself now — the sun round whom an even fairer constellation revolves. Those dainty little coaches lined with brocaded silks, like wonderful bonbon-boxes, contain the maids of honour — eighty giggling, chattering young beauties fluttering perfumed lace handkerchiefs against the dust and holding little velvet half-masks before their eyes to protect them from the sun. The flying squadron — mostly daughters of the smaller landed gentry, brought up to prospects of a humdrum marriage with a neighbour, many children and a great deal of good works; now, thanks to the Queen Mother's fondness for pleasing faces and lively tongues about her, granted lives full of variety, handsome clothes, and opportunities to catch good husbands. Though for a select number there is other occupation as well, such as Mademoiselle de Rouet, or blue-eyed, golden-haired Isabel de Limeuil, whom Catherine has awarded to the Prince of Condé for good behaviour in withdrawing his claim to his late brother's office of Lieutenant-General.

Bringing up the rear of the procession is the supply train.

Waggons bearing arches for triumphal entries into towns, silver and gold plate for banquets, painted barges for use on navigable streams when horse transport palls, a thousand rare and ingenious contrivances for entertainment on land and water. Court furnishers jog along on their donkeys, beside movable shops ready to be pitched at a moment's notice for the sale of gloves, fans, laces, cosmetics, whatever their patrons may run short of — a Rue de la Paix on wheels. Last of all stride in mournful or comic dignity the lions, tigers, bears, and camels to draw the gilded and sculptured chariots for the spectacular entrance of the challengers into the tourneys. The one sort of provision lacking is food, since this picturesque army expects to live on the country; and many a citizen, coming out to hurrah and gape as it enters his village, will mutter ten thousand curses on it before it passes on.

There is a long stop at Troyes to conclude a peace with the English (whom the Huguenots called to their help in the late war and whom Catherine subsequently drove out to make herself temporarily the national heroine), and the daughter of Florentine bankers triumphantly out-haggles Elizabeth, great-granddaughter of a Lord Mayor of London. During the attendant festivities Mademoiselle de Limeuil nearly breaks up a ball through being seized with labour pains and giving birth in an anteroom to a 'fine splendid boy' — an event which Condé hails with transports of fatherly though quite mistaken delight. On May first Catherine embraces Claude at Bar-le-Duc and Charles holds his nephew, the future Duke of Lorraine, at the baptismal font. Then, with much clanking of harness and creaking of wheels, the eight thousand horses are again yoked or saddled, the dogs bay, the menagerie roars, and the cavalcade sets off for the farthermost corner of France where the Pyrenees run down to the sea.

In all two years are spent on the journey. Long before the end tempers begin to give out and also funds; the Queen

Mother cheerfully pawns her jewels and sends home various retainers who, sick of the sight of one another's faces, come to blows. She has to sleep on the floor of abandoned monasteries; flee from Lyons because of the plague, to her ladies' infinite disappointment, since the town is a hive of rich Italian bankers, Catherine's protégés; submit to a damp rescue when an overloaded barge founders in the Rhone during a storm, drowning a number of her suite. Undaunted she proceeds; a hunter of big game must not be put off by flea-bites.

At Valence she learns that Elizabeth has given birth to stillborn twins; she is unhappy for her daughter and grieved that she will not behold, as she had hoped, her grandchildren of Spain, but, as she writes philosophically, 'you are young — and better luck next time.' Still worse news follows: her son-in-law, afraid of rousing suspicion amongst his Protestant Dutch, refuses to meet her. For a few weeks she is suspended without a purpose, till Philip relents so far as to allow his wife and the Duke of Alba, his first minister, to keep the tryst. Ignoring the plain lesson to be read in the King of Spain's caution, Catherine consoles herself with the thought that Elizabeth and Alba may be more amenable than her gloomy son-in-law. Why did not Nostradamus, whom she stopped to see at his home, Saint-Remy in Provence, warn her of her error? Perhaps he did, but in words that made 'as ambiguous as a prophecy of Nostradamus' a contemporary proverb.

Usually the King, Anjou, and Margot ride separately with their own households; and often Catherine, bored with her carriage, changes into the saddle. (Though it is not every horse that can carry her now. In ordering two new hacks from her ambassador in Venice, 'because I have worn out most of mine on this voyage,' she added frankly in a postscript, 'Above all they must be strong.' Her body is black and blue from her falls and her face wears a permanent 'sheep's mark,' as she described it with utmost good-humour, yet she never

Interlude on the Way

thinks of giving up.) Not infrequently, however, the children join their mother in the great coach adorned with the fleur-de-lys: and on those occasions the procession adds another, and not the least remarkable, to its many odd sights. For the four together have extraordinarily the air of three young aristocrats on an outing with their governess. Or three bright-plumed cygnets dutifully paddling to market in the wake of a noisily proud plump black duck.

Even in the neutral simplicity of her mourning, Catherine looks like the relict of a prosperous merchant; even in rags the features and bearing of her three companions would betray their high origin. Her voice is loud, her speech ungrammatical and thickly foreign in accent after all her years in France, she agitates her hands (fine white hands, surprisingly, of which she is childishly vain) and whole body for emphasis when she talks. Charles's voice is gruff, Margot's manner vivacious, but both reveal a cultivated refinement in every gesture, look, word — as for Anjou, beside him ordinary princes seem commoners. While the thoughts the passing scene evokes in the three sleek young heads are so different from any of which the fond matron in charge of them is capable as to be quite beyond her understanding.

Charles, a little nearer the earth and his mother than his two juniors, sees good hunting of stag and boar in the forests and plains through which they ride. But he also observes the terrible havoc left by the late war, the charred houses and gaunt ruins of churches, and vows that when he is old enough to rule such things shall not happen. Alternately he has visions of himself leading armies across some such countryside against France's enemies, in the manner of his father and grandfather. His keenest memory of this whole voyage is the sudden deep snowfall at Carcassonne, which furnished the occasion of a glorious snow fight, with elaborate fortifications and inexhaustible ammunition, between two sides, of which he captained one to victory.

It is harder to know what Anjou thinks, because his thoughts are not of the sort that easily find words at thirteen. The ironic wit hinted at in the corners of his sensitive mouth is not yet ready for expression, nor is his the nature to allow him to say a thing unless he can say it well. Only in later years will the man, remembering this journey, reveal what the boy observed. In a phrase now and then from a verse or a letter recalling the fields golden with corn and the vine-rows marching in green and purple files up the hillsides. For Henry's heart is not a straightforward soldier's, like Charles's, but a poet's seeking against prohibitive obstacles to find itself.

Eleven-year-old Margot, her head full of her history and geography books, excitedly notes resemblances in the changing landscape to the Attica of Themistocles (which is, of course, much more real) or wonders whether it differs greatly from that puzzling area marked on her maps as *Terra Incognita*. Then, being a healthy young female, she speculates on what gowns Elizabeth will wear, for the Queen of Spain is said to have the most magnificent on earth and never to appear in the same one twice; and weaves a romance about the sister who has become a misty legend. Margot has not Henry's mind, hers being more active than his and less subtle, but she is in many ways near him in spirit; too near for their happiness....

Catherine, when she takes time to observe the landscape at all — for being an industrious and conscientious soul she often has with her a secretary to whom she dictates letters until the poor fellow topples over with fatigue and has to be replaced by another — diverts herself with selecting building sites. She cannot see an attractive piece of ground without wanting to put a house on it; or if there already is a house she itches to pull it about and surround it with a formal garden full of avenues of trees and lawns sprinkled with majolica gargoyles. She has already started adding to the Louvre, improving Blois, and creating for her private use the Tuileries. During the current progress, full as she is of schemes and business, she nevertheless manages to buy an orange grove near Hyères and an old farmhouse elsewhere, paying a deposit on the purchase price (which she will afterward have to forfeit) and writing her cousin Duke Cosimo to send her some experienced farmers, since she is determined as soon as her children are settled to take up the simple life. Meantime she has the fun of adding the new houses to her already considerable collection.

But then she has a mania for collecting everything — books in languages she cannot read on subjects in which she has no particle of interest; furniture, glass, tapestries, bric-à-brac, in fact any movable species of object until she grows tired of it and turns to something else. Only to one hobby will she always remain faithful, her collection of portraits of her family and friends and of those unknown brothers and sisters united to her by the mystic bond of kingship. The artists as well as the astrologers have reason to thank their stars for the Queen Mother. She commissions their works by the dozen, pays generously, and makes no other aesthetic demand than an accurate and pleasing likeness of her sitters. In this last representative of the Medici the temperament of that versatile stock has at last boiled down again to its original middle-class essence.

Chapter VI

THE GREAT MATRIARCHY

ON A TORRID June day, fifteen months after leaving Fontainebleau, Catherine stood on a bank of the little river marking the international boundary waiting for Elizabeth to cross over to her as by the protocols arranged; but, unable to bear another ten minutes' delay, she put off in a small boat and the joyous meeting took place precariously in midstream. Endless caresses and many tears both of joy and sorrow. Elizabeth wept for the children she had longed to place in their grandmother's arms and Catherine to see her daughter so feeble still from her illness and sorrow. The mother recovered first: for as they disembarked together on the French side, a sigh went up from the waiting throng at sight of her daughter's queenly beauty, and the practical matron reflected that the possibility of further children was anything but remote.

Why had she come those thousand miles and more, through freezing cold and choking heat, discomfort, dust, and flood, pouring out her own money and that of an already overburdened people, leaving behind her a dangerously unsettled country? To obtain the eldest daughter of the Holy Roman Emperor for Charles, Don Carlos for Margot so that whatever happened to Philip Spain might not be lost to the family, above all to marry Anjou, her *délice*, the apple of her eye, to Philip's sister, the dowager Princess of Portugal, and induce her son-in-law to carve an estate for him out of Spain's vast dominions.

An ambition may be selfish and yet possess grandeur; what made Catherine's merely preposterous was its banal vulgarity. The impulse behind her dynastic greed was nothing more or less than a driving and ravenous snobbery. She would pore for hours over her maternal genealogy because it alleged a king somewhere in its remoter branches and imposed it as an article of public faith that the Medici were ancient Gaulish conquerors of Media who had quitted Asia Minor for Italy in the fourth century before Christ. Despite her rise in the world, she never succeeded in shaking off the traditional Florentine awe of the Habsburgs, before whose glory her native Guelf city had prostrated itself for so many generations. It was with a barely concealed sense of inferiority that she tendered her children, upon whom sat so easy a pride of race, to the House of which Philip and his cousin of Austria were the twin heads; in the very spirit of a social climber, caring little how much she grovelled, only how much she would have to give.

She had a hard customer to deal with. Philip was not the man to part lightly with what was his: he had already engaged Don Carlos to his cousin the Holy Roman Emperor's daughter in order to keep their marriage portions in the family. No thoughts of love, or courtship and marriage either, had induced him to send his wife and his first minister to Bayonne, but the hope of persuading his mother-in-law, by threats if necessary, to do what he conceived to be her plain duty: revoke the Edict of Pacification, accept the decrees of the Council of Trent,[1] and thus finish off Huguenotry in her realm for good.

---

[1] The reactionary forces in the Church had prevailed at Trent, and the Council, despite many reforms of abuses, had left the fundamental dogmatic complaints of the Protestants unanswered.

Catherine simply would not, could not believe that he meant it. How could anyone fail to see that if there were Valois on all thrones all Christendom must obviously live at peace forevermore? For peace would then simply be a matter of the matriarch keeping her own children from quarrelling with one another — a feat of which in her innocence (and their present state of it) she felt herself amply capable. For hours on end during the next three weeks she sat closeted or walked in the garden with Alba — a tall, fierce, silver-bearded figure from El Greco's brush — or Elizabeth or both, pleading, arguing, swearing large vague promises that religion should be seen to when her heart's desire was accomplished. The Duke murmured that she was putting the cart before the horse: off with the heads of such trouble-makers as Condé, Coligny, and his brother Dandelot... with such exhibits of good faith Philip might conceivably welcome closer matrimonial relations... certainly not before. Catherine considered the suggestion, concluded that it was impracticable, and filed it away in her mind without comment.

She had no better luck with Elizabeth. The girl was gentle and deferential as ever, but firm as Alba himself; even in her disappointment Catherine shone with pride at her daughter's skill in this tortuous game of diplomacy. 'You have become very Spanish, my daughter,' protested Catherine sorrowfully. It was true, but how often had not Catherine urged her to be an obedient wife to Philip for her little brothers' and sister's sakes; she could not have it both ways. 'Oh, please, my daughter...' the mother was finally reduced to exclaiming over and over, in her efforts to make her child realize that the greatness of her father's House, her very duty to God, positively required her to bring about those marriages. Elizabeth wept, but stood her ground: could not her mother see that she had no right to set conditions, even her children's welfare, upon *her* duty to God and His Church?

Catherine reshuffled her cards. Revoke the Edict of Pacification or accept the decrees of Trent she dared not, since France would have been ablaze in an instant. But there might be other ways of giving Philip what he wanted in return for what she wanted. She proposed a League, a Catholic League, its cornerstone to be her children's marriages, its immediate object a joint expedition with Philip against the Turks, its ultimate aim the extermination of the new religion throughout Europe, including France. It did not matter to the infatuated matron that France had an old and valuable alliance with the Sultan; she would not have spurned an advantage to her children from the Grand Turk himself — and in fact at that very moment was weighing Suleiman the Magnificent's offer of his daughter and a substantial dowry for Anjou — just in case... It did not even matter to her that the League would commit her to the very persecution she had always avoided and France to a general war that could bring it no benefit; nor that the one enemy whom France had decent cause to fight was the Spain who was threatening her internal peace and strangling her growth: who that very year nailed to the gibbet the first French settlers in the New World. Nothing mattered beside her obsession; the Great Matriarchy had taken so firm a root in her determined, shallow soul that it would have been hard to say which was the obsession and which the soul.

Yet Philip showed no hurry to close even with an offer so dazzling. 'I cannot trust her...' he noted in his precise hand; 'neither her Leagues nor her marriages.' This was the answer which, suitably wrapped, was handed to Catherine by Alba before they parted. A really ironclad infatuation is the best of all buffers for the self-esteem. How could anyone really mistrust the intentions of a good mother? Philip was a little coy, that was all: Elizabeth would no doubt talk him round to the League in time... and she herself might presently be in a position to improve her offer.... In this wise Catherine reflected as she took farewell of her daughter (neither suspecting that it was forever), and with as much optimism as she had started led her travel-stained cortège home again.

One item did not appear in Catherine's accounts for the expenses of the voyage to Bayonne — the natural construction put by a suspicious world on her long secret conclaves with Philip's Queen and His Catholic Majesty's celebrated man of blood. Nothing she could ever do for the Huguenots again would make them believe they had not been sold to pay for her children's marriage portions....

Untroubled by such subtleties Catherine once more took up the pursuit of the elusive formula which should painlessly transform stubborn Huguenots into acceptable Catholics. The old laws having failed to achieve the miracle, she cheerfully drew up new ones: excellent laws passed to please one side and left unenforced so as to please the other. The Guises and Coligny were brought together again and made to renew their oath of reconciliation; though Catherine suffered an unexpected repulse in following up her victory when the flying squadron fell back defeated from an assault upon the Admiral's Calvinist morality. Her reports to Elizabeth indicated that she was making progress, would soon have France in shape for the most searching catechism: 'Thank God, everything is as peaceful as we could wish.' Whereupon a new civil war broke out most perversely and spread with disconcerting instantaneousness into Philip's Netherlands. It appeared that the inhabitants of Europe had other preoccupations besides good matches for Catherine's children.

The war began with another attempt by Condé, uninvited this time, to kidnap the King; though more serious than the first one, it failed because the Queen Mother called out the Swiss mercenaries to beat it off. The incident was significant: no longer was Catherine neutral between the parties, seeking only the quickest possible peace. She had begun, though unconsciously as yet, to play with the idea of crushing the

Huguenots once and for all, of standing forth as a Catholic champion for the sake of those coveted Habsburg marriages. The temptation was all the stronger since such a policy seemed less dangerous than at the beginning of her Regency. Guise was dead, his heir a boy, and the ultra-Catholic party without a strong leader; Condé and Coligny were only too much alive. Nor were the Queen Mother's personal sentiments to the Reformers as friendly as they had once been. They had passed out of fashion, the polite world no longer affected their ideas as a sort of intellectual liberalism nor diverted itself with their hymns as a kind of aesthetic novelty. They had become a grim reality, a party of opposition critical even of the monarchy, gathering three adherents to their discontents for every convert to their creed. A fine gratitude, in Catherine's indignant estimation, for all the kindness she had shown them.

The war dragged on. Condé besieged Paris and was driven off at the battle of Saint-Denis, when the old Constable ended his long service to France after accounting with his own sword for a heap of antagonists fifty and more years younger than himself. Catherine immediately made the seventeen-year-old Anjou commander-in-chief in his place with the title of Lieutenant-General of the Realm, both to forestall the Guises in the leadership of the Catholic forces and to enhance his matrimonial value abroad. Before he could win his spurs, Catholic and Protestant, still capable of horror at the misery their quarrel was bringing in the country, agreed to make another effort at a peaceable solution. While the truce was in force, Catherine attempted to have Condé and Coligny kidnapped — a new style of adventure for her. She failed, because the man charged with the enterprise, the Marshal Tavannes, Anjou's chief of staff, let the pair slip through his fingers in chivalrous disgust, but her act of treachery finished the Queen Mother for the time being with the Huguenots. The war broke out again with increased fury, and the disappointed matriarch had to put off her quest to a more propitious time.

Before that time came both she and the quest together suffered the cruellest of possible blows. One morning, in the autumn of 1568, she tottered from a sick-bed to the Council Chamber for an important meeting on the conduct of the war. The Council were already assembled, the King in his place as she crossed the threshold — and halted there abruptly as they dropped their eyes before her. What had happened? No one answered. Anjou — who had just left for the front? A fit of trembling seized her and she sank into a chair. Someone behind her muttered a few words in Spanish, she wheeled sharply around. Elizabeth! For weeks she had had a premonition that the girl's confinement would turn out badly. But it was impossible... She had been safely delivered of two daughters in the past two years... And then Charles, who had known the truth since late the previous night and reserved the sad duty for himself, told her that Elizabeth was dead.

The best and the deepest in Catherine — they were sometimes the same and sometimes very different — came out in the next few hours. 'Gentlemen,' she said quietly, 'God has taken away all my hopes in this world...' and without a sob or tear directed the meeting to begin. Only after the more urgent business had been disposed of did she retire to her own room and the solitary company of her sorrow. To weep over Elizabeth, so young and lovely... from whose body she had so eagerly hoped for an heir to Spain and the Indies, for Carlos had died three months before... The support of her dreams for her old age... 'always the best and dearest of daughters to me.'... Two hours later Catherine reappeared in the Council Chamber with the crisp announcement that 'The King of Spain cannot remain a widower. I have only one desire, to see my daughter Marguerite in her place.' Nor did she resign that desire even when she came to half-believe that Philip had poisoned Elizabeth out of jealousy born of the fact that she alone had been able to soothe the poor lunatic Carlos in his deliriums.

There was no mistaking the change in Catherine now. Often she talked and acted as if another woman had taken possession of her body. Patience, caution, moderation went overboard as the sense of power grew more ravenous and opposition continued to frustrate her ambitions. 'Moderation!' she snapped at her great Chancellor. 'It is your moderation that has brought us where we are,' and without a scruple sacrificed him to the hostility of the Cardinal of Lorraine.[1] Death haunted her thoughts: fear of it for herself and her loved ones before her schemes were matured, an unsuppressed craving to see it strike down those who opposed her. 'We have just been rejoiced to hear of the death of So-and-so,' she could announce exultantly when one of her adversaries disappeared: they could not die fast enough for her. Alba had not altogether wasted his hint.

In her eagerness to hasten her enemies' deaths, she had resort again to her old friends the magicians. She hired an Italian necromancer who, with the aid of a moulder imported from Strasbourg, cast life-sized bronze statues of Condé, Coligny, and Dandelot in a laboratory specially fitted up at the Queen Mother's expense in Paris. Every day for six months, while the Italian studied the horoscopes of the doomed men with his astrolabe, the assistant turned and unturned screws in the sides of their effigies to make them sicken and die. Dandelot (who had long been ailing) gave up the ghost without resistance. Condé, crippled from a horse's kick (a cunning turn of the screw, that), dashed in to save his side at the battle of Jarnac in March, 1569, crying, 'Nobles of France! Observe the state in which Louis of Bourbon enters battle for Christ

---

[1] L'Hôpital had never departed from his and Catherine's first policy of toleration: despite the turmoil of the civil wars he carried through administrative reforms that were to last to the Revolution of 1789 and are by far the finest achievement of her Regency.

and his country!' fell from his horse and was treacherously shot from behind. Coligny still held out, however, though the magician positively reported the same morbid symptoms in his statue as those that had heralded the decease of his two colleagues; but he turned out this time to be mistaken and his client had presently to see to the Admiral herself....

It is little wonder that Catherine was becoming sinister. Wizards or no, those who stood in her way had an extraordinary tendency to die young. First the Dauphin Francis, the obstacle to her husband's succession, and his younger brother Charles who, had he lived, would have been the natural Regent in her place; her own eldest son at a critical moment, and her rivals Navarre and Guise; now Condé and the gallant Dandelot and a German duke who perished from overeating while bringing reinforcements to the Huguenots. The coincidences were too striking: and many saw the Queen Mother's perpetual black no longer as a symbol of mourning but as the livery of evil.

The third civil war ended, as had the other two, in a draw. There was no other way for it to end if anything was to be left of France. But it was not by the Queen Mother's will that a peace was made in August of 1570, for she opposed it with all her art, against the advice even of her Catholic ministers; it was the young King himself who commanded a new Edict of Pacification to avoid the further shedding of his subjects' blood. Time and nature have crept up on Catherine almost unawares, introducing a new and serious complication into her management of her children's estate — the children themselves, now grown up. Henceforth she will have to reckon with the fact that the good she desires for them may be quite different from what they will choose for themselves, may even be fatally irreconcilable.... She cannot, like other parents, make the struggle to rule their lives and retire to her own if she loses: she has no other but theirs. Nor as Queen Mother has she any position by right or law, nothing but what she can make for herself through her wits, her energy, and the filial devotion of her royal brood. To keep her power — for their sake, of course; who can doubt it? — against any who may rise to challenge it, she must still be ready to lie, scheme, kill if necessary....

BOOK III

CHARLES

Set in the midst of evil, we must needs do evil too.
SOPHOCLES, *Electra*

Chapter VII

THE CHILDREN

THE most striking collective fact pertaining to the children of Catherine and Henry was that practically nothing had been overlooked which might ensure their discomfiture in this world or their damnation in the next. To give them existence at all, Nature had achieved the improbable feat of blending two thoroughly decadent and worn-out stocks. Syphilis, the Black Pest of the early sixteenth century, had ravaged, and an obscure phthisical debility (perhaps derived from it) wasted away the unresisting bodies of grandfathers, uncles, and cousins on both sides; not a Medici of Catherine's generation nor a Valois of Henry's, they two excepted, had lived to see thirty. Heredity, passing on down, had already accounted for Francis at seventeen and Elizabeth at twenty-three, staked its claim on the twisted bodies of Charles, Claude, and Alençon, and even registered its impress upon Anjou and Margot in nerves as taut as lute-strings.

Their early environment was planned by their mother (with the initial collaboration of their father's mistress) according to the same formula that she applied to the government of their realm — a minute attention to detail combined with a total absence of principle. Nothing was omitted from the daily curriculum that would contribute to the improvement of their minds and bodies, nothing included that might indicate their having souls. Under Catherine's vigilant supervision they were drilled in the humanities, arts and graces, all the various accomplishments she had so enviously admired at Francis I's court; neither by word nor even less by precept were those budding young minds instructed in such things as honour, self-control, or even common, everyday piety.

Not that Catherine was silent upon these topics. She penned eloquent though unparsable rules of conduct for her young from the moment they could read, and declaimed lengthy homilies, with no other punctuation than the emphatic beat of her plump white hand, almost as soon as they could listen. But the virtues she inculcated had nothing to do with their moral or spiritual betterment; they were designed solely to assist the little princes and princesses to hold their own in a sadly unscrupulous world. 'Trust nobody but your mother without reservation; show no man or woman favour without equivalent return; conceal the truth and your feelings (except, again of course, from your mother) when to reveal them would serve no useful purpose; lie gracefully and convincingly when your family's or individual interests may be furthered thereby.' And to make sure that her pupils properly understood her instructions she set her spies to watch and report. They lurked in the schoolroom, amongst Charles's and Elizabeth's intimate attendants; and the moment any child showed symptoms of indulging a dangerously disinterested, merely human affection, down came the maternal reprimand with the suddenness of a thunderclap.

Perhaps the greatest danger in that one-sided discipline was its neglect of such natural good qualities as these children possessed. They were ardent, imaginative, generous — virtues which, if carried to excess by private persons, the police could be called in to check before they incommoded the public; but against which in princes, for whose caprices and extravagances a whole nation might suffer, no defence was available except the somewhat drastic one of insurrection or homicide. Catherine never pointed out this simple distinction because she never grasped it herself. It remained a lifelong puzzle to the whole family that just such impulses of generosity as pouring out the revenues on deserving friends could bring the evil it did to themselves and everybody else.

The royal adolescents entered upon a world which contained no surprises; a world in which greed, if not immediately visible, could always be found by stripping off enough layers of deceit. Even in their relations to one another they knew they must forever put away childish affections and quarrels and reconciliations like outgrown toys and regulate their dealings amongst themselves on a basis of unsleeping suspicion. They had no choice in the matter; each must hack out a place at the expense of the others if he or she wanted a place at all. The necessity of their positions drove them, the variety of their temperaments compelled them — and there was an abundance of people with motives of money or place to keep reminding them.

Charles was King, nominally lord and master of them all, yet he was fiercely jealous of Anjou. Poor Charles knew only too well that the world rated his brother higher than himself and would consider it no great loss if he were to die so that Anjou might succeed him; even his mother, whose partiality for her favourite son was a secret torment to him. When he regarded his own ungainly body, he could not help hating Anjou's slim grace, all the more that Anjou seemed so maddeningly indifferent to it. Above all he hated him for having stolen his career.

It was the irony of his fate that the death of his elder brother Francis, who also had not wanted to be a king, had prevented Charles from becoming a soldier. He had been trained to arms by his father almost from the cradle, with a general for his first tutor. When Catherine gave the command of the royal army to Anjou, the King implored to be allowed to go instead, crying that his life was of no greater importance to France than his brother's, who would remain to succeed him if he were killed. But Catherine had her own plans for all her children, and patiently explained to Charles that it would not look right for him to lead troops against his own subjects. He had to content himself with fighting battles in his reveries — one night as his gentlemen were undressing him he pointed to a birthmark on his shoulder and instructed them to take note of it so that his dead body might be identified when picked up on the field of honour. In hungry misery he read the bulletins of Anjou's victories against the Huguenots in 1569, and when the court poets wrote their stale verses in honour of the 'King Victorious,' he turned on them bitterly with 'Don't bother writing your lies and flattery for me. Save them for my brother, he'll cut you a better pattern.'

With the whole world around him serene, he would yet have been at war with himself. Every part of him, body and soul, was at odds with every other. A large handsome head sat askew upon a feeble neck, muscular arms dropped from deeply bowed shoulders, a powerful trunk overburdened a pair of long thin rickety legs. Pleasant of manner and easy of speech, an innate shyness and the face permanently twisted away from his listener nevertheless gave an impression of indifference and evasiveness, while the intelligence and sympathy that readily lit his brown eyes could be veiled only too quickly by a brooding melancholy or erased by blind anger.

His temper was terrifying, to himself as much as to anybody. If kept waiting a moment he raved, if crossed in anything the palace rang with profane allusions to the blood and body of his Saviour or the more private members of the lesser saints — to the horror of his mother, who deplored rude language in any form. Once his schoolfellow the young Duke of Guise began playfully thrusting at him with a blunt pike used for opening windows. Charles ordered him to stop; when

CHARLES IX

the Duke persisted, the King flashed out his sword and only Guise's strong swift legs saved his blond head from being split in two. After such outbursts Charles would fall to weeping, vow the most frightful oaths to control himself thenceforth, sternly forbade himself even the one glass of choice wine he so enjoyed with his dinner; and continued to live in the awful shadow of fear that one day passion would lead him to an act that no remorse could ever repair.

He was mad about hunting, literally mad. He loved the danger, the call upon his strength and nerve, the blood.... When other game was missing, he would set the dogs on grazing cattle or slash away till he was exhausted on deer trapped in nets: the sight of blood seemed to soothe the hysterical violence that possessed him. Only out-of-doors moving at breakneck speed could he both find and run away from himself. Houses he contemptuously called 'the sepulchres of the living' and wished he could be condemned to spend all his days in a forest. There he was afraid of nothing: when a fiery phantom appeared in a wood and the other huntsmen ran away in terror, the King pursued it sword in hand till he drove it to ground. Within walls he would hammer out his surplus energies making his own implements for the chase — pikes, guns, swords, horseshoes; or shut himself up for long hours with his secretary to dictate a book (still extant) on the Art of Venery, or verses on the same subject. Then, the black demons exorcised, body and brain exhausted, he would finish his day with music — the art so specially beloved of melancholy violent men.

Henry of Anjou was a still water running deep. On the surface all languid brilliance, in the depths troubled doubt and conflicting possibilities. He could not help knowing what the world and a doting mother expected of his 'heaven's gifts' of brains, wit, and charm, and the knowledge disturbed as well as pleased him. Looking into himself he was not quite certain that he could live up to so much expectation -- nor that he altogether wanted to. Pride and ambition he had in abundance, like other young men of his age and station, but another set of values as well, which tormented him with their constant demand whether the prizes he had been set to win were really worth the winning. The blood of the Medici and the Valois in him loudly answered yes: his own imagination and sense of proportion wondered....

He could no more have shared Charles's single-minded longing for glory than his meaningless violence, Catherine's mania for power than her bustling energy. When sent out by his mother to be a soldier, he made a good one, winning the affection of his men and the praise of his mentor Tavannes. He could in one battle show unthinking cruelty in success, in the next forbid, with ringing voice and flaming eyes, the slaughter and despoiling of prisoners (the victors' immemorial privilege and often their only pay), because 'he would not suffer Frenchmen to kill Frenchmen.' No one, not even his mother, had greater satisfaction in his laurels — not for an instant did they solve the puzzles that were revolving in his head. More than he wanted to win the world he yearned to understand it, and there seemed no way of doing both.

A little vain, a little spoilt, somewhat frightened of his self-knowledge, he did what many sensitive young men of talent have done since the beginning of time — struck an attitude and interposed it as a barrier between himself and the people about him. When alone or with a few intimates, he could be happy in the study of the poets or in the practice of religion; for, ironically, Catherine's favourite son was growing queerly devout. But in public he played the fop and even the fool with reckless abandon. He invented bizarre clothes; strutted about the court casting the spell of his charm 'with those eyes and that mien that no one can resist,' for the mere fun of the thing — making the dull look even duller with his sharp-edged wit; stopped to banter with a clever woman or pull the ear of a pretty one; led a crowd of madcaps out into the street fairs of Paris in disguise to create riot and disorder and knock about his brother's police; then returned to the seclusion of his poetry, his religion, and his own unsatisfactory thoughts. The world began to mutter unpleasant criticisms: he did not care so long as it kept its distance. All of it, that is, but his sister Margot.

Ever since they could remember this brother and sister had held for one another an excitement shared by nobody and nothing else on earth. Isolated by rank from any close intimacy with their inferiors and by temperament from their few available equals, they entered young manhood and womanhood as a little secret society of two from which the rest of humanity was automatically excluded through inability to master the passwords. Each revelled in the other's passion for the original, impatience of the banal; they possessed the power, through a profound attunement of instinct, taste, and associations, to pass thoughts and feelings back and forth as if through some subtle conversation of the nerves alone: a perfection of response that made all other human intercourse by comparison gross and flavourless.

The world drew back before them in tacit acceptance of their unique fitness for one another. If Margot and Henry felt moved to an encounter of wits, the whole court would fall into silence listening — 'for whether in seriousness or gaiety nothing was more entrancing than to hear those two talk when they wished....' As they entered a ballroom, the other dancers would withdraw to watch the brother lead the sister, 'one body, one soul, one will,' through the steps of the Spanish *pavanne*, 'all eyes on them, ravished by the lovely sight... unable to decide whether to admire more the grace of the movement or the dignity of the pauses, representing now gaiety, now a grave and beautiful disdain.' Two radiant young figures creating, against the background of flutes and viols, melodic statuary upon the black and white squares of carpet... conscious, and superbly indifferent.

If in Henry Catherine had borne a changeling, with Margot she had produced a miracle. For to the daughter she had transmitted her own features, yet Margot's was a beauty to take one's breath away. Twice as beautiful as her queenly sister of Spain, men said: a Polish paladin who saw her at the Louvre took a vow on the spot to spend the rest of his days fighting the Turks, since there was nothing left on earth to see. All the rigid convention imposed upon her by duty was no more than a foil for her flaming independence. One day she would appear before the startled eyes of the court in crimson glittering with jewels, her hair a high curling pyramid like her sister of Spain's, as if she had just stepped out of a painting by Coello; barely had the court recovered its breath and the other ladies rushed off to get themselves up likewise when Margot would reappear in a simple white frock with her tresses 'strewn loosely and naturally' down her back, *très première communion*. And the very next day she would turn up in some daring mode exposing her white breasts and her shapely legs — these last another inheritance from her mother. Henry not only encouraged her in such freaks of originality, but emulated them so far as a man could — which in those days was very far indeed. From him also she acquired her taste for books, especially new books, often reading one straight through without food or sleep. But an accomplishment altogether her own was a talent for composing polished little songs which she sang in a voice of quite professional quality to her own accompaniment on the lute.

The love of brother and sister was not of the earth, a thing impossible to fit into any earthly scheme, so it could not last, but it was a pity for both of them that it had to end in the way it did. So long as they were both children, Margot did not perceive or care that she worshipped and he suffered himself to be worshipped; it seemed in the natural order of things that he, the male and the elder, should stand on a footing to her of sole idol and favourite idolatress. But Margot at sixteen, her emotions matured to self-consciousness, could not but demand what Henry at eighteen, with no equivalent emotion to awaken and a man's interests beginning to occupy him, was as little able to comprehend as to grant. And in refusing her the equality she asked, he thoughtlessly inflicted the one unforgivable injury upon her imperious spirit....

It happened on the eve of his departure for the front in the autumn of 1569. He took her aside in the garden at Plessis-lès-Tours on the bank of the Loire to make a secret compact with her. Charles might grow tired of hunting, he explained, be smitten with ambition, desire to substitute men for beasts as his game: being always with their mother, and being King after all, he might prevail upon her to remove his younger brother from his command.... He would rather die, pursued Henry, than suffer such a dishonour. She must lay aside her fear of their mother, keep him in her good memory while he was away. After God, Margot was all he had to trust: and with a smile, he gracefully deposited his fortunes in her hands as if they had been a bouquet of flowers.

Margot promised, joyfully, 'with all my courage to face our mother for your service... and be your other self with her while you are gone.' Meaning that she would be his spy as well as his advocate. And then he went directly to Catherine and told her of their conversation. It may be that he dared trust his sister no more than anyone else; but more likely he hoped to draw together the two women who loved him by their single common interest, and so to overcome Catherine's dislike of Margot and Margot's fear of Catherine through the comfort they could give one another for his absence. Catherine apparently understood it thus, for she at once summoned her youngest daughter and bade her gently to speak without fear in anything that concerned Henry.

And of course Margot, finding that Henry had betrayed their mutual confidence to their mother, leapt to the conclusion that both were mocking her. So Henry made mischief, whatever had been his intention, and there was no time to repair it; while in the end Margot feared her mother no less and Catherine loved her daughter no more. Catherine could not humanly help resenting the fact that the very perfections she most cherished should have been lavished on the child whose strong resemblance to herself emphasized an unflattering disparity; and deeper than that lay her jealousy of her second son, almost like a mistress's. Of such things the mother never spoke, but the daughter felt them none the less.

Meantime Margot's suitors had all reached a state of suspended animation, including the latest, Sebastian of Portugal, whom Catherine had added to the list when Philip showed no indecent haste to marry his dead wife's sister. A daring thought fluttered and took focus before the alert retina of the Cardinal of Lorraine. Margot still a spinster at seventeen... his nephew the Duke of Guise a bachelor... Henry away, winning victories of which Charles was insanely jealous... Margot's husband as the future successor to Anjou in the leadership of the Catholic armies... Not since his brother the late Duke's death had the Cardinal observed an opportunity to do so good a day's work for the clan's drooping fortunes.

To offer the young man formally as a suitor demanded more nerve, however, than the fond uncle possessed. There were too many dangers; Catherine's idolatry of her second son, the fierce Valois pride that might take a murderous turn at Guise presumption. The Cardinal excogitated a better, or at least safer scheme, based upon his extensive first-hand knowledge of the frailties of the flesh. Win the young lady's affections first, ran his advice to his nephew, as he affectionately computed the assets printed by Nature upon the ducal countenance; she is warm-hearted, impulsive, and at a loose end. When you have succeeded, we can present the Queen Mother with the *fait accompli* and trust to her fear of the outraged conventions to do the rest. For the honour of our tribe go in and win.

The Duke set out upon his wooing with the confidence of a man who has known ever since he was breeched that he is the most presentable male in the kingdom. Six feet four in height — 'an oak in the forest of men' — brave as a lion and nearly as strong, he had further to assist him the Guise arrogance and his own lofty conceit. There were not too many brains inside his comely blond skull, but their absence was more than compensated for, at least for such purposes as love, war, and politics, by a gracious affability of demeanour that brought crowds swarming and women swooning at his feet.

He really was handsome, outstanding even amongst that generation of handsome men. His portrait alone proves it: and illustrates as well how the ideal of masculine beauty had changed since the Middle Ages. The strong outlines and rugged planes have given way to an almost effeminate regularity and delicacy of feature; instead of the calm self-confidence looking out of those earlier eyes, one is struck by a puzzled uncertainty, a grave distrust... the expression with which men scrutinized their fellows in the late sixteenth century. At least men in high place.

The first part of the Cardinal's plan went forward swimmingly. Once upon a time Margot had not looked with any favour upon young Guise: when her father Henry II had teasingly offered the lad to her as cavalier servant, the seven-years-old spitfire shook her curls with a determined 'No! He's never happy unless he's doing somebody a bad turn and he always wants to be master.' But circumstances and Guise were both different now. She was burning to do some act of spite on Henry for his frivolous breach of their secret compact. She was also bored; she had not the least desire 'to go to Portugal and eat figs.' Guise was devoted, adoring — genuinely so, to his own surprise — and it was extremely agreeable to see the arrogance melt out of his blue eyes as they sought to placate her capricious brown ones. Not being the sort to do things by halves, she took him for a lover.

Catherine's spy system had evidently broken down, possibly because Madame Curtin, Margot's governess, adored the daughter more than she feared the mother. The first news of the intrigue came to Henry, laying siege to the town of Saint-Jean d'Angeli in the south, through the good offices of his dependent and friend — and hence Margot's enemy — Louis de Bérenger, the Sieur du Guast.

What Henry felt he said neither then nor ever; it was not his way. However much he yearned to punish his sister and her lover, he was first of all Catherine's son, disciplined to place the family's welfare before private revenge. Unless the affair were hushed Margot would be compromised, Catherine's schemes for her and them all imperilled. He waited until his mother, who could never bear to have him long out of her sight, paid him a visit in camp, bringing along Charles and Margot, and then he told her. Only in her brother's freezing courtesy, her mother's cruel slights, had Margot any reason for guessing that her secret was discovered. She fell ill of sheer nerves. Henry lingered by her bedside day and night, anxious but silent. She tried to drive him away with taunts of 'Hypocrite!'

The Cardinal guessed, too, on Catherine's return: he had only to watch how Catherine treated his nephew, for she was a genius at killing by pin-pricks. 'Your eldest son is in grave trouble here,' he wrote sorrowfully to his sister-in-law, 'and you and I will catch our share of it, though no one breathes a word of it yet. Never have I seen a longer or more cruel anger.' He could plan the strategy, but not fight the battle; as always at the first smell of danger, he turned and fled from court.

It was the worst thing he could have done. Staying, he still had his weapon of blackmail; fleeing, he not only flung it away, but made exposure certain. Though Catherine stuck pins into young Guise, she would rather have been torn by hot pincers herself, once the intrigue was nipped, than let a scandal get abroad to depreciate her daughter's marital value. The Cardinal's flight took matters out of her capable hands, set tongues a-wagging, sent a rumour creeping up the back stairs of the Louvre to the King's ears — and Charles went mad. The upstart Guises to sully the honour of the Valois... fling their arrogance once again, as they had been doing for two generations, into the face of the House that had made them!... He rolled on the floor, tearing his hair, screaming curses....

At five o'clock in the morning he burst into Catherine's room, woke her and demanded to know the truth. There was no standing against him in that mood: in a few seconds she had blurted it out. Turning to the Gentleman of the Bedchamber who accompanied him, the Count de Retz, Charles despatched him to fetch Margot forthwith. She came in with her hair down her back and a robe lightly flung over her shoulders, followed by Madame de Retz, whom the Count had roused and brought along with some vague hope that her presence might act as a restraint. Charles ordered her back to her room, directed her husband to keep watch outside the door, then flung his sister on the floor and beat her till she was senseless, Catherine showing her sympathy by lending an occasional hand. Suddenly the King left off and flung out in an agony of exhaustion and remorse — for in his own way he loved his sister. Catherine, poignantly mindful that her daughter must not be seen in such a condition, gave a solicitous hour to repairing her toilet and dressing her wounds.

Then, like sensible women, they joined forces to save whatever was left to save. In the morning Charles sent for Angoulême, his bastard half-brother by the pretty Scotswoman, and handed him two swords with instructions to use one on Guise or the other on himself. Angoulême, indisposed to either method of suicide (for Guise was a noted swordsman), dallied. Meantime a frantic letter from Margot to her sister Claude resulted in Claude's husband, head of the House of

Lorraine, recalling Guise to his own country; while Claude herself, with the young man's mother, hurried to Catherine and patched up an arrangement for saving everybody's face in a marriage between the unfortunate Duke and a rich young widow to whom he had formerly been attentive. Guise mourned, but having no choice — as his uncle the Cardinal eloquently explained — obeyed.

It was a splendid wedding. Charles, his wrath spent, gave the groom a costly present. So did Anjou, after murmuring with his congratulations, 'If you so much as look at my sister hereafter, you will find a knife between your ribs.' Guise obeyed the caution, but received the knife nineteen years later. Margot was also there, smiling, exotic, and unforgetful — biding her time till Henry was in a position to be injured and until she had an instrument for revenge upon him and upon Du Guast in the ugly little brother Alençon of whom no one yet took any notice. One serious flaw in the Great Matriarchy, had it materialized, was the matriarch's exaggerated estimate of her ability to keep the peace amongst her offspring.

In any event the Great Matriarchy had had to be withdrawn for drastic revision. The Peace of August, 1570, with its grant of extensive rights to the Huguenots, extinguished Philip's last spark of interest. His sister of Portugal flatly turned down Anjou, though her son Sebastian continued unable to make up his mind (or his monks to make it up for him); until Charles IX called the marriage off with the proud declaration that he would allow no sister of his to be kept dangling by any prince alive. Philip took for himself the elder daughter of the Holy Roman Emperor, to Catherine's loud grief, but Charles contented himself very well with the younger, an amiable little thing and very pretty despite a pronounced Habsburg jaw, whom he married in November of this same year. Catherine may have felt a little bitter when she reflected that the entire fruit of the voyage to Bayonne was a daughter-in-law who had been offered her before she started.

She had no time for regrets, however; events were rapidly bringing her to the crisis of her life. In the next twelve months she saw the whole of her so carefully cherished combinations turned hopelessly topsy-turvy. The Huguenots, released from occupation at home, marched by the thousands into Flanders to help their co-religionists in the fight against Alba's savage tyranny. To have stopped them would have meant a renewal of trouble at home. She dared not try, nor would Charles have permitted her to, for Charles had begun courteously but firmly to show that he meant to be king. Bewildering new combinations emerged, not her own. Spain, her old standby, threatened war and Charles answered with defiance; England, the enemy she had put down in 1563, became the necessary friend of 1572; and the King, flinging out of the window his mother's whole system of marriage schemes, sought to cement the peace in his kingdom by reviving an old project of his father's — the union of his sister Margot with the nominal head of his Huguenot subjects, young Henry of Navarre. Strange transformations, indeed, were these that Catherine was forced to contemplate in this the twelfth year of her rule and the fifty-third of her age.

Having no particular principle of her own and any amount of resiliency, she might have adjusted herself. But as she groped to find the new balance of which she herself would again be the fulcrum, the worst of all disasters occurred. Charles gave his imagination to a great idea, his confidence to a great man, and in despite of her set out with his new guide for a high place whither she, with her bundle of intrigues, fears, and snobberies, might not venture even to follow. What could she do but struggle to hold him back, cost what it might? During one breathless hour the fate of France, indeed of all Europe, would hang on the success or failure of a woman to master a boy's will.

Chapter VIII

MOTHER AND SON

THE man was Gaspard de Châtillon, Lord of Coligny....

For a year Catherine managed to keep her son and the Admiral apart. She was shrewd enough to know the highest when she saw it, though she felt under no compulsion to love it. She feared the man as she did the Devil; probably more. But finally she could resist no longer, since Coligny's help was necessary to bring about the marriage of the King of Navarre with Margot, to which the Queen Mother had reluctantly become converted in the absence of anything better. At Blois the King, pale with excitement to behold the most illustrious of his subjects, whom he had not seen for seven years, raised the Admiral from his knees, embraced him, called him 'my father' — and promptly succumbed to an ecstatic hero-worship.

Apart from the special circumstances it was an emotion that Charles shared with most of the youth of his realm and not a few of their elders. Time and his character had raised the Admiral to a place absolutely unique: 'the first subject in the world.' Last of the famous soldiers who had served Francis I, the only great party chieftain to survive the civil wars, he walked amongst his contemporaries like some grand figure remaining from an epic past. He was not popular in the sense that his enemy the Duke of Guise had been (or his son now was) popular with the Paris mob, since he knew or cared nothing of the arts that win such popularity. But more than any other living man he fulfilled the new ideal that was capturing the late sixteenth century: that of 'the Soldier of Christ.'[1]

He was a warrior who hated war for the evil it encouraged, a partisan leader who loved his country more than he hated his adversaries, a statesman who believed in and tried to practise honesty and just dealing. Alone of the Huguenot leaders of the First Civil War he had opposed the surrender of Havre to the English for mere party advantage, yet at the end he was the only one who stood out for honouring the pledge his colleagues had signed. No other commander would have dared as he did to forbid his wild troopers to loot the burghers and peasants and to hang them with their loot at their feet when they disobeyed him. There was something of Cromwell in him and something of Lincoln — an iron sense of duty fused with a profound capacity for pity.

He was fifty-four at the time Charles summoned him to Blois, spare and very erect, his brown hair and beard already deeply silvered. His aspect was stern, his speech brief, though rich with the accent of one whose language has been formed on the Bible. Not a man to be approached easily by other men or moved to passion without grave cause, yet despite his formidable exterior very tender to the few who were close to him.

[1] One of the most significant effects of the Reformation upon the Renaissance was the change in the style of popular hero. Barely fifty years earlier, the ideal had been the knight steeped in the courtesies or the learning of the past — Francis I, '*le roi chevalier*,' Bayard, '*le chevalier sans peur et sans reproche*.' The hero of the new age came to be of an entirely different sort: the earnest violent man, the crusader who carried a Bible in one hand and a sword in the other — William of Orange, Sir Francis Drake, Don John of Austria. Whereas Sir Walter Raleigh, versatile and highly lettered but of indifferent enthusiasm in the matter of religion, was the most hated man of his time in England. 'The causes of Atheism,' wrote Francis Bacon in an illuminating passage on his own age, 'are learned times, especially with peace and prosperity. For troubles and adversities do more bow men's minds to religion.'

He brought with him to court a new bride, whom he had married the previous spring after remaining many years a widower. She was an heiress from Savoy, the Lady of Entremonts, who had fallen in love with him by reputation and gone into France resolved to become 'Marcia to this new Cato.' The Duke of Savoy, a rigid Catholic, threatened to confiscate her estates unless she returned; Coligny's had already been confiscated or ruined; and so they got married.

Day after day the King and his new Councillor-in-Chief strolled arm in arm down the long tree-lined avenues that radiated from the Château of Blois, in and out amongst the intricate flowered mazes so cunningly laid out by the best landscape gardeners in the world, while the Admiral spoke of the plan by which alone, he had come to believe after ten years of meditation, France could be saved from herself and again made great. The Great Enterprise, as Europe was to call it for a generation and more, as distinguished from the Guises' Great Design to which it was the aggressive answer.

Spain, Sire, is your natural enemy, he explained. She must provoke disturbance within your realm if she is ever to reconquer the Low Countries. 'Better,' he urged, paraphrasing Philip's basic maxim of policy, 'to start the fire in your neighbour's house before he lights it in yours.' Attack before you are attacked. Win back by arms the old French provinces of Flanders which are the Habsburgs' only through the mean title of marriage, regain the natural frontier of France on the Scheldt. Attack on the high seas, attack in the Americas, that half-a-world from which your people are barred by Spain's preposterous monopoly. Thus you will liberate the Dutch from Alba's inhuman cruelty and release your people's energies upon a worthier object than slaughtering one another. Strike for humanity as well as for France, and win for yourself a name worthy of a son of Charlemagne.

It was the Elizabethan vision first held by a Frenchman. Out of his own resources Coligny had equipped three expeditions to settle colonies in the New World: two had failed, the third had been massacred by the Spaniards on grounds of religion and trespass. Alone he could do no more. What he now urged upon the King with respect to the Americas would soon be dinned into Elizabeth's ears with the same eloquence and feeling by a young man at present hanging about Paris waiting for something to turn up; a seventeen-year-old English volunteer in the Huguenot armies named Walter Raleigh.

Charles listened with swelling heart to the plan unfolded to him in simple phrases, step by step — from its solid base of realism to its soaring apex of romance. Here was something at last that a king might live for! To lead his own armies against his enemies, to send his fleets in search of golden domains beyond the seas. No more miserable fratricide amongst his own subjects, with his brother stealing whatever glory was to be got. No more petticoat government....

He laughed aloud in exultation as he remembered his mother's rules of conduct written out for him when he reached his majority. 'Please everybody... give grand balls... be sociable... carry always in your pocket a list of offices and of deserving office-holders... favour three or four of the principal merchants in each town without anybody knowing it so that they will report to you what goes on in the city government and even in private homes... I have seen your father and grandfather do this....' No doubt! But his grandfather had also striven with Spain for Italy, his father had wrested Metz, Toul, and Verdun from the Empire. An end to petty dissimulation, paltry truckling. They were a woman's business — to act was a man's. 'The hour is come for resolution,' he cried, 'my mother is too timid.' He gave secret audience to Louis of Nassau, William the Silent's brother, and through him sent word of good cheer to the illustrious leader of the Dutch rebellion.

It was not until this point that Catherine awoke to the danger that threatened her. Some sort of anti-Spanish policy had been made inevitable by the Peace of 1570; having with a slight grimace swallowed the peace, she had very quickly accommodated herself to the policy. She went farther and made it her own, an easy task so long as she could keep it too tricky for anyone but herself to understand and no one rose up strong enough to dispute its management with her. She had other, quite characteristic reasons for her about-face. One was annoyance with Philip for having let her down so shabbily over her marriages, the other a more dazzling opportunity than any that her unfilial son-in-law had withheld — a share in the throne of England for her son Henry.

The proposal came directly from Elizabeth herself — or at least as directly as that elusive creature ever proposed anything — and the Queen Mother, palpitating with delight, hurried an embassy over to London with two portraits of Anjou, one of the head, the other of the figure, so that their separate perfections might be appreciated independently. At that moment Catherine would have been prepared to look as favourably upon the Great Enterprise as Coligny himself, who was still buried in the country occupied in rebuilding his house and replanting his vineyards with his own hands. She saw her idol — if trouble with Spain had to come — commanding the English armies as their King and squandering Elizabeth's resources in the war rather than Charles's; a most satisfactory picture. To impress her prospective daughter-in-law she gave orders for the building of a French fleet, all the more gladly that it would provide a career as admiral for one of the horde of Florentine relatives who had followed her into France to make their fortunes, Filippo Strozzi. So far Charles, struck principally by the beauty of a policy that seemed likely to establish Anjou in foreign parts, was content to figure as the obedient, somewhat bewildered echo of his mother's complicated ventriloquy. Together they concerted the death in a brawl of one of Anjou's followers who, paid by Spain, was egging on the Duke to refuse Elizabeth; Catherine's first experiment in outright murder.

It was Henry who started the trouble. His friends, headed by his old chief-of-staff the Marshal Tavannes, pointed out to him with painful realism what his exact position as Elizabeth's husband would be: kept man to a middle-aged harridan of the most scandalous reputation, a beribboned stallion with no other duty or responsibility than to beget children upon her repulsive, disease-twisted body. This was the general portrait of Elizabeth in circulation amongst continental Catholic circles. Henry said no, by God, he would not. The French clergy applauded and offered him a substantial pension to stiffen his resistance.

Catherine, desolate at so great an opportunity being flung away and terrified at what Charles would do if his brother crossed him, went after the truant with the whole maternal arsenal. She wept, she stormed, she coaxed. She exhibited the marriage contract before her son's sceptical eyes, emphasizing with vigorous forefinger the honours, revenues, and prerogatives reserved for him therein; she promised to send it back for amendment and improvement. Henry, at bottom the most devoted of her children, in the end agreed to sacrifice himself to her new policy and the family's greatness.

But the whimsical Elizabeth suddenly turned difficult. She could not, she suddenly announced, allow the Duke to practise the Catholic rite in Protestant England. Catherine thought that this might be arranged, and thereby showed how little she had explored certain regions of her children's souls. Henry, having given in on everything else, flatly declined to compromise on religion. In tears Catherine reported to the English ambassador that there was no more to be done: 'He has become so devout that he hears two or three masses a day and observes the fasts so scrupulously that he is losing his colour. I had far rather see him turn Huguenot outright than risk his health the way he is going on.'

It was at this juncture that Coligny arrived at court. He had very little use for Anjou, and suspected with justice that Anjou had very little use for him. How should they, the stern man of righteousness and the supple young pagan (for he was that, despite all his piety), understand one another? The Admiral could not forget — though Catherine had conveniently done so — the four years she had spent in building up her son into the leadership of the Catholic party, the faction that would fight him tooth and nail over the Great Enterprise. There cannot be two kings in the same country, he told Charles; get rid of him: make him marry the Queen of England whether he will or no.

Charles, only too glad to be encouraged in such a course by his hero, summoned Henry and in their mother's presence pitched into him with fury. Called him a liar and a hypocrite, accused him of refusing Elizabeth so that he might stay in France as ruler of an opposition court. 'You, always talking of your conscience; that's not the real reason, but the huge sum the clergy's offering you.... I'm glad to hear they're so well off, I'll remember it when I need money. As for the friends who are putting you up to oppose me, I give you warning I'll shorten some of them by a head.' He stalked about the room raving, his hand on his dagger. Holding back tears of impotent rage, Henry bowed and without a word hurried back to his own apartments, where he locked himself in for the rest of the day, while Catherine hovered round his door like a large disconsolate ghost.

'Not since the death of Henry II has the Queen Mother wept so much,' wrote an interested onlooker. She had never had better reason to weep. The loss of the English marriage — though she did not take it quite so seriously as Charles, since already she had an eye on her youngest son Alençon as an available substitute; the growing hatred between the King and Anjou, which experts on such subjects, including herself, were beginning to anticipate would end fatally for the Duke before six months were up; and her own helplessness as she saw Charles turn from her, more and more give his increasing, indeed his sole, confidence to the Admiral. The latter she could not detest more than she did already, but there was growing up in her something dangerously resembling a dislike for her eldest son. It was all this cursed Huguenotry. ... With a violent longing she regretted the old days, the comfortable well-tried policy of balance, chicanery, and friendship with Spain.

She regretted them more before that autumn of 1571 was out. A Holy League had been formed between Spain, Venice, and the Pope to drive the Turks out of the Mediterranean. The very League she had proposed at Bayonne, with herself missing from it.... The Pope and Philip, anxious to keep Anjou from marrying Elizabeth, first considered him for the command of the joint expedition that was being fitted out, but Charles, for many obvious reasons, declined to allow him to accept. The command was given instead to Philip's bastard half-brother, Don John of Austria, who led the most splendid flotilla ever assembled to the immortal victory at Lepanto. Heartsick with envy when she heard the news, Catherine remembered what it was that had deprived her son of Don John's glory... and at the same time came to the conclusion for good and all that there was no resisting the might of Spain....

Many times had she wished Coligny dead. She had done more than wish; she had distributed considerable sums to bring his death about: to her Italian wizard, to a bravo whose shot missed the Admiral and killed a friend, De Mouy, standing next to him. It is as well to note down the bravo's name — Maurevert — since she may have need of him again; meantime she put him on the pension list and got him a royal Order. During the Third Civil War she had offered a reward of fifty thousand crowns (more than the equivalent of as many pounds today) to whoever would kill the Huguenot commander. But that was all in time of war, when Coligny was officially a rebel: it would scarcely be safe, even for her, to resort to such means in time of peace against her son's first minister. All she could do was keep her own counsel... work as best she could against his influence... and wait, as she had successfully waited before....

The winter was a period of marking time, since no military operations could be undertaken till spring. Coligny left court to resume his farming. Catherine began active negotiations with the Queen of Navarre for the marriage of their children. At the same time she tentatively put forward Alençon, stunted and beardless at seventeen, as a suitor for the exacting virgin whom his brother had declined — 'he is quite well-formed for his years and shows unmistakeable signs of a beard,' she represented, with less truth than motherly hope.

The spring of 1572 came, Coligny returned, and Catherine knew that the struggle of her life had begun. Louis of Nassau, secretly supplied with funds by Charles, raised a company of Huguenot volunteers, and threw them into Valenciennes and Mons in Flanders; Alba drove them out of the former town and the whole French contingent fell back into Mons, where the Spaniards closely besieged them. Quietly, without telling his mother but a small part of what was in his mind, Charles authorized Coligny to raise three thousand men under a captain called Genlis to reinforce Mons, at the same time sending word to Strozzi to be ready to sail for the Netherlands at a moment's notice — a use for that new navy far from anything Catherine had ever seriously contemplated. Under the peculiar rules of the time no act of war had yet been committed, since Charles could still disavow his Huguenots (as Elizabeth disavowed her corsairs when convenient), but everything tended unmistakably in that direction.

Catholic and Protestant flocked to join Genlis, whose destination remained to the last moment a closely guarded secret — but the Cardinal of Lorraine passed the word on to

Alba, the three thousand were ambushed and cut to pieces. The Cardinal had his information from the Count de Retz, the First Gentleman of the Bedchamber, who had accompanied the King on a recent occasion memorable for Margot: and De Retz, born Albert de Gondi, was one of Catherine's innumerable Italian dependants, whom she had placed to spy on her own son from the moment of his accession at the age of ten.... She hurried to Charles with a triumphant 'I told you so.' The Spaniards cannot be beaten... Valenciennes... now Genlis.... Take example by the Queen of England, who is withdrawing her own volunteers from Holland, knowing the venture to be hopeless....[1]

The poor young King, inexperienced and disheartened, had no answer to the inflexible certainty in the hoarse voice he had so long been accustomed to obey. He promised to think it over, to do nothing rash, nothing at all but by her consent. More elated than surprised, for she was well used to extorting obedience from her children when she put herself out to do so, Catherine departed easy in mind for Châlons, where Claude had fallen ill on her way from Lorraine to Paris for Margot's wedding, which had now been definitely set for August eighteenth.

Scarcely had she left when Coligny made up all his lost ground. Calmly he pointed out to his royal pupil that occasional defeat was one of the unavoidable accidents of war... Genlis had been rash (treason was not yet suspected)... it was unfortunate but in effect of small importance... and kings did not so lightly throw over a great cause on account of a slight misadventure. Under the influence of his hero's calm, Charles regained control of his shaken nerves, saw the vision steadily again and whole. He told the Admiral to carry on.

De Retz sent the alarm galloping on to Catherine at Châ-

---

[1] Elizabeth had just made the announcement, for her own purposes, but very soon recalled it.

lons. Without an instant's delay she rushed back to Paris, locked herself in alone with her son, and poured out on him one of her rare rages:

> Is this the way you repay me for all my trouble, in raising you and saving the crown the Catholics and Huguenots wanted to steal from you? After all I've sacrificed for you and all the dangers I've run? You hide yourself from me, your own mother, to listen to your enemies, tear yourself from these arms that nursed you in order to fling yourself into those that tried to kill you. Do you suppose I don't know that you're holding secret conferences with the Admiral? Or that you're planning to throw yourself into a war with Spain and hand over your kingdom as a prey to the Huguenots? Before that happens, give me leave to go away, to my own country and birthplace...

— quivering, scarlet, awful in her injured righteousness.

It was not with compassion or even filial reverence that Charles listened to her now, but with fear and something not far short of hatred. He knew what that last request of hers meant. She would rather die than go back to Florence. What she was telling him in her own way was that if he disobeyed her she would withdraw from court taking Anjou with her, and raise the standard of revolt amongst the Catholics. Thwart the Great Enterprise, fight him, everthrow him if necessary, anything to regain her power and exalt her favourite.

He mumbled that nothing was yet decided. Pressing her advantage she demanded that he take the advice of his Council. He could not do otherwise than agree, and she laughed to herself. *His* Council! Every man in it but Coligny of her choosing. The meeting was held. The Admiral argued for war — ' Whoever is against is a traitor with the red cross [of Spain] on his belly'; the rest voted solidly for peace. Catherine, in one of those accesses of optimism on which she floated aloft when things seemed to be going her way, gleefully departed once more to bring the ailing Claude into Paris.

When she returned, a few days later, she found ' the Admiral holding the helm with a firm hand,' working all through the night in the Louvre with the four royal secretaries at his constant disposal.

It was then Catherine decided that Coligny must die... once Margot was safely married to the nominal chief of the Huguenots.

Chapter IX

MARGOT IS MARRIED

WITH Charles, his mother, and his minister-in-chief working harmoniously together for the achievement of the same object, it had nevertheless taken two full years for the King to thrust upon Henry of Navarre, his vassal, the signal honour of marrying his sister. The delay was in no way occasioned by the strong mutual antipathy for each other of the two principals, since no one, of course, took the slightest notice of that; it was due entirely to the resolution of one small but exceedingly strong-minded woman not to be put upon.

Jeanne d'Albret, Queen of Navarre,[1] consisted of seven stone of bone and sinew charged to bursting point with sulphur and brimstone and held together only by will-power. In her tiny kingdom, perched so precariously on its mountains between two strong and greedy neighbours, her word was not only law but the whole of the prophets as well. She had early made up her mind that Béarn (the only fragment of Navarre Spain had left her) was to become a sort of way-station between this sinful planet and the Calvinist heaven, and, so far as well-stoked fires could cure her subjects

---

[1] She was the daughter of Henry d'Albret, King of Navarre, and of Marguerite of Valois, sister of Francis I and authoress of the *Heptameron*, 'the Marguerite of Marguerites of princesses.' Jeanne after her father's death became queen in her own right, though her son bore the title of king even in her lifetime.

of any hankering after adultery, papistry, or frivolity, she had succeeded in her endeavour.

For over a year she resisted every enticement to come into France and talk over her son's marriage. The alliance was tempting, both for her son's sake and her religion's, but if she came it must be on her own terms. She and her son must be granted full liberty of worship, though all the Catholics in France screamed themselves purple in the face; Margot must be prepared to forgo her own liberty of worship when she came into her husband's kingdom. What could be fairer? The ceremony must be celebrated according to the Protestant rite; a dowry guaranteed commensurate with her son's importance, including certain towns to become spiritual annexes of Navarre. Her Henry must not be expected to come to Paris until all was in readiness nor hindered from going away again immediately after the wedding — she was not going to allow him to stay an unnecessary minute at a court where his morals were certain to be in constant peril. All these things and many more must be promised her or they could keep their princess: she, Jeanne d'Albret, would *not* be patronized merely because France was big and Béarn small.

That anyone should refuse an obviously worldly advantage because of such scruples seemed to Catherine so bizarre that she failed to take it in. There must be another reason... there had been a number of unexplained deaths amongst the prominent Huguenots in recent years... the Catholics were in a vindictive mood... that must be the trouble, thought the daughter of the Medici, and at once wrote Jeanne offering the most ample pledges for the security of her life and her children's. Back came the retort, 'Madame... excuse me if your letter provokes me to mirth; you wish to reassure me of a fear I have never had, since I don't *really* believe that you eat children, despite what people say.' For that, unfortunately, was now the Queen Mother's reputation amongst the lower orders, particularly of the Reformed persuasion.

Perhaps the taunt to her courage turned the scale; or it may be that Catherine's flattering anxiety to receive her turned her head the least bit. She left Nérac, her capital, at the end of 1571, accompanied by her daughter Catherine (on whose moral stamina she counted, justly, more than upon her son's), and after a leisurely two months of travel arrived at Blois.

There she found a Queen Mother much changed from the fulsome authoress of the letters that had set her in motion. Catherine was sick of the Admiral and all his friends, regretful of the lost Habsburg opportunities, annoyed with the difficulties this tiny ruler of a twopenny country was making about allying herself to the Valois. She bowed with all the dignity of her fourteen stone and kissed her guest coldly on the forehead with a perfunctory inquiry as to how she was.

'I am hungry,' replied Jeanne, unperturbed by her reception.

On this point at least she could be satisfied. It was the last for a long time. Over the collation they went at it hammer and tongs, the fur flew; all the matters on which Jeanne thought she had been promised satisfaction she discovered that Catherine had apparently never heard about or meant something quite different from what her letters had said. Liberty of worship... dowries... Protestant or Catholic wedding:

> *Catherine* (in thickly Italianate French): Beauvoir [Jeanne's ambassador] assured me that you would allow your son to marry my daughter according to the Roman rite.
>
> *Jeanne* (in her mountain twang): I find it hard to believe you, Madame, since he told me quite the opposite and will repeat it to you if you ask him to.
>
> *Catherine* (losing interest): In any case he said something on the subject.
>
> *Jeanne:* Quite possibly, Madame, but nothing like that.

Catherine shrugs her shoulders. And so on, through all the items in the nuptial contract.

From corner to corner the small woman drove the large one, poking her evaded promises under her nose one after the other.

Catherine, kept to her work chiefly by fear of disappointing Charles's wishes at this critical time, retaliated as no good hostess ought to have done. 'I am astonished,' wrote Jeanne to Beauvoir, 'at how I bear all that they do to me here. They stick pins into me, insult me, try to lead me about by the nose. In order to spy on me they have bored holes into my bedroom and dressing-room. If this lasts a month I shall certainly fall ill.' Her prophecy turned out to be anything but an empty whimper. Several times she would have called the whole thing off, much as she hated to retreat before her plump but slippery adversary, had not her exasperation with the mother been balanced — most surprisingly — by a growing admiration for the daughter.

It was surprising because the Queen of Navarre was not one of those people who like where they disapprove, and she strongly disapproved of many things in Margot. She told her bluntly, with a glance of cold rebuke at Catherine, that no God-fearing girl would desecrate her body with such whorish clothes and tight corsettings or her face with such shameless quantities of rouge. But privately she wrote to her son that his bride-to-be was 'very pretty, of excellent judgment, and a real credit to her mother and her brothers.' Perhaps the high pure air of the Pyrenees or her ban on loose talk amongst her subjects had protected Jeanne's ears from the defilement of certain scandals.

Looking at Margot and remembering her Henry's very different, though no doubt more wholesome, style of toilet and apparel, Jeanne began to entertain novel stirrings that led her to add various hints for making a good impression if and when he should present himself in the rôle of fiancé. 'Look to your manners; do not be afraid to speak up boldly, for it will depend upon you to inspire whatever opinion they will form of you here; get in the habit of brushing back your hair and curling it, not in our Nérac mode... but in the latest style, which I recommend as my preference.' Aware perhaps that her ambition for her son was giving her thoughts a worldly taint, Calvin's favourite female disciple hastened to tack on the warning that 'You must be on your guard against all enticements for debauching your morals and religion; it is their aim, they do not conceal it. If you remain here, you will not escape corruption.'

Plainly a rift had opened between Jeanne and her devout fears: the first was weakening as the second grew (if that were possible) stronger. She made one more effort for conscience' sake, an exploration into the possibility of Margot's ultimately finding grace. It took a long time, since Catherine, holding a less favourable opinion of her daughter's judgment than the one transmitted to Navarre, was careful never to leave the girl unattended. But finally persistence found a way, and Jeanne inquired of her prospective daughter-in-law in a gracious aside what chance there was of her changing her religion.

There was none. 'I was brought up in the Catholic faith, which I shall never renounce, not even for the greatest monarch on earth.'

'That's not what I was told,' muttered Jeanne. 'If I had known this I should never have come. I have been deceived.'

What to do? Trying to obtain satisfaction from Catherine was like attempting to punch a well-stuffed cushion into a desired shape, from Margot like expending the same effort upon a stone wall. Would religion be better served by contracting this unholy but undoubtedly advantageous alliance with the House of France or rejecting it? After intense communion with her ministers sacred and profane, Jeanne followed the example of many idealists larger, stronger, and fully as obstinate as herself: she compromised, as no doubt Catherine had foreseen that she would once she had been wheedled into coming. She signed a contract providing for a mixed wedding ceremony, Catherine to seek the Papal dispensation (a bitter pill, that, to an upright Calvinist) necessary for the marriage of two cousins of whom one was a heretic, the bride and groom each thereafter to retain their respective liberty of worship in the other's country. Very regretfully she put her pen to the document, believing in her heart that she was doing an evil thing for her religion, trying to console herself with the thought that she was on the whole obtaining a good wife for her son.

Shortly she left Blois for Nérac to bring her son to Paris for his wedding, arriving in the capital early in June; a week later she died. It would have been better not only for her, but for the cause she served all her life, if she had been better able to bend without breaking.... She had said more than once that Catherine would be the death of her, and in a sense she spoke the truth; but not in the sense in which the grief-stricken Huguenots interpreted her words. They accused the Queen Mother outright of having made away with their brave little chieftain by means of a gift, a pair of gloves subtly impregnated with poison by Catherine's Milanese perfumer, Monsieur René, universally regarded as her private toxicologist. The post-mortem certificate was published; it declared the cause of death to have been a suppurated tumour on the lung. The Huguenots laughed bitterly: since the venom had been inhaled, obviously it had lodged in the brain — why had not the head been opened? Actually it had; Coligny knew it and tried to acquit Catherine, but few people in Paris were any longer ready to listen to reason... Jeanne had chosen a very bad time to die.

For Paris was packed to bursting with guests, invited and uninvited, up from the provinces for the wedding, thousands upon thousands of them, eight hundred in the train of Navarre alone. And owing to Jeanne's death the wedding was postponed for two months — the very two months during which Catherine's struggle to regain her power approached its climax. The thousands, idly billeted upon the turbulent and always overcrowded capital, had nothing to do but listen to new and fearful rumours. The old grudges and suspicions mounted to boiling point. Sullen and resentful, the extremer Catholics waited for the declaration of war upon Spain which would reduce them to a subordinate position in the State... from the fetid alleyways that twisted darkly in and out of the marshy quarters to the east the lower classes of Paris emerged after working hours to watch, silent and ferocious, the Huguenot gentry passing lightly through the doors of the Louvre as if they owned the place... the Huguenots in their turn marking Catherine's every expression, distrusting her by instinct rather than from any tangible evidence of her ill-will.

Only the Admiral worked away calmly through the sultry tension, turning a deaf ear to repeated warnings that his life was in danger. Were not he and his there under his King's sacred promise of safety? Had not even the Guises, on their arrival for the wedding, embraced him in token of complete reconciliation?

Enter the bridegroom, the Man of Destiny, his hair standing up every which way despite his mother's careful injunctions, his rakish new clothes already spotted and bursting at the seams, smelling strongly of garlic and, the chances are, a little drunk. Altogether not very different, except that he was not a bridegroom and wore no clothes, from his first entry onto any stage, at Pau nineteen years earlier.

When the onset of labour pains announced his imminent appearance on that occasion, his mother had burst into a suite of spirited native songs, in deference to the theory of her father, Henry d'Albret, King of Navarre, that by these means she would avert the risk of presenting him with a whiner and a mollycoddle for a grandson. As soon as the infant was delivered, his royal ancestor, after one glance, swung him aloft, shouting, 'My ewe has brought forth a lion,' rubbed his lips with garlic and anointed them generously with strong Jurançon wine.

HENRI IV

Thus certified, Destiny's cub was dismissed for a term of years to run barefoot with the mountain peasants' children; until, mindful of his rank and the fact that his grandmother, 'the Marguerite of Marguerites,' had fastened a tradition of scholarship on the family, his parents gave him shoes and a liberal dose of Latin and Greek, all of which he accepted without relish, though not altogether without profit. After that his father took him to the court of France with the intention, not only of continuing the formal part of his education, but of beginning the convivial: at which the young Henry immediately gave evidence of a most precocious talent.

On Antoine's death he reverted again to his mother, who did not know quite what to make of him. She could not conceal from herself that he was a natural hotbed for every imaginable kind of sin, original, congenital, and acquired — in short, a chip of the old block. She did her best, but somehow it appeared that the more she tried to root out of him the love of worldly pleasure, the more abundant the noxious weed grew. Yet she never gave up nor spared the rod; when, at fifteen, it was thought time for him to join the Huguenot forces, she escorted him to headquarters at La Rochelle, where he simultaneously received the title of general and a proper tutor to look after him. Alas! even before she had left for home, she caught him redhanded with money won at dice. Summoning the tutor, she ordered him to turn the new general over his knee and give him a thrashing then and there in her presence. Henry tried excuses, but they sounded weak in his own ears; pleading, which broke off after a scrutiny of the tightening maternal lips. The tutor waited, birch in hand, for the colloquy to end. Suddenly Henry threw back his shoulders and said loftily, 'It will bring but little glory upon you, my mother, to treat me as a child, seeing that I have the honour to command an army and bear the title of general.' The claim of military privilege also failed.... During the next two years, while he learned the trade of war under

Coligny, Jeanne mitigated her maternal anxiety for her only son with the reflection that he was better off on the battlefield than in the company of his Valois cousins.

The little martinet wrestled and prayed in vain. The Lord had afflicted her with one of His rarest visitations, a perfectly natural man. If he felt like having a good time, he somehow managed to have it. If a sermon bored him, he yawned. The most improving society failed to cure his taste for waggery as the best elocution master to correct his common Gascon drawl. It was just the same in Paris as in Puritan Nérac: he could no more be polished into refinement than hammered into virtue. As a lad of eight he rode into a solemn session of the Grand Council on a donkey followed by his contemporaries dressed in full ecclesiastical regalia which he had stolen somewhere. Now, ten years later, he would clump out of the Louvre in the midst of a polite entertainment and be discovered on the steps of a house under repairs swapping yarns with the workmen, eating their onions and drinking their wine as he had shared similar delicacies with the peasants in his infancy. Or, growing weary of some court lady's cleverness, go out into the streets and pick up a prostitute to see Paris with. Or failing anything else have a romp on the floor, like a great shaggy bear, in expensive rumpled clothes that were always too small for his huge frame, with whatever children happened to be quartered in the palace.

Naturally the fastidious Margot and he hit it off like nothing less than a pair of lovers, and all her proud self-control, the sense of duty to the family that had become a second nature, could not entirely conceal her fright and revulsion as the hour drew near for her to be united to the playmate of her youth. The one person who thoroughly appreciated her feelings was the bridegroom,[1] who had a pretty shrewd

---

[1] It is extraordinary that Matthieu, Henry IV's own historiographer, had it from his master's lips that his bride 'had to hold herself in not to reveal how her heart refused consent to the obligations of her body.'

idea of himself and no more use for her physically than she for him. Like a good many sensualists he was sentimental about women, and the hard, haughty, self-contained beauty he had been ordered to marry was not in the least like what he would have chosen to share his bed and his heart's intimate confidences. The kind of wife he would have preferred was soft, easy-going, one who would be content to take him as he was and be happy to sit on a pedestal of his erection instead of remaining coolly poised on her own. There were plenty such ladies ready enough to be his mistresses — not the least valuable of Margot's contributions to their marriage was to consist in preventing him from divorcing her so that he might marry one of them, to his own material hurt.

They were quite frank with each other, and out of their honesty rose the possibility of an understanding. If he was put off by many of the qualities in her that most people admired, he had the quality himself to put a right value on her loyalty and courage; and she saw before anyone else the incorruptible simplicity, the shy belief in himself to command destiny, the sense of life as a gay and exciting adventure, that lay beneath the uncouth exterior of this impossible husband who had been given her. Since there was no avoiding what had to be, the boy of nineteen and the girl of twenty resolved between them (only partly in words) to make the best of what was: and if the relation of man and wife proved as impossible as their fleshly shrinking forewarned them both that it would be, to play fairly with one another as man and woman, and as partners in the great game of power.

On Monday, August eighteenth, they were married before the main portal of Notre-Dame, on a high scaffold draped in cloth of gold. On the scaffold stood the members of both families: the groom and the bride's brothers in lemon and silver; Margot in ermine and violet, wearing a coronet of diamonds and a blue mantle heavily studded with jewels; Catherine in rich black velvet; the presiding priest, Charles,

Cardinal of Bourbon, the bridegroom's uncle, in canonicals of red and white and gold. In the open space below and the adjacent streets, on the near-by bridges and the housetops, the mob swarmed and gaped, a hundred thousand baleful critics who would have their chance to assist actively in the marriage celebrations before the week was over. Bride and groom knelt and gave their assent to be joined in marriage, the former very pale and inaudible.[1] The Cardinal pronounced the benediction. . . .

Four hundred miles to the south the Governor of Lyons, Mandelot, was holding up all communication between Rome and Paris. The Pope, despite the utmost pressure, had withheld his dispensation, and the Cardinal had refused to go on without it. The King swore that the wedding should take place if he had to perform the ceremony himself in full preaching. That would have been too tactless: Catherine concocted a letter purporting to indicate that the document was on the way, to satisfy the Cardinal, and he, a muddle-headed man with a great conceit of himself, the butt of Anjou's best sarcasms, swallowed it. The order to Mandelot was to guard against premature exposure: but whether, despite this ingenious expedient, Margot and Henry were properly married or not remained, and still does, a choice question for canonical lawyers.

Descending from the scaffold, Margot, with three princesses bearing her four-forked train, entered the Cathedral to hear Mass at the high altar, the while Henry retired to the bishop's palace and the Protestant lords strolled up and down the long nave. It was hung with Huguenot flags taken in the Civil Wars and Coligny, pointing to them, said quietly, 'Others more suitable for Frenchmen to display will soon be hanging there.' One can see Catherine drooping her lids over her

---

[1] One account, not an eye-witness's, says that she shrank back and that Charles pushed her head forward in a nod; it sounds more like a Protestant invention than like Margot.

prominent eyes when the remark floats to her ears, careful not to reveal her own inward comment: 'Will they indeed...'

Four hectic days followed; of balls and tourneys, and exotic sports devised by Anjou's fertile imagination, of sinister rumours and growing tension. Charles, who was having the time of his life, begged his chief minister to put off work until the festivities were over; but aware of something in the atmosphere, gradually coagulating whispers of a Guise plot against the Admiral's life, he called twelve hundred infantrymen into the city as a precaution. Paris, gorgeously decorated, was holding a carnival on the flank of a simmering volcano — and knew it.

At eleven o'clock in the morning of the fifth day, Friday, August twenty-second, Coligny left a Cabinet Council at the Louvre for his own house with two companions, walking very slowly so as to study a petition he held in his hand. After a few hundred yards he paused and stooped over to tie a shoelace. At that instant a shot rang out, and another, one bullet lodged in the flesh of his right arm, the second carried off the index finger of his left hand. That loosened shoelace was to cost ten thousand people their lives without saving him his own.

Chapter X

THE EVE OF SAINT BARTHOLOMEW'S

THE Admiral straightened up, motioned to silence his frantic suite, who had rushed forward to screen him from the bystanders. 'This is the fruit of my reconciliation with the Guises,' he said quietly, and looking about him pointed to the blinded window whence the smoke came curling. With a brief direction to two of his followers to break into the house and to another to carry word of what had happened to the King, he walked on with the assistance of his original two companions.

The two who forced the door of the house found nothing but a harquebus, still smoking, on a table and a pair of stupefied servants. Rushing to the back door they were in time to hear the clatter of galloping hooves on the cobbles making off in the direction of the Saint-Antoine Gate to the west. They mounted and followed for several miles, caught sight of the fugitive, presently lost him for good....

Charles was at tennis with young Guise and the Admiral's son-in-law Teligny when Coligny's message reached him. For a moment he stood dumbfounded — the King's first subject to be murderously attacked in broad daylight, within five hundred yards of his palace, while under the royal protection! It was too incredible. Abruptly flinging down his racquet he cried with an oath, 'Shall I then never have peace?' and hurried off to his own apartment where he shut himself in for the rest of the morning.

Catherine received the news just as she was sitting down to her midday meal. Without a word or the least sign of emotion she left the table and retired to her study in the Tuileries, whither she at once summoned Anjou and certain of her confidential advisers. An hour or so later she was informed that the Admiral had sent Teligny and the Marshal Damville, the late constable's second son, to the King begging the favour of a visit and that Charles had agreed to go. Not caring to remain in ignorance of whatever her enemy said to her son, completely in the dark as to how much he suspected, she and Anjou were ready to leave when the King did, and all three arrived at the Admiral's house together at two o'clock.

Meantime, the famous surgeon Ambrose Paré had amputated the stump of the finger and removed the bullet from Coligny's arm — a horrible operation performed with a pair of scissors and an ordinary probe. The Admiral had borne it stoically, but he was very weak and in great pain as the royal party entered the room. The King hurried to the bedside and exclaimed brokenly, 'Oh, my father, the pain is yours, but the grief and outrage are mine.' Catherine, following closely, chimed in with 'They are all France's. Why, the King will soon not be safe in his own bed.'

Coligny spoke a few words of regret that his wound incapacitated him for the King's service at this crucial time, and went on to exhort Charles neither to be dissuaded from the Great Enterprise nor to hearken to those who might try to make him out a rebel if he should die — for the doctors thought it likely that the large copper ball Paré had extracted was poisoned.

Charles, too stricken to think of anything but the immediate present, implored the Admiral to leave Paris under an armed escort until things were quieter. The other shook his head: God knows, he returned, what such a move would precipitate — an attack on his followers who remained behind — retaliation — 'Better a hundred times to die than live in this perpetual suspicion. I had rather my body were dragged through the streets of Paris than see another civil war.' At least, begged the King, come to the Louvre, where your enemies will not dare pursue you. Again the Admiral declined; if the King felt uneasy, he might throw a guard round the house, but it would not do to involve the Crown in his private feud. There was still such a thing as the King's justice in France and he put his full trust in it. The Huguenot lords standing by — including the new bridegroom Henry of Navarre and his cousin the young Prince of Condé — nodded their agreement.

Facing them, Charles swore a mighty oath by all he held holy to track down the guilty and punish them for this dastardly crime whoever they were, 'in a way that will be remembered forever'... and turned to his mother and brother to witness his vow.

The Admiral thereupon asked for a few moments of private speech. Charles, motioning the bystanders to withdraw from the bed, bent over to listen. Catherine and Anjou stood alone in the middle of the room — the Huguenot lords, gathered into knots or pacing back and forth, looking at them in silence with grief, hostility, and suspicion — while they, outwardly seeing and hearing nothing, strained eyes and ears to catch Coligny's murmured syllables, or at least a glimpse of the King's averted face....

Unable to bear it any longer, Catherine abruptly stepped over to the bed with a solicitous rebuke to her son for keeping the patient talking so long. It would give him a fever — she appealed to the doctors in the room, 'whose task it is to guard this precious life,' whether it was not so. They agreed that it was; Charles reluctantly allowed himself to be led away.

They were in the carriage again, Catherine trying to draw out of Charles what the Admiral had said to him. Had he any theories regarding his assailant... had he mentioned the Guises, whose name was on everyone's tongue in that connection? Charles returned evasive answers or none, his face twitching. All at once, as if maddened by her persistence, he turned on her and his brother with 'God's death, he only told me the truth! You *have* always managed somehow to get the power into your hands — he warned me to take care — before you ruin both me and my kingdom.' All this in gasps, mingled with shrill oaths and hardly suppressed tears. 'That's what the best and most faithful of my subjects wanted to tell me in case he should die before... well, since you wanted to know it, God's death, there it is.'

So that was all. A curious glance of relief passed between Catherine and Henry as they began a vehement argument to prove that the Admiral wronged them, underrated their loyalty. The arrival at the door of the Louvre cut them short. The King passed into his cabinet to institute an immediate commission of inquiry, the other two proceeded on to the Tuileries.

The rest of the day passed quietly. In the evening various of the younger Huguenots went to hurl insults and threats under the windows of the Guise mansion near the Porte Saint-Denis. They were answered by a small mob of townsmen, but the city authorities had been ordered to make ready for such a demonstration and it passed off in words. Though Paris slept that night with one eye open behind barred doors and windows.

The morning of Saturday, August twenty-third, dawned hot and sultry: a foretaste of the heavy summer weather Strozzi was at the moment reporting from Brouage on the western coast, where the fleet rode at anchor. At an early hour the surgeon Paré sent word to the Louvre that his patient was out of danger; the news passed on to the Tuileries, whither Catherine hastily summoned her councillors of the previous day. A little later the commission of inquiry waited upon Charles with a preliminary report. The house from which the shot had been fired (it ran) belonged to a Canon Villemur, a former tutor of the Duke of Guise. The two servants testified that on Thursday evening, during their master's absence from Paris, one Chailly, known to them as Master of the Household to the Duke of Aumale, Guise's uncle, had introduced into the house a soldier by the name of Bondol or Boland — they had not caught it very well — who had installed himself for the night by the heavily curtained window giving onto the street. Chailly (went on the report) was already under arrest and ready to talk; so was the man who had brought round to the back door of the house the horse on which Bondol or Boland had escaped; the animal had been identified as one missing the previous day from the Guise stables.

Left alone, Charles paced the room and tried desperately to see his way ahead. If the report pointed to the true solution of the crime... and he were called upon to prosecute the heads of the most powerful family in his realm — the idols of his turbulent capital, which was already spoiling for trouble... He cursed the whole house of Lorraine, provisionally, if they had really given their word only to break it... and as if in answer to his imprecation the two special objects of it, Guise and Aumale, materialized in the room to beg his gracious permission to be allowed to withdraw from court, 'seeing that our services have not apparently been pleasing to Your Majesty for some time past.' He studied them with a scowl. Confession? Funk? A ruse? 'Go where you like,' he answered brusquely. 'I shall know where to find you if I want you.'

They rode out of the Saint-Antoine Gate with a flourish, doubled on their tracks, and at nightfall re-entered Paris in extreme secrecy, safe from immediate arrest or Huguenot revenge behind the fortress-like walls of the Hôtel de Lorraine, conveniently at hand to assist in whatever plan of action their friends at court should have decided upon in the course of the day.

There was no sign on this, the morning of the most crucial day of his life, of the Charles whom responsible men had so long accused of neglecting his duties for his sport. With a heavy heart and grim determination he worked away to make his capital safe from any mischance that might arise out of the blood-feud that had apparently come to a head after so many years of quiescence. 'They shall *not* embroil my people in their quarrels,' he wrote to his ambassador in England, and meant it from the very depths of him. He summoned the Provost of Paris and instructed him to assemble the captains of the militia at the Hôtel de Ville, 'quietly and without giving cause for excitement,' so as to be ready to restore order if the followers of the Guises and the Châtillons clashed in the streets. Worked away depressed and wretched, but resolved that peace shall be preserved and justice done so long as he is King of France — and his own master....

Shortly after noon another request comes to him for an audience — from his mother on behalf of the Council. She appears, filling the doorway for an instant before crossing to her seat at the King's right hand; like some looming black shadow taking on the semblance, the very substance of the evil it portended. After her comes Anjou, visibly holding on to himself as he takes his place on his brother's left. Then the Marshal Tavannes, grizzled and bent, with the half-absent intentness of the partially deaf; De Retz, dapper, hawk-like, and palpably nervous; the new Keeper of the Seals, Catherine's destined Chancellor, René de Biragues, born Birago, famous for his pithy advice that for disposing of political opponents 'cooks are more useful than soldiers'; the Duke of Nevers, a soldier by profession and a Gonzaga from

Mantua by birth. The inner Cabinet of State, all present except Coligny and the Cardinal of Lorraine, who is in Rome for a conclave; all appointed by the Queen Mother, all except Tavannes Italians.

Without delay Catherine proceeds to the business that caused her to convoke this meeting: evidence which has come into her hands of a Huguenot plot to overthrow the King and seize the government.

Charles looks at her as if he could not have heard aright. Did the Admiral conspire to have himself shot, by any chance?

The shooting was a mere coincidence, she returns, the result of a private row, as Charles no doubt suspects. Very likely he would find the Guises at the bottom of it if he pushed his investigations. Though it would have been far better if their bullet had found its mark, she adds pointedly, since the Huguenots are about to use it as a pretext for the rising they have long had in mind. 'They stand armed and ready to kill you and me and your brothers — in order to secure themselves in power and so be free to go ahead in Flanders relieved of all future danger of hindrance at home — from you or anybody else.'

Ignoring equally her son's surprise and his scepticism, she unfolds her story. It is a staggering one, but she has it completely documented. The exact words spoken by the Huguenot lords in the Admiral's house: some favouring a direct attack on the Louvre for the extermination of the Guises in the King's presence, with open sneers at the King's intentions or his power to compel justice; others clamouring for the removal of the Admiral from Paris, secretly if possible, forcibly if necessary, so as to raise the standard of insurrection in the country. The genuineness of the speeches is beyond doubt; they are attested by a man who has free access to the Huguenot councils, the clever spy Bouchavannes whom Catherine skilfully introduced amongst them; confirmed in many

The Eve of Saint Bartholomew's 123

details by her other spies, Messrs. Caviani and Petrucci of Florence. Facts and figures relating to ten thousand Germans and six thousand Swiss the Admiral is raising for the invasion of France, down to the exact number from each commune and the precise sums available for their payment, with the source of every franc. Damning facts, damning figures. Where her memory or knowledge fails, Catherine calls on the others to bear her out or upon Birago to read from his sheaf of documents.

Every separate item is true: and the whole is a masterly lie. With a little artful editing the threats uttered by the Huguenot hotheads in the first hour of suspicion and panic after the Admiral was brought home bleeding have been made to wear the appearance of premeditated rebellion. No one present cautions Charles that the guilty phrases shoved under his eyes were spoken in hot blood and taken down in cold; nor that Coligny and the more responsible of his colleagues had overruled the speakers and soon won them to calm. No one explains to the bewildered young monarch that the ten thousand German and six thousand Swiss are no more than a prudent minister's preparations on paper (cunningly extracted from his files) against his King's ultimate orders to go ahead with the raising of mercenaries for the needs of the Great Enterprise.

The exposition of the evidence takes over an hour, each link being carefully turned round and round before it is riveted onto the chain of proof. The King listens with lowered head, saying little, the tip of his tongue moving to and fro over his thin under lip. Before it is over he is standing by the window, his breath coming in short gasps. Dazed, incredulous, convinced; above all passionately hurt. One thing is certain, Coligny has kept things back, deceived him. (It does not strike him that a great party leader with many irons in the fire, many men to reconcile, cannot tell everything to a sovereign who has wobbled so constantly as Charles has done, who is constantly surrounded by that leader's enemies.) His hero... those dreams of glory... all an illusion like everything else. Nothing but selfishness and treachery, pious or smiling, it was all the same. As he had always been instructed.

Instructed in the same hoarse voice that now passes on to the inexorable conclusion. The Admiral must die and his principal colleagues with him. Else his followers will strike tonight on the pretext of avenging the outrage on their chief. The Paris mob, glad of any excuse for killing Huguenots, will strike back to protect their idols the Guises. 'With the sacrifice of five or six lives you can nip the plot against yourself and appease the mob at one blow; otherwise your capital, your kingdom may become a shambles, your throne itself totter.'

Granted the premises, the conclusion is irresistible. But she goes too fast for him. He turns, pours out a stream of hysterical oaths from which emerges one thought over and over: 'The Admiral must not be touched. He came to Paris under my protection — on the word of a king. Some other way must be found.' He looks round at them wildly as if for help — still desiring in his heart to doubt the truth of what he has heard.

Catherine shrugs her shoulders and lets the others speak, his trusted servants, as she remarks, until his recent strange infatuation for those who all these years have been his rebels. The ministers give their opinions one by one, all affirming there is no other way — until a surprising thing happens: De Retz, the Florentine, the spy, breaks down and shrilly confesses that he cannot advise the King to an act that will make his and France's name stink in the world's nostrils, and 'bring such calamities that neither we nor our children will see the end of them.'

All turn on him, and for a moment there is furious argument round the table where until now such complete concord had reigned: De Retz tries to hold out, but the mysterious impulse that moved him, some weird flash of the imagination, weakens and he bows before the collective certainty of the rest. Ere this the hope that kindled in Charles's eyes as the man first spoke had already died out. Of all those present he most distrusted this Florentine, whom he by now more than suspected of having been the source of the intelligence that sent Genlis and his men to their deaths. Another dodge, thinks the King wearily, whose meaning he is too distracted to fathom.

The Council is again unanimous and Catherine resumes. 'You see there is no other way. The Huguenots are already armed. Here in Paris the quarters are arming ——'

At this Charles rouses himself. 'How can that be?' he breaks in angrily. 'I have expressly forbidden them to arm.'

'You will find they are doing it nevertheless,' his mother answers evenly.

She is quite right. The rumour has been spread through the city that the Duke of Montmorency, the late Constable's eldest son, was advancing from Chantilly at the head of a large force to the Huguenots' assistance. Anjou confirms her — his first contribution to the discussion — and he ought to know, since he and the Bastard of Angoulême toured the quarters in person a short while ago.

'You see? You have no choice. Either you assert yourself or become a puppet in your own kingdom, an object of contempt to the whole world. To protect a handful of rebels who have made a horror of your reign. Surely,'' she adds ever so quietly, as he still does not answer, 'you are not *afraid* of the Huguenots?'

She is wise enough neither to plead nor threaten, knowing these devices to be exhausted. She speaks with the impersonal detachment of an Elder Statesman called in to advise on a grave matter of public interest; with the authority of the Crown's oldest councillor, as indeed she is.

Charles returns to his place and buries his head in his hands. It is not for nothing that Catherine has made her children's characters her first study. All his violent instability, the dark uncertainty of himself, the highstrung vanity in Charles, that responded intuitively to Coligny's leading, quiver under the impact of her subtle taunts. Old memories come up — of Amboise, of Condé's and Coligny's attempt to kidnap him five years before, the terror he felt and the oath he swore on that occasion to be even with them. There is no escape: either the Huguenot chiefs must go or he must resign himself to be crushed between his old enemies and the riff-raff of his capital....

Dully he hears the others, speaking in order of rank, dot the i's and cross the t's. Suggest that unless he acts his Catholic subjects, rather than suffer a change in the government that will drag them into the war in Flanders, may take matters into their hands, elect a Captain-General to lead them — Guise himself, perhaps — against the Crown rather than submit. Very likely that is what Coligny is counting on. A man cunning and unscrupulous enough to exploit his sovereign's inexperience for his own ends would scarcely stop at provoking a civil war.... Until all have spoken and pause for the King to decide.

If it were only his mind that had to decide, the word would be spoken: the mind which his mother has worked upon so mercilessly for two hours after preparing for twenty-two years. But his score of kingly ancestors still have something to say: and though the struggle has lit an insane glare in his eyes and brought a froth to his lips, Charles still manages to gasp, 'I cannot, I cannot. I have given my word.'

The Councillors look furtively to Catherine, who rises and says with an air of finality: 'Then you must give me and your brother leave to go away. You cannot expect us to remain where our lives are in danger, and watch you plunge this state I have worked so long to preserve for you into ruin.'

How he would love to be able to say, 'Go where you like,' to both of them, as he did to the Guises, but he dare not; he is too alone, too terrified, before the dangers that grow more inscrutable the more he faces them; too young and much too far gone in his wits to detect the ghastly fear that lurks behind her impassivity lest he take up her challenge and let her go — to what? He begs her not to desert him... to stand by him a little longer... he will take action immediately....

A little shiver of relief passes through the company. Catherine is unable to repress a flicker of triumph as she resumes her seat... a flicker that quickly dies as Charles announces in short, jerky phrases his decision: to arrest the Guises for the assault on the Admiral, so as to appease the Huguenots — use the troops to keep the mob in order — until everyone's guilt can be sifted ——

Then she lets him have it. 'Very well, arrest the Guises; they will only turn around and accuse your own mother. And they will be perfectly right.' As unemotionally as if she were relating some trivial domestic incident she describes how she enlisted the widow and children of the late Duke of Guise to revenge themselves upon their sworn enemy. How Anjou hired Bondol, or Boland — whose real name, she discloses, is Maurevert. Yes, the same Maurevert who missed Coligny and shot De Mouy instead three years ago. The man upon whom she induced Charles to bestow a pension and the collar of the Order of Saint Michael, with the result that the public has given him the nickname of 'the King's Assassin.' 'Yes, we struck down the Admiral. To save you. But unless you finish the job, we all go down together. After all, better to fight here in Paris, where you hold all the keys, than run risks in the open country.'

Not a bad scheme of reinsurance for a desperate woman to have worked out in twenty-four hours. With the Admiral still alive she was in worse case than ever — till by the masterly elaboration of her Huguenot plot she found a way to make her son, already innocently involved up to the eyes, finish her work on his own responsibility.

'So pursue the Guises if you like, but if you hang them you hang your mother, your brother, and yourself along with them.'

Charles stares at her with unseeing eyes, a foam bubbling out on his lips. Suddenly he leaps from his chair screaming: 'God's death, if you must have the Admiral's life, take it! But kill them all, every one — don't let a Huguenot live to reproach me.' And still screaming rushes from the room.[1]

[1] Three of those present at the conference that led up to the Massacre of Saint Bartholomew's left some form of record of their part in these transactions — Anjou, Tavannes, and Nevers. (Margot, in her *Memoirs*, also presents an account, but as she was not a participant, her evidence must be heavily discounted.) Nevers is not worth much, since he is very sketchy and on the defensive. Tavannes, though very full, did not write down his account (or rather pass it on to his son) until years later. Anjou, when King of Poland, dictated his to his doctor, Miron, during a night of insomnia not very long afterward, in 1573-74. There is much division of opinion on the reliability of his narrative, some scholars urging that it is suspect as a bit of special pleading. I do not see the grounds for this criticism: Anjou places a full measure of responsibility on his mother and himself, thoroughly acquits Charles (whom he disliked) of any premeditation, and on most substantial points agrees with Tavannes, even though their confessions were separated by many years. Both, curiously, agree in making De Retz (in Margot's story Catherine's principal tool for Charles's conversion) the one remorseful conspirator. Both, though they knew the plot to be a fiction, genuinely believed they were doing a good thing for France in keeping her out of a purely Protestant quarrel with Spain.

The order of the final scene is my own reconstruction based upon a compromise between the available accounts. Both Tavannes and Anjou agree that Catherine began with the 'revelation' of the plot before confessing to her part in the shooting of Coligny, though just at which point she made her confession it is impossible to say with certainty. Charles clearly attempted further resistance before his frenzied exit as above, but nothing occurred that was not mere repetition of what had gone before.

Chapter XI

A SLIP OF THE IMAGINATION

The remaining six drew up again round the Council board, the Queen Mother now presiding, to consider the next question: who shall live and who die. Catherine ruled out her son's parting injunction as ill-considered; in all things moderation, including slaughter, and the Guises, with no one left to balance them, might get above themselves. As cool as she had been while conducting her children's classes in sight of the swinging corpses at Amboise, she went down the list of Huguenots in Paris for her daughter's wedding, Charles's own list drawn up the previous day for his guests' protection. The Admiral first. Her son-in-law of Navarre? No; she hoped through him henceforth to manage his party, though for that very reason his intimate suite must go. Condé? Several spoke for him, including his brother-in-law Nevers, and he was spared. Rochefoucauld, the King's dear friend? Yes, he was a close kinsman of the Admiral. And so on down.

Then the means. The Duke of Guise, of course, to look after his family's blood-foe. The Royal Guard to take care of those of the proscribed who were lodged in the palace. The twelve hundred infantry brought into the city a few days before, the civic militia, each given their section and their duties, both as police and executioners. For though Catherine, now that she had her enemies conveniently in a cage (as she aptly described their congestion in Paris for her daughter's wedding), meant for her own security to lop off more than the five or six heads she had mentioned in opening the delicate topic to the King, she meant also to avoid general disorder, which made her as uncomfortable as did high words in her hearing. Once the more troublesome chieftains were got rid of and such of their followers who chose to interfere, she would be quite satisfied. She forgot that she was not the only person with a grudge, that there were at least two hundred thousand more within the radius of a mile or so in the same mind.

Now to wait on the King. Unless he consented to provide the means, and by so doing assume the responsibility, there could be no going ahead. They found Charles in a kind of stupefied frenzy, like a man sleep-walking in a delirium. Without discussion he agreed to everything. The Provost of Paris, Charron, was sent for, ordered to lock the city gates so that no one might enter or leave, remove all boats from the Seine, mass the artillery in front of the Hôtel de Ville, hold the militia ready and armed for further orders. In a state of collapse the man departed to carry out his instructions. After him entered an ex-Provost, Marcel, leader of the Paris gangs, who was told to pass the word on to his lieutenants that

> by the King's command an armed man, provided with a torch and wearing a white scarf, shall be waiting in every [Catholic] house this night and a candle burning in every window. The signal will be given from the tower of the Palais de Justice at dawn.

Marcel ran to carry out *his* orders as to a feast.

Catherine, too, gave orders, unknown to her son. So did the Guises, restored the privilege of the Louvre. It was a triumph of over-organization.

A Slip of the Imagination

There was the usual assembly for conversation, dancing, supper, in the King's rooms that evening,[1] but no one seemed to have much appetite for gaiety. The atmosphere was close; everyone a little tired, perhaps, after the continuous festivities of the preceding week. The Catholic lords whispered to one another in corners or, remembering themselves, made too hearty conversation with the perplexed Huguenots — many a man bidding a cordial good-night to another who was inscribed on his own particular list for visiting a few hours later.

At ten o'clock the guests dispersed. As the young Lord of Rochefoucauld took his leave of the King, Charles roused himself to say in a low voice, 'Don't go, Foucauld; come and sleep in my room tonight.' But Rochefoucauld, having brought along to Paris his new bride with whom he was very much in love, laughingly declined to take his friend's request as a royal command and bowed himself out.

In another room the bridegroom of the previous Monday, apparently uncured by the maternal birch, played at dice with his brother-in-law the Duke of Alençon, and the Duke of Guise. Suddenly, after a throw, Navarre called the attention of the others to drops of blood on the dice. All three examined their fingers for cuts, but found none and proceeded. At the next cast the blood reappeared. Rather white-faced, the three gamblers decided to give up their game for the night.

Catherine withdrew to her room followed by her daughters and the ladies whose duty it was to undress her — the ceremony of the *coucher*. Margot, who knew nothing of what was afoot, but had felt the heavy constraint in the air all evening, sat down on a chest with her sister Claude, who did

[1] In what ensues it must be remembered that the sixteenth century lived on a very different time schedule from ours, in order to take the maximum advantage of daylight. The usual hour of rising even for the wealthy was six A.M., or earlier in summer, of dinner eleven to eleven-thirty, of supper five to five-thirty P.M., of retiring nine to ten.

know and unconsciously tantalized Margot with her expression of worry and sorrow. Presently Catherine, catching sight of the two, broke off her own conversation to order the younger immediately to bed. Margot rose and made her curtsy, but as she was about to leave Claude seized her arm exclaiming, 'Dear God, sister, you mustn't go.'

Frightened, the bride looked at her mother, who called Claude to her and scolded her in a sharp undertone: 'Not a word — do you want her to give it away?'

'But you can't sacrifice her like that,' pleaded Claude humbly; 'if they find out they are certain to revenge themselves on her.'

'God willing,' returned Catherine piously, 'she will come to no harm. But in any event she must go, lest the Huguenots suspect something through her not being with her husband.'

Margot went. Strangest part of the story, she and Claude continued to love their mother slavishly.

At half-past two in the morning — it is the festal day of Saint Bartholomew, patron of healing — Catherine goes to call her son, but finds him already dressed and striding up and down muttering to himself. A few moments later, Henry joins them and the three go along the dim corridors of the Louvre to a window facing the church of Saint-Germain l'Auxerrois to the east. It is still well before the hour given for 'the executions' to begin. They can see the troops, evenly spaced shadows, motionless in the courtyard — waiting. They take their seats and wait too.

Catherine composed and alert; Charles feverish, unheeding what is said to him; Anjou — on both of them there seems to dawn for the first time the full implication of what it is that they are about to do. It is their first chance, now that all the hectic activity of the forty hours since the Admiral's shooting has narrowed down to these dreadful minutes of quiet, to think. Of the thousands of simple men sleeping peacefully in the darkened city who lay down in the serene belief that so long as their King, 'God's image on earth,' watched over them, no harm could come to them or their wives and their children in the night. Of what this act may breed, 'calamities' (as De Retz said a few hours before) 'of which none of us may ever live to see the end.' Henry gasps. Charles jerks round on him and they stare into each other's eyes, reading the same thought. Catherine turns, too, half-rises and opens her mouth to speak, but falls back as if their mood of horror had in some form communicated itself to her. She hears Charles order one of the servants behind them to hurry to the Admiral's house and bid the Duke of Guise 'to undertake nothing against him' — a message that will automatically cancel what was intended to follow Coligny's death. The man runs off... he needs barely five minutes... at least fifteen remain before dawn gives voice to the bell on the Palace of Justice....

When abruptly the silence is shattered by a clanging in the tower of Saint-Germain l'Auxerrois over the way. A pistol shot rings out — another — a scream — more shots — shouting and the scuffle of running feet — bell echoing bell in every direction — and suffusing the whole the most dreadful of all sounds on earth, the roar of a mob loosed upon a congenial work of destruction.

The messenger returns to report he was too late — Guise's men have already broken into the Admiral's house — two of his servants lie on the doorstep in their blood. Charles goes entirely off his head, grabs a harquebus from a member of his guard, rushes to his own room and blazes away into space, screaming, 'Kill! Kill!' Anjou goes out into the streets, Catherine back to the Tuileries. She knew her sons' natures too well to take any unnecessary risks — earlier the previous evening she advanced the hour for the signal on her own initiative and ordered it sounded from the neighbouring church instead of the more distant Palace of Justice.

In the courtyard of the Admiral's house the Duke of Guise waits, flushed and excited, for his men to throw his enemy's body from the window. It falls face downward on the cobbles, the velvet dressing-gown round it oozing blood from a hundred stabs. Guise turns it over lightly with his foot to make sure and stares at the dead face for a moment with a smile... one day one of those responsible with him for this night's work will turn *his* body over in just that way — without smiling.

The mob breaks into the courtyard, hacks off the Admiral's head, drags his body through the streets — he has his wish: he will not see another civil war — and hangs it on the public gibbet. Guise, his brothers and the Bastard of Angoulême, now partner of the man he had been set to poignard not so long before, rush out into the streets shouting, 'Kill! Kill! It is the King's wish!'

Kill! Kill! From the window of the Louvre the royal maniac raves his confirmation. Within ten minutes the ex-Provost Marcel and his stout lads have made a ghastly farce of the tidy plan drawn up so painstakingly by a lady and five gentlemen sitting round a table the previous afternoon. A list! They never heard of it. *Their* business is to kill Huguenots — this chance may not come again. They drag them out of the houses, men, women, and tiny babies, cut the throats of those fleeing blindly for the fields or the river. A lady of quality borrows a nun's robe and tries to steal away toward the palace... they observe her little red velvet shoes, catch her, stab her.... Hundreds of fugitives throw themselves into the Seine — attempt to climb the piers of the bridges — have their hands hammered loose by men standing above — fall back into the water to be pounded to death by oars swung by boatmen with white bands round their arms. And not only Huguenots.... In the general orgy second sons murder their elder brothers, cousins despatch cousins who stand a step nearer an inheritance.... France's greatest living philosopher, Ramus, is murdered by a rival whose pretensions he has insulted.... Shopkeepers perish protecting their wares....

In the Louvre Margot lies wakeful the entire night behind the drawn curtains of her bed, listening to the murmur of a conversation her husband is carrying on with the gentlemen of his suite regarding Friday's outrage. At dawn he comes and tells her that he is going to meet the King by appointment for tennis, where he will press for instant justice on those who plotted the Admiral's life. He goes out with his suite and she tries again to sleep, but cannot for memory of her sister's agitation the previous night. A few minutes later, someone comes running down the corridor shouting, 'Navarre! Navarre!' She tells the old nurse with her to open the door and see who it is. A man bursts in and flings himself on her bed, bleeding from several wounds and after him four archers of the guard. Without understanding what it is all about, Margot takes the man in her arms and shields him against his pursuers with her body, until the captain of the guard, Nancy, enters and draws his men off, smiling despite himself at the Queen of Navarre's predicament. Margot puts the man to bed in her cabinet and throwing on a dressing-gown runs to Claude's room. On the way she sees a man hacked to pieces by the halberds of the guard and faints into the arms of Nancy. Recovered, she staggers on, slithering in blood, shutting her eyes as best she can to the horrors round her... Huguenots pursued through the corridors and cut down then and there or driven outside to run the gantlet of the Swiss guards in the courtyard.... In Claude's room a gentleman of her husband's suite, fleeing from his pursuers, begs her to save him; she hurries to find the King, pleads on her knees, successfully....

Charles's bosom friend Rochefoucauld is not so lucky. He

opens his door to a knock, finds himself confronted by some masked men, thinks it is one of the King's pranks and smiles — as a sword runs him through....

The little Queen, Elizabeth of Austria, who has been kept in ignorance, wakes to learn from her ladies what is going on around her. 'Does the King know?' she asks — her first thought. They tell her that he ordered it. 'What does it mean?' she moans, 'and what councillors can have advised him to do such a thing?' Falling on her knees she sobs out a prayer for her husband's forgiveness....

Piles of naked corpses, like carelessly stacked logs, stare up into every window of the Louvre; and the groans indicate how little care was exercised to separate the dead from the dying. In the city the work still goes on, despite frantic orders from the King to stop, until the capital of the civilized world looks 'as if it had been sacked by an enemy.' On and on into the suburbs, across all France by hysterical contagion, until the dead are beyond counting....

Catherine returns from her early morning walk to hear Mass in the chapel of the Tuileries, eats her usual hearty dinner and sits down to her letters. 'She looks ten years younger than yesterday,' wrote an ambassador who saw her that day, 'and gives the impression of one who has recovered from a grave illness.' Undoubtedly she owes a candle to the patron saint of healing whose day it is. In the fulness of her heart Catherine drafts a letter to the one man she knows will rejoice with her at what has occurred, the one man whose sympathy she most values, His Majesty of Spain:

> My son, I have no doubt that you will share with us our joy at God's goodness in giving my son the King the means to rid himself of subjects rebellious equally to God and to himself, and that it pleased Him to preserve us all from the cruelty of their hands, for which we feel assured you will praise God with us, both for our sakes and for the good which will result to all

Christendom and the honour and glory of God... and I rejoice still more that this occasion will confirm and augment the friendship between you and the King your brother, which is the thing in this world I most desire.... I send my greetings to my grandchildren the Infantas....
 Paris, this 28th day of August, 1572
 Your good mother and sister
 CATERINE

To accompany this epistle she dictates an official announcement of the massacre, the document which is said to have given Philip II the one good laugh of his life.

She has only one serious regret, that the Count of Montgomery, next to the Admiral the most formidable Huguenot chief on her list, has got away: she has an old score to wipe out with him for having had the bad luck to be her husband's opponent in the tourney that ended his life. One small sorrow, that in its excitement the mob killed some of her women friends, though she early sent her great painted coach to pick up various of them and bring them to the Tuileries for safety. And one real worry: by what means simultaneously to convince the Catholic sovereigns of Europe that Saint Bartholomew's was a holy design and the Protestant that it was a regrettable accident. Cheerfully the reinstated mistress of France sets to work on this impossibility. Some say that Philip's laugh was provoked by the thought of her trying....

There is nothing on her conscience, nothing whatever. Her mania for power has become almost a force of nature in its blind irresistible strength. How shall a flood or an earthquake feel pity or guilt for what it destroys? To her last day Catherine will contend that she only meant to get rid of five or six persons who richly wanted getting rid of. Those five or six, she considers, were merely inferior players in the game for whose winning they as well as she had to be prepared to lie, scheme, kill if necessary.... The ten thousand remaining victims expired, so far as she was concerned, of a mere slip of the imagination.

An excess of that quality accounts for the last victim. 'So much blood, so much blood,' murmurs Charles as he lies dying twenty-one months later in the Castle of Vincennes, where he so often played at soldier as a boy.

His nurse, a Huguenot, whom he clings to like a child in his illness and will not suffer to leave him day or night, wipes the feverish sweat from his forehead and tries to soothe him to sleep.

'Oh, nurse, nurse,' he moans, 'what bad advice I have listened to.... Oh, God forgive me... I don't know where I am any longer.... What will happen to me, and to my people... I am lost, lost...'

She continues her ministrations, saying gently, 'The murders are on the head of those who urged you to them. Since you repent of them, you must believe that God will not charge you too heavily.'

He shakes his head and stares at the dark, lofty ceiling. He is yellow and emaciated as an old man, though his twenty-fourth birthday is still a month away. The malady of his race has caught him up, with the assistance of another disease that is not of the body. Memory... since that morning nearly two years ago when the firearm dropped from his hands and he sank unconscious to the floor, no man has ever seen him smile or even raise his eyes to another's for more than a fleeting instant, and then only with evident pain. Round him has swirled unceasing civil war, not only the old quarrel, but rebellion against himself, his mother; murmurs even against the dynasty.... Danger, not sentiment, has chosen the great fortress for him to die in.... He lies there more eager for death than for anything in his whole life except the vision of glory that was taken from him. 'Thank God,' he ejaculates suddenly, 'that I leave no son to succeed me.'

A Slip of the Imagination

Catherine bustles in, all agog with a piece of news she is sure will cheer him up. Montgomery, the new Huguenot leader, the cause of Henry II's death, has surrendered to the royal troops on the promise of his life being spared. He is on his way to Paris for instant trial and execution. Beaming she waits for Charles to echo her delight.

He looks at her impassively before turning his face away. 'It doesn't matter. Nothing on earth matters any more.'

He died at four o'clock the next morning, May 31, 1574. Catherine found consolation in the thought that his last words were, 'My mother.' At least so she wrote; without mentioning in what tone the words were uttered.

BOOK IV

HENRY

It is a miserable state of mind to have few things to desire and many to fear; and yet that is commonly the state with kings.... Hence it comes likewise that princes many times make themselves desires and set their hearts upon toys; sometimes upon a building; sometimes upon erecting of an order; sometimes upon advancing of a person; sometimes upon obtaining excellency in some art, or feat of hand....

BACON

Chapter XII

INTERREGNUM

Long ago, and more than once, the stars had promised Catherine that all her sons should be kings; and in the very act of renewing the promise, at the time of Francis's death, had apparently nullified it by announcing the family's extinction in the current generation. Nothing seemed less likely on the morrow of Saint Bartholomew's, with the Protestant part of Europe shrieking for a holy crusade against her and the Catholic part complacently certain that she had delivered herself into their hands beyond any further need of purchasing, than that anyone would offer a throne to Anjou or Alençon; just as nothing appeared more improbable, with Charles's Queen expecting a baby within a few weeks, than that the seed of Henry II could fail to replenish itself into the indefinite future. Nevertheless, the twenty-one months following the massacre saw both promises well on their way to fulfilment: and the family, from the peak of its grandeur, looked for the first time upon the specific shape of its doom.

In May, 1573, two very different events were taking place at opposite ends of Europe. On the Atlantic coast of France the royal forces under command of the Duke of Anjou laid siege to La Rochelle, where the Huguenots, risen in rebellion after Saint Bartholomew's, were making their last stand. On the plains round Warsaw thirty-five thousand horsemen in bearskin helmets drew up in battle array to acclaim with voice and sabre the new King of Poland chosen a few hours before by the assembly of nobles. Fast riders brought the news across three kingdoms to Fontainebleau, where the Queen Mother, bursting into tears, hurried to fall on her knees before her private altar; then rose to dash off a note to her son directing him to drop the siege and make ready to claim his new throne. The Polish nobles and their ballot-box had simultaneously saved Huguenotry to fight another day and justified the matriarch's faith in her astrologers.

Never was faith better combined with works. For eight years she had jealously counted every pulse-beat in the ageing frame of the late Sigismond Augustus, studied minute reports on the ages, characters, and dispositions of his marriageable female relatives. Taking time well by the forelock she had despatched over a year earlier two of her ablest servants, one into Poland and the other into Germany, to pull wires amongst the Teutonic Princes who had a commanding influence in the election. She had pawned her own jewels and the Crown's for necessary expenses — and nearly threw her money away when Saint Bartholomew's all but finished Anjou's chances with the Protestant Germans. To counter that setback she flung in everything else she could think of to promise — all of Anjou's patrimony to the Polish treasury, free trade between France and Poland with a French fleet especially built to protect it, an expeditionary force to fight Russia, the endowment of a Polish University at Cracow, complete toleration to the Huguenots, and an immediate renewal of Coligny's enterprise in the Netherlands. Some of the ablest masters of contemporary fiction were drafted to explain how completely Saint Bartholomew's had taken her by surprise: indeed, most of it was a sheer myth (it appeared) invented by the Spaniards to favour their own candidate, the Archduke

Ernest of Austria. The opposition turned out to be her biggest asset. Central Europe had no desire to see Spain's power extend farther than it did already; and the Poles, not knowing Catherine very well and thinking she might keep at least part of her promises, chose Anjou for their king.

Even then her troubles were far from over. She had still to get him to go. Henry had at least two excellent reasons for not wishing to leave home at this time. He was head over heels in love and he had an enemy who, he was reasonably certain, would do everything possible to damage his interests while he was gone. The lady was Marie de Clèves, the Duke of Guise's Huguenot sister-in-law, married the previous year, to Henry's grief, to the Prince of Condé: a young woman who rippled her way into men's hearts because she found the world such a deliciously funny place. The enemy was his brother Alençon, in whose nineteen-year-old head were beginning to fester strange delusions of grandeur.

Again, as two years before over Elizabeth, Catherine strove to make her son sacrifice himself for the family's glory; and just as on that occasion she had Charles on her side — Charles, who could not look at his brother now without remembering what he wanted to forget, and from whom Catherine still dreaded some irrevocable gesture of rage against her darling. She promised Henry to make his interests her first thought while he was gone (and nobly kept her promise); held before him the great ambition of her own life, the crown of the Holy Roman Empire, which the German princes who had now favoured him would one day have in their power to bestow by election on a son of France; and as she pled she also wept in anguish at the thought of being separated from him — but 'I love your honour and grandeur more than my own pleasure, for I am not one of those mothers who love their children selfishly; I love you that you may be first in splendour and esteem among men....' And as before she had her way with the most dutiful of her children.

In the autumn the whole court accompanied the new monarch and the Polish delegation sent to fetch him — strange fellows accoutred like wild Tartars and speaking like the most cultivated of Europeans — as far as the castle of Blamont in Lorraine near the German border. To enable him to make a proper showing before his new subjects, Catherine bought him a collection of pearls on a year's credit; all her own jewels were in pawn and she had been compelled for the expenses of this journey to scrape together a million crowns from the clergy: but at least no one could say she did not do things royally.

Yet even his brilliant send-off failed to lift the weight from Henry's heart — regrets for the past, despondency over the future, a deep sadness to be leaving the country which he loved. Before the parting he took Margot aside and tried wistfully to light in her some spark of the old feeling between them: begging her at least not to think too unkindly of him nor lend herself to the intrigues of his enemies when he was gone. He was truly in love himself now, so he knew how much she had to forgive. But she, trusting not a word he said, looked at him quizzically and wished him a cool Godspeed.

Early next morning the first of the Valois to be called to a foreign throne waved his jewelled cap at the company on the terrace as he slowly trotted with his retinue down the wooded slope toward the Rhine.

At no moment of her life would Catherine more gladly have called quits with Fate. She had achieved, in Henry's election, her supreme triumph; France was at peace, Charles had shown himself quite capable of perpetuating the dynasty (since there was no reason in nature why the wife who had already borne him a daughter should not bear him a son, as his mistress had done). But Fate's concern was with the family, not with her nor with any of them as individuals.

For it was upon the family that Fate had lavished greatness — not greatness in the modern, personal sense, but in the sense in which Aeschylus and Shakespeare understood it, that of membership in an ancient, divinely established House; and it was against the family, therefore, as collective representatives of the House, that Fate held the reckoning for the sins and follies charged upon that greatness through the generations. That is the tragedy of Catherine and her children, as it is the theme of all tragedy in the exact meaning of the word: like the House of Agamemnon, and all the descendants of Atreus, they were granted the privilege of determining the time and manner of retribution's coming, but the retribution itself they could not possibly hope to avert, since it was already entailed upon their inheritance before they were born. It is not often that an episode in the incoherent jumble of the casual and irrelevant which we call history conforms so obediently to the pure canons of classical tragedy.

By the time the court, travelling with painful slowness because of the King's health, had arrived at Saint-Germain for Christmas, the signs of approaching death in his face were visible to all the world. Catherine, an acute diagnostician in such matters, had apparently detected them even earlier: for amongst the arguments she had used to Henry in prevailing upon him to leave for Poland had been a cryptic 'Go, my son, it will not be for long.' By February all the hatred she had stored up against herself — amongst the friends of those she had caused to be murdered, amongst the hundreds of thousands of moderate men who sympathized with them and detested her rule [1] — had crystallized into a resolve that when the crown passed for the third time to one of her sons, it should not be the adored one through whom she

---

[1] These later formed themselves into a middle party, under the leadership of the Montmorencys, and took the name of *Politiques* to distinguish themselves alike from Huguenots and rabid Catholics.

might be expected to continue her power, but the last, the ugly duckling untainted with the crime of Saint Bartholomew's.

Hercules, Duke of Alençon (he had already been rechristened Francis and would presently bear the title of Anjou, thus acquiring his elder brothers' names as in humbler circumstances he might have been awarded their old clothes), had not outwardly improved with the years. His nose, fulfilling its early promise, had swollen into an enormous porous bulb, which to the startled onlooker's first glance seemed extraordinarily like two noses either one of which would have been more than sufficient for the thin, brown, deeply pockmarked face that wore them. A tight, uncommunicative little mouth and a plump body precariously strutting on twisted legs completed more or less the picture he offered to the world.

It differed very materially from the one that he hung up for his own inward gaze. What are a few physical blemishes to one who knows himself to be born with the soul of a king? To be a king is what Alençon lived for, and only that. Unlike Francis, Charles, Henry, he never had a doubt of his vocation nor any interest apart from it. When Elizabeth of England was transferred to him from Anjou, he embraced her, so to speak, with a lover's ardour: she — or rather what she stood for — became from that instant the romance of his life and remained so till the hour of his death; the nearest that the royal coquette ever came to inspiring romantic sentiment in a masculine heart she inspired in that hideous boy's — even after he had a good look at her, and she at him. Silently — for he had a rare knack of keeping his mouth shut — he followed the plans for the Great Enterprise, envying Charles his chance, impatient of his hesitations; and when the Admiral died, Alençon in the seclusion of his own mind slipped on the great man's shoes and stood up in them ready to go out and wrest the Netherlands from Spain for the endowment of France's portionless younger son. For a dozen years, heedless of the world's laughter and his family's annoyance, he hugged that vision of a Gaspard de Coligny, fleshed as Francis, Duke of Alençon, laying a kingdom at the feet of the red-haired, hawk-nosed Gloriana of England and they two ruling their joint empire happily ever after.

Charles he tolerated, mildly despised and stood a little in awe of. Anjou he openly hated; had hated him with growing intensity since early childhood because he suspected the airy Henry of laughing at him; hated him with additional fervour as their mother wrestled for and finally won him a throne. 'Why should he be a king and not I?' he demanded wildly of Catherine. 'Am I not of the same blood as he?' and implored her to make Charles let him collect an army forthwith for the conquest of Flanders. But Catherine, with many other preoccupations and only too glad to be out of Flanders, dismissed him with an absent caress.

He turned to Margot and begged her to befriend him, offering to do anything on earth for her in return. For a while she held him off, not knowing quite what to make of him. When they were both children he had been her devoted slave, over whom she had capriciously tyrannized and whose infant tempers she alone, with one firm word, had been able to quell; but they had seen very little of each other since she left him behind in the schoolroom to go on the voyage to Bayonne. Moreover, being a good Catholic, she had an instinctive scruple against interfering in Flanders. But he followed her around like a dog, pressing awkward little gestures of good-will upon her, until all at once she melted. He seemed so infinitely pathetic, with his gnome's face and figure trying to give utterance to his grotesquely heroic ambitions. How unfair that he should not have his chance in England through a crime of which he was innocent![1] In a warm

---

[1] Margot's sentiment was shared quite generally, since it was believed that Elizabeth would have had Alençon in 1572 if not for Saint Bartholomew's. Some historians still think so.

uprush of pity, a pity that never thereafter forsook her no matter what he did, she took him in her arms, kissed him, promised to do whatever she could for him. And as she took the ugly brother to her heart, something stirred in that impetuous organ — 'the sole oracle of my good or my ill,' according to its owner — the old love turned to hate for the beautiful one, whispering to Margot that perhaps the hour was at hand for the squaring of accounts.

With a secret and driving energy worthy of her mother she welded Alençon's ambitions abroad and the discontent at home into a purposeful effort to bar Henry from the throne. The human material for the task lay scattered all over France and beyond: Montmorency at Chantilly, his brother Damville in his southern government of Languedoc, Navarre's followers in the angle between the Atlantic and the Pyrenees, Louis of Nassau on the far side of the Flemish border, Montgomery and his expedition equipping in the Channel Islands with English money, the Huguenots of La Rochelle under their captain La Noue, nicknamed *Bras de Fer*. It was Margot who brought leader and followers together, watched over her brother and warned him of danger, guarded her husband's complicated interests in the matter... for if Alençon became King, Henry of Navarre emerged as his heir by virtue of the old title dating back to Saint Louis.

Someone was needed to act as liaison officer between the conspirators and the brother and sister upon whose every move poured the blazing limelight of the court. Someone equally devoted to both, whose judgment both could trust. A rare bird, indeed, but Margot found him in the person of a Provençal gentleman, La Mole, who enjoyed Alençon's intimate confidence, and whom, to make doubly sure of his fidelity, she took for her lover. For ten years, so long as Alençon lived, she never deviated from her policy of choosing her lovers by the criterion of their usefulness to her brother's service; it is surprising how many qualified.

La Mole was one of those men born with so much charm that they are certain sooner or later to get themselves into trouble. The fascination he exercised over her youngest son had for some time caused Catherine to suspect sorcery and meditate assassination. Nevertheless, she had sent him to England to plead Alençon's cause with Elizabeth, a mission he carried out so capably that he nearly displaced his principal: if this is the man, ye gods, what must the master be like, shrilled the ladies of the English court, while the Queen covered him from head to foot with jewels, and Leicester, her Robin of a now almost historic scandal, stalked through the corridors of Greenwich Palace biting his nails with jealousy. It may be that La Mole ultimately did the Duke's courtship more harm than good by arousing too great expectations in Elizabeth. On his return he entered into a successful rivalry with Anjou for Marie de Clèves's smiles — an additional reason for his preferring Henry to remain permanently in Poland — and after her marriage to Condé attached himself, though not exclusively, to Margot. He was very devout: Henry said of him, 'If you want to count La Mole's debauches you have only to watch how often he goes to Mass.'

La Mole worked swiftly and thoroughly. It was a race with time, for no one knew how long Charles would last. By the end of February a plan was complete for Alençon and Navarre to ride out on March fourteenth as if for a day of hunting, when a detachment of cavalry under a captain called Guitry would kidnap and carry them off to Sedan, where Louis of Nassau would be waiting for them with ten thousand men. Meanwhile, Montgomery would join forces with La Noue, the Montmorencys would declare themselves at the same time, and confronted with this combination Catherine would be summoned to resign and Charles to recognize Alençon as his heir.

But Guitry's precipitancy and the Queen Mother's furious energy balked the arrangement as set forth in the schedule.

The cavalry leader, riding too fast, was sighted in the vicinity of Saint-Germain ten days too early. Fearful of finding himself and his master implicated in treason if the raiders were caught, La Mole urged Alençon to go to his mother and confess to an intention of running away to make a career for himself in the Netherlands. Catherine, doubtful whether to believe him or not, elected to proceed on the safer assumption that he was lying. At two o'clock in the morning she thrust him and Navarre into one coach, herself and Margot into another, and set off via Paris for the mighty fortress of Vincennes, Charles moaning as he followed, 'Why couldn't they at least wait for me to die?'

The insurgents were shaken, but only momentarily; within a few days Catherine learned to her dismay that they were still standing to arms everywhere, in plain expectation of near developments from Vincennes. She called Alençon and Navarre on the carpet and put them through a wringing cross-examination. What were they really up to? Who was in it with them? Her son-in-law put a bold face on it, frankly admitting his boredom at having nothing to do and his intention of running away the first chance he got, while Alençon, though 'disheartened and half silly,' stuck to his first story. Really terrified now, as much by the mystery as the danger surrounding her, Catherine put them both under arrest and set grimly to work unravelling the threads of the plot.

As fast as she picked them out cunning hands snarled them up again. Alençon mysteriously came into funds, transmitted from England to help him escape. A sudden search of his rooms brought to light a woman's dress secreted in readiness for a flight in disguise. When questioned, he laughed lamely and said it was a joke on Navarre. Fiercely the Queen Mother peered around for someone else to put under lock and key: scarcely heeding the daughter sitting next to her with the demure expression proper to a well-bred young female confronted with wrongdoing she has no business to understand.

Margot walked with the two culprits to lighten the tedium of their detention and in the evenings danced with, among others, La Mole; who next day found means of seeing the new set of accomplices he had assembled after the flight from Saint-Germain. Within three weeks another escape had been contrived for April eighth.

It was averted by Margot's old enemy, Du Guast, whom Henry had left in charge of his interests while he was away. Du Guast temperamentally suspected Margot of any deviltry that might be afoot and sagely decided that in any business where a woman was involved he could not do better than call in the help of another woman. He had exactly the right one to hand in his mistress, Charlotte de Sauve, a hardy perennial of the Queen Mother's flying squadron. The wife of a high court official, Madame de Sauve — tawny-haired, tranquil, timeless — had already buried one husband, grown bored with another, seen her first lover's children grow up: fifteen years hence the Duke of Guise would choose her as the pleasant companion of his last night on earth. Dismissing her other suitors at Du Guast's request, she concentrated her smiles upon the youthful prisoners who had long been hovering on the outskirts of her court. Margot tried to tear them away, without success. She could only stand helplessly by as 'that Circe' artfully planted jealousy between the brothers-in-law, separated them, pumped them. 'How shall one refuse one's confidence to those one loves?' inquired the crestfallen Queen of Navarre despondently of her *Memoirs*.

The Circe had it out of them; enough at any rate for the Queen Mother, when Du Guast passed his findings on to her, to supplement what she already knew and arrive at a fairly accurate answer. In a trice the indiscreet pair found themselves secluded from the world in their own rooms behind barred windows. Montmorency, enticed to court through his wife, Diane de France, Henry II's natural daughter, continued on to the Bastille in the company of the Marshal Cossé, his confederate. He expected immediate death, nor would he have been disappointed had Catherine dared to kill him so long as his brother Damville was free in the south to retaliate; she sent one of the royal secretaries south with a bravo named Martinengo, to overcome that difficulty, but Damville, protected by a wolf whom he kept in a state of semi-starvation and a Turk who could cut an ox in half with one stroke of a sword, proved harder to assassinate than she had anticipated. So did La Noue, but that was because she insisted on employing again that uniformly erratic marksman Maurevert: who presently got himself killed instead by the son of the De Mouy he had once shot by mistake.

Nearer home Catherine's net did better. It hauled in La Mole first thing; then his chief adjutant, the Count of Coconas from Savoy, who was dragged out of the house of a lady sheltering him, 'little to her credit'; and finally the renowned astrologer, Cosimo Ruggieri, whom the Queen Mother had imported from Florence and heaped with benefits for his knack of wringing only the most genial responses from the stars.

This last turned out to be the most important capture of all. In La Mole's house had been found a little wax figure stuck full of pins. As Ruggieri was led out of the Florentine ambassador's house, whither he had been tracked in defiance of diplomatic immunity, he asked with interest whether the King had vomited. The whole plot stood revealed! La Mole had clearly hired the wizard to conjure a swift end for Charles before Henry could be summoned from Poland, so that Alençon might take advantage of the interregnum.

Frantically Catherine ordered the public prosecutor to put La Mole and Ruggieri on the rack: 'Make Cosimo talk. Find out the truth about the King's illness. If he has cast an enchantment on my son Alençon to make him love La Mole, that he undo it immediately.' Spluttering fragments of agitation.

The prosecutor carried out his task to the best of his ability, but with no success. La Mole persisted in denying that the figure had anything to do with the King's health. Torn almost limb from limb he finally gasped that it was only the image of a lady whom he wanted to make fall in love with him. Plain nonsense — with the King vomiting blood as Ruggieri had foreseen he would. The Florentine stoically backed him up. La Mole was sentenced to death, Ruggieri to the galleys, the wax figure to the flames — as it began to sizzle the people by the King's bedside noticed the first improvement in his looks for many days.

Alençon fought desperately to save La Mole, but Charles and Catherine refused even to listen. On his knees he then begged his mother at least to order a private execution. She promised — but somehow, through the offices of the Italian perfumer, Monsieur René, the gates of Paris were locked as La Mole went to the scaffold and the royal messenger gained admittance too late. Perhaps Catherine judged that it would be unwise to deny the public so salutary a spectacle. Alençon writhed on the floor calling the heavens to witness the humiliation of a Prince of the Blood powerless even to spare his friend this final disgrace....

He himself got off, as did Navarre, thanks largely to an extremely able defence written by his wife; apart from a natural reluctance to proceed against her own kin, Catherine had no desire to advertise the discord within the family. She made them both, however, sign a declaration of loyalty disavowing their Huguenot connection and fetched Alençon to dance at a ball that the English ambassador might observe how utterly carefree he was. Only Margot, inscrutable and unreachable, went quietly her own way, so quietly that no one ever learned how she had got hold of La Mole's head, which she thereafter kept by her for a time in an embroidered bag: a gruesome reminder of things past and of the vengeance she hoped was still to come.

With his realm, its humours temporarily bled out of it on rack and scaffold, once more quiescent, Charles IX gratefully resigned his crown to his brother Henry and his soul to whoever would care to claim it.[1]

Catherine, Regent of France for the second time, sat down and poured out her heart to Henry as she had poured it out to Elizabeth on a very similar occasion nearly fourteen years before.

> To Monsieur my Son
>   The King of Poland
> Monsieur my son, I sent you yesterday by special messenger the tidings of the terrible affliction that has befallen me who have already lost so many of my children. I pray God that He send death to me before I see any more of them die, for I thought I should go out of my mind at the sight, and the love he [Charles] showed me at the end, not wishing to leave me and praying me to send for you at once and until your arrival to take over the government of the realm... saying that he knew his brothers [Alençon and Navarre] were unfriendly to him, which caused him to think they might be more obedient to me and to you... and then said farewell and begged me to embrace him, which almost caused my heart to burst. Never did man die in better possession of his understanding... commanding his brothers and all those who served him to obey me as yourself till you came, confident that you would wish it so, speaking constantly of your goodness and that you have always loved and obeyed him so well and never given him a moment's pain, only great services; for the rest, he is dead, the best Christian that ever was, having received all the sacraments and the last word he spoke was 'my mother.' In this extreme anguish I find only one consolation that you will soon be here.... The world was

---

[1] He left a daughter of nineteen months by his wife and a son of thirteen months by his mistress Marie Touchet — the one love affair of his life. The girl, Marie-Isobel, was of course barred from any part in the succession by the Salic Law; she died at five, after her mother was sent back to Austria. The boy, Charles, became a protégé of his uncle Henry III and lived to see Louis XIV. What an extraordinary difference it would have made to history had the two infants been changed round!

big enough, God knows, for you both to have had honour and grandeur... without this great calamity... of having lost your so good brother; but since it has pleased Him that I be tried so often, I praise Him and pray Him for patience and the consolation of soon having you here, for your realm has great need of you, and in good health, for if I were to lose you, I should have myself buried alive with you in the same tomb.... I am dying of longing to see you, for the one thing that can console me and make me forget what I have lost is your presence: you know how I love you, and when I think that you will never leave us again, I am enabled to bear everything with patience....
From the Forest of Vincennes, this last day of May, 1574.
Your good and affectionate mother, if ever there was one
CATERINE

Indomitable woman! To be able, in the very agony of her motherhood, to rise to ever sublimer optimism. All the evils that had threatened when she wrote the earlier letter to Elizabeth had come to pass and many more. Four civil wars had demonstrated with terrible conclusiveness her inability to win obedience by persuasion or compel it by force: even the scant intervals between had degenerated into a chronic anarchy in which both sides bloodily violated the edicts they had accepted until one or the other decided that it had received sufficient provocation to start all over again. The Crown, compelled to assume the cost of each struggle in order to buy peace, was caught in the vicious circle of being unable to tax a country impoverished by disorder without risk of starting another war. The House itself stood divided, the conduct of its younger members an ominous example in disrespect to the principle of legitimate succession on which its very existence rested.... The blood spilled on Saint Bartholomew's Day still cried for justice, the Paris mob had been initiated into the dangerous secret of its own power... And the people, weary and hopeless, were letting themselves go in riotous extravagance and blamed their demoralization upon the Queen Mother's Italian parasites who had brought in the new fashions of dissipation, gambling, lewdness, and furtive murder in the streets....

A few weeks earlier Catherine had been 'so depressed because she begins to suspect that her mode of government no longer satisfies' that she had considered abdicating. No thought could be farther from her now. Henry was coming home! He had only to show himself to his people as she saw him, in his natural majesty, for everything to be all right again. With renewed zest for life and its central meaning, power, she came to the mid-point of the family's story — the halfway mark between the fifteen years allotted by the stars to Charles and Francis and the fifteen promised to Henry.

Chapter XIII

TWO CROWNS AND A RIDE

Late in the forenoon of June 15, 1574, the Imperial ambassador to the court of Poland brushed peremptorily by the sentries at the door of the royal bedchamber in the palace of Cracow and demanded of the courtiers clustered round the table on which the four tall night tapers burned an immediate audience with the King. The group directed his glance to the drawn curtains of the bed and the two motionless pages on duty either side of it, the spokesman adding in a courteous whisper that His Majesty, tired out after the ball given in his honour by his predecessor's daughter the night before, had left orders on no account to be disturbed: he had been sleeping very badly, as His Excellency was no doubt aware.... With an impatient frown the ambassador drew from his sleeve a letter which he handed to them: a communication of such importance that in order to save a few hours his master had sent it express immediately the Queen Mother's weary courier had waited upon him in Vienna. One glimpse was enough; those tidings had long been awaited. The Frenchmen knelt facing the bed as the ambassador awoke the sleeper and, kneeling also, congratulated him in the name of the Holy Roman Emperor on his accession to the throne of his fathers.

Henry III, by the grace of God Most Christian King of France this fortnight past, raised a tousled head and stared blankly before him. Deliverance! Day and night for six months he had prayed for it, vowed with passionate sincerity that he would exchange crown, freedom, everything, to go home to France — 'Gladly would I be a prisoner there rather than a free man here.' His lips quivered, two tears rolled down his cheeks; in a convulsion of sobbing he flung himself face down on the pillow, more miserable than he would ever have dreamed possible during those long months of anticipation. For Charles... just as Charles dying had yearned for him. Once, long ago, before the wretched conflicts and jealousies of adolescence divided them, they had loved each other with the easy understanding of two brothers separated by nothing more serious than fifteen months of age. And now Henry in exile wept heartbrokenly for Charles dead, repenting many things and in vain. When his mother's letter arrived a few hours later, he read over and over the passage in which she related Charles's last kindly words of him.... One can forgive Catherine much for remembering to repeat those words.

An hour and more Henry lay there struggling to recover his shattered poise. The first grief past, a whole whirlpool of memories, resolutions, desires twisted and leaped inside him. The gruesome posters thrust under his eyes as he passed through Germany on his way hither, to remind him of Saint Bartholomew's... the veiled insults at his hosts' tables, sometimes even at his own. Pictures and words had risen again, often, to mock him in the long hours of darkness; even full confession, made to his doctor, Miron, during one of those nights of wakefulness, had failed to exorcise them.... He would atone, he would redeem, Henry told himself, let him but see France again. Strive to be a king, a good king....

Not as kings in Poland were, a symbolic ornament.... Tavannes had warned him it would be so, but Catherine in her expansive way had refused to believe. An ornament? People paid for their ornaments... it was *he* who had paid, lavishing with free hand everything he had brought with him as well as all that devolved upon him as king — gold, lands. ... He had not minded, he loved giving... if only he had been able to make good what his mother had promised before his election — and then failed to deliver, to the daily laceration of his self-respect.... And though his subjects had been wonderfully considerate of him personally in this as in all other matters, their ways had not been his — their orgies of eating and drinking that revolted his fastidious soul.... Nothing had really hurt so much as that unending throb of homesickness....

A spasm of longing shot through him, for France, for his mother — and, more than either, the woman over whose image he had brooded ever since leaving Blamont, for news of whom he had thrust incessant couriers across half Europe. Sitting up, he called for pen and ink and forthwith wrote a letter to the Princess of Condé offering her, if she would now deign to accept them, both his heart and his kingdom — 'You shall be Queen of France if you so desire' — and signed it, according to a quaint custom he had learned from the native nobility, in blood drawn from his own finger.

He rose, dismissed the ambassador under oath not to divulge his news for the moment and sent for his cabinet of intimate advisers to attend him while dressing. They filed in: Bellièvre, Charles's ambassador extraordinary, now automatically recalled by his master's death; Souvray, Keeper of the Wardrobe and Henry's most intimate friend ('had God willed me to have been born in another state I should have wished to be Souvray'); Villequier, First Gentleman of the Bedchamber; Pibrac, the Secretary; Larchant, Captain of the Guard; Du Halde, the Valet-in-Chief; Caylus, a soldier, and next to Souvray the King's closest friend; and several others. They were nearly all young, all but Bellièvre attached to

Henry's personal fortunes: there was scarcely a man present who would not cheerfully have laid down his life for him and more than one who did; all of them would live to be scurrilously blackguarded for their devotion to him, some to share his degradation and downfall, a few to shine under his successor amongst the most honoured servants of France.

The King told them the news and asked their opinion on what was to be done: depart in secret at once (presuming that were possible) or try for the Poles' consent. Half, led by Bellièvre (who was going in any event), favoured staying; if an arrangement could be made to have the crown transferred to Alençon, it would both enhance the family's prestige and enable the King to rid himself conveniently of a nuisance. The rest urged that France needed her sovereign as soon as possible to avert the perils of an interregnum — even as they debated came the messenger with Catherine's letter, '... as to your departure from Poland, do not in any way delay it and take care that the Poles do not hinder you for their own purposes.... We have need of you here.'

Two duties in balance. An irrevocable decision to make and a very brief time to make it in. At any moment the news might leak out and the Poles put the King under polite arrest. For, having solemnly prayed Heaven for enlightenment on the eve of the ballot, they considered Henry as much God's anointed in Poland as in France, and might with justice object to having their state thrown into anarchy through the abrupt removal of its central pillar. If he tried and failed, he would be brought back in humiliation, their permanent captive. On the one side temporization and boredom, on the other danger and overwhelming inclination. 'We go,' said Henry.

The rest of the day was spent in preparation. By evening the rumour of Charles's death had spread through the palace and the town. To attempt to keep it a secret any longer could only arouse suspicion: taking the bull by the horns Henry summoned the members of the Polish Senate, then in residence at Cracow, to meet him on the following morning. Their response to his announcement was brutally direct. He would not in any circumstances be allowed to leave nor even assert a nominal claim to his inheritance by signing himself King of France as well as of Poland. Without protest he declared himself ready to comply with their wishes. Meantime, Bellièvre, having presented his letters of recall, set out to arrange for the passage over the Austrian frontier and the relays of horses from that point on to Vienna, while Neuvy, Catherine's returning messenger, departed separately with the King's personal jewels and other objects of value.

The populace of Cracow, with the curious instinct of crowds, were the first to suspect the King's intention, and all that day drew a milling cordon round the palace. Count Tenczynski, Grand Marshal of the Household, came to Henry and frankly asked him what there was in the popular report. The King answered with a shrug that he had disclosed his whole intention to the Senators: 'Let the people talk if they like. I am only concerned with my own honour and reputation.' Tenczynski, temporarily disarmed, went off to a banquet — an absence that had been counted upon in setting the escape for that night, since the Grand Marshal's surveillance was the thing above all else to be feared.

But disquieting remarks were dropped at the banquet. Tenczynski rushed back to the palace, where he found the King still at supper. On seeing him enter breathless, Henry laughed with a quizzical 'Still doubtful of me, are you? Well, you'll soon see me slumbering peacefully and then you can go and do likewise.' He joked and drank until, at the usual hour of retirement, his eyes began to droop, his head to nod. The servants helped him off to bed, where he chatted drowsily until the curtains were drawn. Tenczynski listened for a few moments to his breathing, peeped in once, then took himself off.

By another door entered Souvray and Larchant, booted and

spurred. The King slipped out of bed, Du Halde swiftly drew on his clothes — a service he was to render fourteen years later in preparation for a far different kind of flight — and together they glided through the adjoining apartments, occupied by the physician Miron, and out by a service staircase that led to a postern gate and some swampy fields beyond. Miron went ahead to test the gate, returned to report that it was locked. The little party, squeezed against the walls of the palace kitchens, consulted in anxious whispers: Souvray the dashing swaggered out to the keeper of the gate, transferred a piece of money and the confidential information that he was on his way to a very secret tryst with a very great and very pretty lady. The sympathetic porter remarked that in that case he would probably be staying out late and handed him the key to let himself in with on his return. Souvray opened the gate and sauntered out; a few seconds later a series of shadows followed him through.

The four ran three quarters of a mile across the fields to a little chapel where the others had been appointed to meet them. The men detailed to bring up the horses were already there, but no Villequier, no Pibrac: the pair charged with responsibility for the pack-animals and — of greater importance even — the guides. What had happened to them? Someone replied that Villequier had been observed by the crowd outside the palace leading his party to the rendezvous, giving him no option but to dismiss both horses and guides. To go on without them was awkward, to wait for them fatal. 'Let's trust to God and our luck,' said the King, and leaped into the saddle. His mount, an Arab of Souvray's, wild for lack of exercise, bucked and reared beyond hope of control. He changed to a mare — a gift of Tenczynski's! — and the little band galloped away.

A pitch-black night; not one of them with the least notion of the road or a word of the language; and fifty miles of dense forest to be traversed before dawn if they are to have the least chance of shaking off pursuit. They strike an opening in the woods, take it. Soon their horses plunge breast-deep into a marsh, emerge two hundred yards later with all sign of a trail gone. They spread out, find another, assemble and gallop on. At the end of fifteen miles the river Vistula, noisy but invisible, brings them up short. Which way is it flowing? Henry dismounts, trails his staff in the water, swings and races off upstream: the other way lies Cracow.

Again in the forest. And presently an insurmountable obstacle looms up — piles of new-cut logs strewn about in every direction. Once more they separate to find a road, this time without success. But Souvray and Larchant come on a wood-cutter's hut, knock imperiously on the door. The frightened peasant climbs into the loft, dragging his ladder after him. The impatient Frenchmen break in, scramble up by toe and finger, haul him out and by means of signs and a dagger at his throat indicate that he is to come along and guide them — a little ashamed, as they later confess, of their inability to speak a word of Polish after seven months' residence in the country. They mount the man on the crupper of a saddle, call together the rest of the party, and through the pine-scented dawn make for the town of Zator, where there is a bridge over the river. Luckily somebody left the night-barrier open. They cross, make for another town, Oswiescin, a dozen miles away — where they find Villequier and Pibrac, exhausted but triumphant, waiting for them with guides and luggage.

The whole party stops a few moments for rest and refreshment — until someone's quick ear detects the roll of hooves in the distance. The Poles! Again they mount, dig their spurs into their steeds' dripping flanks. Soon they can see over their shoulders Tenczynski leading what seems to be a flight of eagles' wings — a hundred of his Tartar cavalrymen, the best in the world.

The race for the frontier is on. Villequier, Pibrac, Caylus, drop out, calling to the King not to mind them, but go on; Pibrac jumps into a marsh up to the ears in order to avoid the notice of the pursuers, but they ignore both him and his two companions; they are after bigger game. Miron next falls behind, crying, 'Spur, spur, the whole of Poland is after us!' The King and the others almost hold their ground; the Tartars, with three hours to make up, are winded, too. Now another stream, the Oder, close beyond which lies the international boundary, draws in sight. In a final whirl of dust the royal party thunders across a frail wooden bridge — safe: for Larchant, Souvray, and du Halde throw themselves out of the saddle, rip up a row of planks, fling them into the water. Henry's mare topples over, stone dead. Tenczynski and his Tartars draw rein on the opposite bank, half-turn and trot slowly upstream to a ford five miles away, while the King is escorted smoothly by Bellièvre into the territory of the Holy Roman Empire.

The laggards straggle in and the journey is resumed, though with a strict watch still for the pursuers. Presently Tenczynski and a few of his Tartars appear on their flank.

Souvray rides toward them and calls out, 'Do you come as friends or enemies?'

'Friends,' answers the Pole.

The King joins Souvray. 'Then send away your Tartars,' he commands, 'and speak without dismounting.'

'Sire, return to Poland. You will find us as always your most obedient subjects.'

'Count,' returns Henry, 'in going to claim the crown of France, my lawful inheritance, I do not renounce the other. When I have fulfilled my duty, you will see me again.'

'Sire, you will not find in France subjects as faithful as your Poles.'

'I beg you not to insist, Tenczynski. If you had an army you could not drag me back. I have this' — drawing his dagger — 'for whoever tries. Go back and watch over my people till I return.'

Without a word the other draws his own dagger, opens a vein in his wrist and sucks the blood in token of eternal fidelity. Amid a complete stillness he rides forward unclasping a bracelet of rare cameos: 'Take it, Sire, and give me in return one of the glass ornaments from your tunic.'

Henry sits mute for an instant, holding the bracelet and looking at the giver. Then with an impulsive gesture he wrenches a valuable diamond ring from his finger and extends it, saying, 'Keep it in memory of me.' They embrace and ride away in opposite directions, and Henry confides to his companions his dream of leaving Poland as a perpetual inheritance to his seed by his second son. But no Valois would ever follow him on the throne of Poland — any more than on that of France.

He meant to press on. His mother, his country, his heart, all called urgently to make speed. There was a long way to go — Vienna, Venice, Turin, the passes of the Alps, Lyons, Paris: the route he had chosen to avoid a repetition of that nightmare passage through Germany seven months before. But the matter was taken out of his hands. The Archdukes Ernest and Matthias met him halfway bearing their imperial father's welcome; Maximilian himself rode out to greet him a league from the gates of Vienna, where, after a long and courteous argument, the old Emperor made the young King precede him into the capital to receive the triumphal reception that had been prepared for him. Despite the shortness of the notice, balls, banquets, tourneys had been arranged for every hour of the week to follow: and no amount of tact could get Henry out of them without offence to his host's feelings. He bowed to necessity, but wrote at once to the French ambassador in Venice, Du Ferrier, asking if it would not be possible to pass through the Republic's territory incognito. Du Ferrier wrote back at once:

> Though Popes, Emperors, and Kings have sojourned in this city, nevertheless they say that they have never been so delighted as at the prospect of seeing a King of France, whom they have always honoured above all other princes of the earth, and to come here incognito, Sire, would be quite out of the question, for apart from the fact that there is no prince in Italy who will not come to do you reverence, there is no man or woman in this city who does not look forward with keenest anticipation to seeing you, as well as all the lords of the provinces through which you are to pass, who have sent command to their subjects and ministers to honour and obey you as if you were in your own realm.

After all, there were many worse things than being King of France and twenty-two years old, and free as one must never expect to be again once this holiday was over; than having beauty spread out on every side solely for one's pleasure and approval; than feeling the power in oneself to gratify and more than gratify every curiosity and expectation.

The world went mad about him. 'It is his misfortune that none of his portraits do him justice,' an observer wrote, 'not even Janet himself [the master of contemporary French portraiture] has been able to render that indescribable something he has received from nature. His eyes, that lurking charm round his mouth when he speaks, the spell he casts over those who have the honour to be received by him in private, can be rendered neither by pen nor brush. His hands are so fine and beautifully proportioned one... can only imagine them holding a sceptre.... He conquers wherever he goes and is unconscious of a hundredth part of his conquests.'

There was a time to come, and soon, when the multitude, seeing his weaknesses magnified and distorted through his natural reserve as through a powerful lens, would loathe him: but never, even when he injured them, did those who served him in any intimate capacity cease to adore him for

HENRI III

the blend of unpretentious dignity and gay, unaffected familiarity with which he conducted his relations with them.

'Stout fellow,'[1] he wrote to the Duke of Nevers, who happened to be in Italy at the time, 'here I am, having managed by the grace of God to get out of Cracow, and making merry at the Emperor's expense. I shall be in Venice in six days or thereabouts.... Wait for me there, since you are so close by; I can't think of a better Pantaloon [the good companion of contemporary Italian comedy] than you, and you must come with me on the Bucentauros [the Doge's famous ceremonial galley]. Trusting that God will keep you and not let you die before I see you, I sign myself Henry, at present King of France, the same you once knew as Duke of Anjou.'

He left Vienna at the end of June, and two weeks later reached the sea. At the little port of Marghera the whole body of Senators, the venerable directors of the mighty Venetian oligarchy, stood waiting to receive him, at their head Giovanni Correr, ambassador to three French kings, his aged frame bent nearly double under his mantle of cloth of gold. Three gondolas were drawn up at the quai, one draped in black velvet, the second in violet, the third in cloth of gold. The King embarked in the last and asked for the canopy to be furled. And as the eight oarsmen, yellow-skirted and white turbanned (the colours of his House), sent the craft ploughing forward, he stood up and feasted his eyes on the loveliest vision in the West. The splendid, semi-barbarous masses of Venice gleaming in the midsummer heat — the Venice that had lorded it over and largely fabricated during the four centuries past a whole civilization — the Venice whose afternoon glory Veronese and Tintoretto and the ninety-six-year-old Titian were at once depicting and creating.

A fleet of gondolas belonging to forty young patricians who were to do the honours of the city for him met him mid-

---

[1] This is a rather free rendering of *bon homme*, but it seems to me justifiable in the context, particularly considering his relations with Nevers.

way and escorted him to the palace in Murano where he was to spend the night. He was exhausted from a long day's travelling, the crowd brought him out on the balcony twice to respond to their cheers, he had to grant several interviews: yet, after retiring, he rose again, dressed himself simply in black and slipped out unseen through the garden to the water's edge, where the Duke of Ferrara was waiting for him with a plain gondola. During the next four hours the King of France enrolled himself amongst the countless millions of tourists and the Duke amongst the ageless fraternity of guides who have passed up and down the Grand Canal asking and imparting the names and histories of the fairy palaces along its banks.

Next day, a Sunday, at three in the afternoon, the Doge Mocenigo came in the great galley of state to conduct the King to the Lido, where the high dignitaries of the Republic stood drawn up on the steps of the Podestà's palace to be presented before escorting him across the lagoon for his ceremonial entry. Henry leaped lightly from the galley, embraced the Podestà Lippomano before he could kneel, exchanged a few easy words with the others. Then all took their places in the brilliant fleet, the King once more on the state galley, the Doge on the freshly gilded Bucentauros, the rest following in fourteen ships-of-war and a hundred liveried gondolas, till the procession reached the quai at the foot of Saint Mark's Piazza, where towered the great triumphal arch specially designed by Palladio and decorated by Tintoretto. Henry, dressed in black velvet, jewelled cap in hand, passed under it with the Papal Nuncio on his right and the Doge on his left, knelt at an altar before the Cathedral as the *Te Deum* was sung, waved to the crowd packed in, round, and above the Piazza, and then, amidst a salute of the guns from the ships and the forts, was borne by the Bucentauros to the Foscarini Palace, where he was to lodge as guest of the Republic.[1]

[1] The scene of Henry's debarkation is preserved in a fresco by Vizentino on the walls of the Room of the Four Doors in the Doges' Palace.

That evening after dark he stood on the balcony of the palace to receive as lovely an homage as was ever offered to any man in the whole history of the world. On every housefront and every roof facing the Grand Canal, against the very heavens themselves, shot from ten thousand rockets, there blazed the Lilies of the Valois and the Lion of Saint Mark's, the arms of France and of Poland intertwined, antique columns and pyramids and stars. Venice had dressed herself in light in his honour. It went on the whole night through. From the windows along the serpentining waterway ladies borrowed from the canvases of Titian and Veronese fluttered their handkerchiefs, from the drifting gondolas below they flung up to him flowers and laughter. At two o'clock a barge passed from whose deck the sweetest-voiced choir on earth gave a serenade in his praise. Henry turned away with a little catch in his throat, muttering to those who stood next to him, 'If my mother were only here to receive her share of these honours, which I owe so entirely to her.'

Yes, it was good for once to be a king and young and free — with a fond mother to scrape together a nation's reluctant pennies so that one might repay hospitality as befitted a prince. To bestow diamonds worth thousands of pounds upon the Doge, gold chains worth three hundred upon one's hosts, tips of twenty upon the musicians that sang and played for one, and ten or more upon the domestics in the houses in which one stayed. To roam in disguise through the incomparable bazaars of Venice like another Haroun-al-Raschid, buying pearls and musk in staggering quantities for one's friends, little curly-haired white dogs for oneself. To visit incognito the famous courtesans and exchange lettered conversation with them, collect the little books in which they noted down their names, addresses, and rates, and inspire a sonnet from Titian's immortal friend and model Veronica Franco. Or visit the museums attended by an escort of thirty ladies in trailing robes and collars of heavy pearls, ready to walk straight into the pictures. Or call upon the great painters in their studios and buy three Tintorettos from the master himself (who had been on the Doge's galley disguised as a sailor in order to make a sketch of the royal visitor). Or at the arsenal watch the keel of one of the galleys that had transformed the life of Europe laid in the afternoon, and mount it for its maiden voyage to one's own door at dusk. And in between have Venice pour out its wealth and genius to provide one with entertainments each more gorgeous and exotic than the last. . . .

But all good things must end. A final service in Saint Mark's — then on to Mantua, where the splendours of Venice were repeated on a smaller scale; Turin, where Henry outdid himself in generosity by giving away three of his frontier towns to his aunt's husband, the Duke of Savoy, because she asked him to; and finally the Mont Cenis Pass, on whose heights Henry paused to look down upon France and exclaim, 'No, there is no country on earth worth this one.'

Meantime Catherine, fretted into an illness by her worries at home and her yearning for her absent son, debated with herself whether she should go to meet him or not. She put the question to her ministers, who advised strongly against: with the country in such a precarious state it would be most imprudent for the Regent and the sovereign to be away from the centre of affairs at the same time. She had no answer, she merely remained unconvinced. Suppose the people who were flocking to greet Henry in the south, even in Italy, should put ideas into his head detrimental to her power? She could not bear it; early one August morning she ordered her coach without telling anyone in advance, packed Alençon, Navarre, and Margot firmly into it, left word for her escort to follow and told the driver to make for Lyons.

She arrived there on the twenty-seventh. A week later, Henry crossed the frontier, where his brother and brother-in-law awaited him, by Catherine's stern instructions, with a confession of error and an application for forgiveness; he granted it, subject to their future good behaviour, and embraced them both. A gun boomed its welcome: another a long way off took up the signal, and another, until the echo of the King's homecoming had travelled across France and died out in the distant oceans. Catherine, too, could put up a good show when moved to it.... Next day she was holding Henry in her arms, so happy to see him she could hardly speak.

Chapter XIV

THE ELEGANT MISFIT

A GOOD reign, in the heyday of monarchy, was considered to resemble a fortunate marriage, in that both arrangements, though originally made in Heaven, depended for their subsequent success on mutual devotion and harmony of disposition. ' "I marvel that ye have forgotten the pledge of this my wedlock and marriage with my kingdom," ' exclaimed Queen Elizabeth to her turbulent Commons, ' and therewith drew the ring from her finger and shewed it, wherewith at her coronation she had in set form of words solemnly given herself in marriage to her kingdom.' She herself proved the force of the analogy up to the hilt: for forty-four years, while her consort swaggered over the earth redistributing the ownership of its valuables to his better liking or shut himself up with a quill to relieve his pent-up humours in blank verse, she tended his house and abetted his career with wifely thrift, loyalty, a humorous understanding of his foibles and an unscrupulous way with those who hoped to take advantage of him.

They ordered the thing differently in France only to the extent made necessary by the reversal in the sex of the parties. France, for some inscrutable reason of her nature the eternally, uniquely feminine amongst nations, demanded to be ruled by a husband in place of being guided by a wife; the very fundament of her constitutional being, the Salic Law, stated her instinctive recognition of that quality in herself early and forever. She had proved through all her history, and would go on doing so increasingly, that to put forth the best that was in her she needed a master — a man to love her, pamper her, but above all to keep her in order with an iron hand lest she fall into hopeless disagreement with herself. That was why on the whole she had been happy in her submission to the Valois, whether to Louis XI, who had alternately tricked and bullied her into a fruitful surrender, or Francis I, who had been able to circumvent her gathering petulance by overstimulating her imagination and focussing it upon himself; that, essentially, was why Catherine, a woman, had never captured her trust; and why her son Henry's return took on so strongly the air of a joyous nuptial.

As a bridegroom he fell scarcely short of perfection. The lean, thoughtful face, the dark, lustrous eyes and whimsically turned mouth; the 'fine, beautifully proportioned hands that one can only imagine holding a sceptre'; the low musical voice with its gentle overtone of irony... his soldierly background, the glamour of his recent kingship .. and more than all, his manhood, an attribute of transcendent importance after the miseries accrued through the unhappy sequence of the two children his brothers. Dowered in his person with every charm, bearer of the world's golden opinions like a universal felicitation upon his kingdom, France, who from his earliest youth had yearned in her distress, 'Ah, if Anjou were only King!' could not but fancy that in him she saw renewed the qualities in his ancestors which had freed the land from foreign domination, united it, made it great and rich.

Yet, even through the epithalamion of din and flame at the gate of Lyons, a still, small voice, speaking in accents of doubt and a kind of sardonic melancholy, made itself heard in the knot of old servants of the Crown packed to suffocation behind the ecstatic bulk of the Queen Mother. Weary and sceptical from a long experience of humanity's ways, they had lost the imperishable illusion that love, however strongly founded upon a reciprocity of romantic desire, could sustain the burden of conjugal vicissitude. They knew both the high contracting parties so well, Henry from his cradle, France from a lifetime spent in her intimate service: their grey heads shook with forebodings as they reflected upon her present disorder, the self-torturing tantrum of the nerves which made her crave a master as almost never before in her history, yet would compel her to resist with a pathological fury any effort to reduce her to obedience... and upon the picturesque young man who had never exhibited the least will to mastery nor made up his mind about anything of importance in the whole of his twenty-three years.

He had his popularity only, an asset of inestimable, perhaps insuperable value; but the old men, appraising it, were not reassured, perceiving that it consisted of two insubstantial elements: the elusive charm that was so like a perfumed emanation of his decadent heritage and the dual glamour of his warrior's laurels and his crown, both vicarious achievements. So long as he had been merely Duke of Anjou, it had not mattered greatly that he thrived by his mother's energies, since he had not to bear the odium of her mistakes; now that he was King, he must find an alternative force within himself to surmount his inertia, his speculations, his prayers, and his extravagances. A force great enough to override hers if necessary, the responsibility for everything, including the esteem of his people, being henceforth his alone and indivisible.

Muttering thus together the old men observed that he had drawn near, smiling, to receive their obeisances. From under furtive brows they scanned his face, hoping for some sign that the ten months of his absence had discovered to him the indispensable attribute of his royalty. But what they read in his features and the easy, languid gestures of his body only deepened their presentiments for him and for France.

The small voice whispered to him, too, in his private ear, constantly and far more articulately. The self-knowledge which is the beginning of all wisdom was with Henry the very end of it, a virtue swollen to such excess as to be an organic disease of the spirit for his own undoing. To the finest shading of a degree he knew what the time expected of him and wherein he fell short. How was he, the curious amateur of the far-fetched, to choose a common good for (let alone the manner of imposing it upon) opinionated millions under his rule when he had never succeeded in selecting one for himself out of the infinite variety offered? By what means did one set about transforming an irresponsible dabbler in the wayward into a trained scavenger after facts, a dogmatic oracle of decision, a lusty engine of applied power? The feat of his great namesake, Henry V of England, in casting out of himself the ebullient Hal he frankly recognized to be beyond him: he remained fettered to the truth whimsically implied in his greeting the Duke of Nevers from 'Henry, at present King of France, the same that you once knew as Duke of Anjou.' Yet, if he could not be a strong king in the accepted definition — a part as abhorrent as it was profoundly enviable — he saw no reason why he should not follow the bent of his own nature and be an original one. That way, too, might lie goodness.

For characteristically there lodged in him, in the place where most men would have kept ambition, a theory — a high vision of kingship derived from his reading in the classic masters of political thought, moulded gradually by his tastes and the sense of his own limitations. Nominally the throne was still supreme: he meant to make it actually so by surrounding it with such an atmosphere of grandeur as to compel the whole imagination of the people, leaving no room for rivals to magnify themselves by proximity to it save in humble usefulness as its servants and courtiers. Rejecting the rôle of the Man on Horseback, he would deliver his realm from the evils of faction, not by the futilities of violence, but by the subtleties of reverence, and rule it as he imagined his great forbears had done, as the Patriot King high above the greed and clamour of the parties. Actually no Valois, in the long course of laying the foundations of the royal supremacy, had ever contemplated raising it to such heights; though Richelieu and Louis XIV would take over Henry's vision on which to build the grander and happier France of the century to come.

From time immemorial the aristocracy had been accustomed to go to the King with their wants whenever it struck their fancy — when he put on his shirt in the morning or took it off at night, lay in his bath or in bed with his wife, ate his meals or sat on his elegantly carved *siège percé*. The right of intrusion had evolved, in fact, into a proudly displayed badge of rank. To Henry the practice seemed intolerable, an offence not only to the royal dignity but to his jealous love of solitude. By the first decree of his reign, published within twenty-four hours after his entry into Lyons, he set up a new code of etiquette more rigid and elaborate than any yet seen in western Europe. It forbade any lord, no matter how exalted his rank, to enter the sovereign's apartments without previous summons; prescribed the exact order and style in which the nobles might approach him, hand him his food, his napkin, his basin of water when he dined, all without speaking unless first spoken to; set up a velvet railing and a special detail of Household Guards to screen his person from the importunate — detail upon punctilious detail fitting in together to emphasize the aloof splendour of the throne.

At the same time and as part of the same general policy he set about demolishing a long-standing injustice. It had been

The Elegant Misfit 179

the custom amongst his predecessors to have their subjects' petitions for favour or redress passed upon by the royal secretaries, the King himself merely receiving formal notice of the answers returned. Apart from saving the monarch's time the more obvious virtues of the system seem to have been the profits it placed within reach of the secretaries and the power it gave the great nobles of strengthening themselves with their followers by seeing the latter's requests through to a happy conclusion: the nobles still keeping in reserve, in the event of failure to come to a satisfactory arrangement with the relevant secretary, an appeal to the King when they saw him familiarly in his bedroom, at dinner, or in Council.

Henry's reform was drastic. He ordered all petitions to be deposited in the green velvet sack traditionally kept for the purpose, a brief of the contents of each to be made for him by special, anonymous deputies, and 'the sack to be emptied every Saturday after dinner' in his presence, when he himself would examine and grant or reject. No one was to be allowed henceforth to press a petition upon him either before or after hearing, whether privately or at the Council table — all were to be treated on a basis of absolute equality. As an additional novelty he ordered the Chancellor and secretaries to draw up an agenda for the guidance of the Council's meetings so as to eliminate still further the confusion between private axe-grinding and the public business.

A riot nearly followed, and Henry's popularity with the great vanished overnight. Ritual and ceremony had not yet lost their old passionate significance as indexes of actuality; men killed rather than tolerate the slightest tampering with the form of the sacraments and appealed to the rapier on high solemn occasions to decide who would walk or sit before whom. Hence the very air of the age uttered a warning to the aggrieved nobles not to pass his new ceremonial lightly by as a mere exuberance of youthful vanity. Nor did they. The country rang with their laments for the good old customs put in peril by 'these apish tricks imported *ab ultimis Sarmatis* into our country of France.' Their pamphleteers accused him of having had his head so turned by foreign flattery as to disdain the society of his own good subjects, of hankering after an Oriental despotism which might do for Poles, but would never go down with free-born Frenchmen ... in short of plotting against the whole social order. As indeed he was.

The attacks hurt and angered him, but he affected not to notice them. With the reserved man's sensitiveness to criticism he possessed also the unaggressive man's frequent stubbornness where his imprescriptible rights are involved, and to Henry the right to privacy was very nearly the first of them. A little dissimulation would have gone a long way, a pretended heartiness to cover up his ulterior design, but he had no more appetite than aptitude for heartiness and a very feeble talent — strange lack in an heir of Louis XI and the Medici — for dissembling even in trifles. If he felt like staying in bed in the morning to read, he stayed, and if indisposed to exercise, took none. Every now and then, when the mood seized him, he would break out with some extravagantly original freak in entertainments that set the town by the ears; but many more hours he passed in a small windowless room, painted black and lit only by candles (spicy food for the charge of necromancy, though actually his eyes were weak and supported glare badly), presiding over philosophical séances to which he invited such intimates as the Duke and Duchess of Nevers, Souvray, Margot (when on momentarily good terms with her), and four or five young poets of his acquaintance: the guests assembled, he would invite one of them 'to speak in praise of one of the virtues, exalting it above all the rest; when he finishes, each person in the room argues against the proposal.' His pleasure in the debates of this neo-classic Academy was perfectly sincere, devoid of any mere affection for fatuous dialectics. Once he invited a noted preacher, who proved 'by most excellent argument' the existence of God. Henry complimented him and made him a present, whereupon the flattered cleric declared that 'If Your Majesty will invite me again tomorrow, I will prove by equally excellent argument that there is no God.' Henry directed him not to show his face at the palace again.

Even Catherine was aghast at these eccentricities in the son she had done her very best to spoil. 'It is no time,' she stormed plaintively, 'for you to say you cannot put any constraint on yourself or dissimulate.' To offend the great whom she had so assiduously courted — it was like taking an axe to the legs of his throne. His father and grandfather, she wailed, had *always* encouraged the nobles to hang about, danced with them, taken exercise in their company religiously.... 'I have often heard your grandfather say that two things are necessary to live in peace with the French: keep them amused and occupy them in athletic exercise.' The meagre success of her prescription hitherto she attributed, not altogether unjustly, to his brothers' youth, her sex, and a run of ill-luck.

The cry went up that he was effete, unhealthy, overaddicted to the enervating indulgence in poetry and theology because incapable of clean, manly sport — 'While France, crushed everywhere by civil war,' ran one Latin epigram, 'lies half-buried in her own ashes, our King practises grammatical exercises so that the high-souled may be able to conjugate "I love." He is able to decline it, truly he does decline the verb too well, and he who was twice a king may yet end up as a grammarian.' It was about the most unfortunate reputation he could have gained with a country longing for a master... and just because it seemed to him so unreasonable he failed to grasp its danger. Later, when the report came to his ears that he was fit only to be a monk, he mounted the wildest horse in his stable, rode him over an almost impossible hurdle, and cried gaily, 'Ask the Duke of Guise if he ever saw a monk take a jump like that!' But by then it was far too late....

The ceremonial half of his reform survived and ever flourished, the attempt to deal justly with the petitions ended in dismal failure: the disparity between the two marking exactly the twin poles of his character. The secretaries had spent their lives mastering the intricacies of the relation between Crown and subject. They had at their fingers' ends a dozen reasons in law why the majority of applications could not be granted; they also took the burden of the disappointed applicant's displeasure on their own shoulders. For Henry to have acquired even the rudiments of the business would have demanded a prolonged period of the most intensive application and he was simply not up to it. His indolence groaned at the mass of detail; his exuberant paganism refused to be chained to the grindstone more than so many days a week. All he could do was fluctuate haphazardly between a policy of economy that made him unpopular with the petitioners and one of openhandedness that made him unpopular with everybody else, besides leaving him without the money to meet the awards he had made. For of course the bulk of the requests related to that commodity in some form — pleas for estates, pensions, the right to levy special taxes ... the ingenuity of people in detecting merits in themselves deserving of reward from the Crown.

He carried out the reform of the court and failed in the reform of the petitions because he believed in his ideas but not in himself. The one found instinctive expression in his feeling for manner, whether the style of a gesture or the cut of a garment; the other could only express itself in conscious doing and he had no faith in the validity of his deeds. The serious thought somehow emerged invariably in the frivolous act. He was the introspective man whose agile reason dodged action with fear and a faint self-mockery because of its unpredictable and hence irrational consequences: the genuinely decadent man constrained to lean upon intelligence while all too aware of its futility for his purposes, and therefore glad to escape the burdensome large in a finicking concentration upon the more responsive small. A type as recognizable in this present time as his sister Margot, the inverted vestal immolating public considerations on the fiery altar of her personal loyalties....

His unfortunate beginning drew tighter round Henry the vicious circle of self-knowledge, that fog-walled prison in which each inmate is condemned to grope alone as his own hapless gaoler. He might have broken out of it in time, when experience had toughened him sufficiently for the venture — had not Fate chosen to strike him down from behind with a blow so cruel that the rest of his life was barely long enough for him to struggle to his feet again....

Not long after his return Henry and Catherine sat in his study reading and minuting the newly arrived despatches together. She opened one which, after a glance, she tried to tuck unnoticed in amongst a heap of finished documents before her on the table. The gesture caught his eye, her expression told him that something was amiss. He retrieved the letter, read it, and learned that Marie, Princess of Condé, was dead.[1] He rose, took a step, and without a word toppled unconscious to the floor. They carried him to bed, where for three days he hovered on the edge of a brain-fever.

It is probable that he himself had not known till then how much he was in love with the laughing girl whom he had asked to be his Queen. Catherine knew; that was why she tried to hide the letter and to keep Marie from court as long as possible. But Henry had half-believed it a pose —a literary passion stimulated by loneliness and her indifference —

---

[1] Some authorities hinted poison, implicating her husband. What response she made, if any, to Henry's proposal from Poland is a mystery: did Condé suppress his letter? or Catherine her answer?

until it turned out to be, like some of his other poses, a shattering reality. It was too late now to verify the might-have-been, to learn whether she would have left Condé to become mistress of France or not. She had been compelled, along with her husband and many other Huguenots, to forswear the reformed creed after Saint Bartholomew's. Condé had recanted and run away, but his wife had grown into a fervent Catholic. Faith might have held her from divorce: it might equally have drawn her to her King and away from the apostate husband who neglected and was jealous of her. In any event she was gone... and with her went forever the love of woman from Henry's heart. Margot would occupy her niche of hatred in it to the end, Catherine hers of filial devotion; he would presently marry and treat his wife with an unfailing tenderness. But even of little loves there would never be any more.

Undoubtedly, as the shrewd old men who observed him surmised, Henry stood on the verge of a moral crisis after his exile in Poland and the excitement of his return. Marie's death hastened and brought it to light before responsibility had the chance of arresting or usefully diverting it. His character seemed to split up almost overnight into its diverse elements — as if the still water running deep had churned upon a rock and thrown off a vivid spectrum of its component colours. But human character is the fusion and not the sum of its parts: mere characteristics, once dissolved, tend to lose proportion and become parodies of themselves. Henry's taste for the original, thus cut adrift, turned into a craving for the fantastic and forbidden, his piety into morbid religiosity; the pose of indolence into indolence itself, and self-doubt into a creeping paralysis of the will that could alone have arrested and repaired that process of inner disintegration.

The age ran to extremes, and Henry, who had always outrun the age, henceforth outstripped even himself. When he appeared again in public after his illness, his costume consisted of a suit of funereal black from every part of which — his hat, the laces of his tunic and shoes, the chaplet round his neck — dangled rows of carved ivory death's heads; even his books were henceforth stamped with them. No one underestimated the violence of his grief because of the grotesque shape it took; quite the contrary.

Catherine, alarmed for his reason if he went on in this way, sent for Souvray, the Keeper of the Wardrobe, and demanded, 'Does he own anything of the princess's that might call her to memory?'

'Yes, Madame, he wears a cross that belonged to her under his shirt, and a pair of earrings that she gave him.'

'Then manage to get them away from him,' the practical woman directed.

Henry made no inquiry after the missing objects — very likely he suspected what had happened to them — but their owner he never forgot. In Paris he always went out of his way to avoid the abbey of Saint-Germain 'because her heart is buried there,' and the chaplet clicked its reminder of mortality thereafter no matter how flamboyant the new costumes he delighted to invent and wear. A strange combination the little skulls must have made with the suit of mulberry satin he presently wore four days running — the cloak slashed with white and scarlet, its folds set with coral buttons and streaming parti-coloured ribbons, a brooch of gems on his cap, pear-shaped pearls in his ears, a carved bracelet of coral round each arm.

He knotted emeralds in his hair; he ran through the streets during carnival the wildest madcap in his kingdom; he broke into his own prisons to release inmates for whom he was sorry. Fifty devils drove him down every road of folly, flamboyance, generosity, and self-abasement: while all the time there eluded his discernment that one road of kingly action he so anxiously sought. Not because there was none, but because there were too many, all beginning in a maze and ending in a bog....

Very soon the grinning death's heads were transferred to the girdle of a quite different garment: the monk's robe which Henry first adopted that autumn and wore alternately until near the end of his life. The two styles of dress symbolized perfectly the conflict long joined in his soul between an acquired piety and a congenital pagan hunger for the immediate world; a conflict that neither could win, that served only to strengthen both of them. More and more the sense of the early doom none of his House might reasonably hope to avoid intertwined itself with a sense of sin he knew himself too weak to resist. The exotic semi-Oriental influence of Poland prepared the outlet, Marie's death achieved it: and Henry, like many another mystic sensualist, tried to ease his soul by giving his body over to the ecstasies of self-mortification. That autumn the court moved from Lyons to Avignon, and there, in the ancient city of the Popes, the King of France, one of a long procession of cowled figures walking two by two, exposed his bared and bleeding shoulders twice weekly to the whip of the man behind while he administered similar penance to the man in front of him.

The thing, of course, became a fashion. All the court insisted on joining one of the three flagellant orders, white (the King's), black, and blue. Catherine joined the second, where apparently the whips were laid on gently. Navarre, bored with doing nothing and ready to try anything once, proposed to attach himself to the King's. They had already made him go to Mass: if he could swallow the holy wafer why strain at a mere haircloth gown? But the King only laughed and told him that he was not at all cut out for the rôle of penitent. The Cardinal of Lorraine would have been wise to heed his Church's official frown upon flagellation, but he was a politician first and anxious to please: with the result that he caught cold of exposure, contracted pneumonia and died. As he breathed his last a terrible storm burst over the city, which the Catholics interpreted as a sign of God's wrath on the kingdom, the Huguenots as a witches' sabbath convoked especially to fetch away the Cardinal's soul.

Whichever it was, the Cardinal brought off a *coup* for his House by dying which he could never have hoped to achieve by staying alive. It was of the utmost importance that Henry should marry, since an infant heir would infallibly bind the people's hopes and enthusiasms to the dynasty for at least another generation. The whole of the previous summer Catherine had been scouring Europe, particularly the unworked Scandinavian portions of it, for suitable princesses, and on Henry's return had portraits, pedigrees, and health certificates ready for his inspection. But Henry would have none of them: since he could not marry for love, he had determined at least to choose a mate who would be personally sympathetic. He had such a one in mind in Louise de Vaudemont, a tranquil, fair-haired girl of twenty of the House of Lorraine, whom he had met at Blamont before leaving for Poland. While the Cardinal lived the alliance would have been unwise, as throwing too much weight toward the Guises, but his death, by depriving them of their head and most of their brains, restored the balance, and Henry made his choice known to his mother.

At first she wrung her hands in dismay that her adored son, with all the world to choose from, should descend to such a mediocre connection. But though she could sway him altogether too much in matters of state, he stood firm, as usual, where his private feelings were involved: the girl was charming, intelligent, and promised to bear him healthy children; so that within two days Catherine was announcing, with the air of having made the marriage herself, 'what a beautiful and abundant progeny the King would soon have from so lovely and well-formed a princess,' and reflecting with satisfaction that 'she will devote herself to praying to God rather than mixing in affairs of state' — all as it should be.

On Sunday, February thirteenth, a year to the hour after receiving the crown of Poland, Henry was anointed with the sacred oil brought to Clovis from Heaven by an angel nearly eleven hundred years before. On the following day he and Louise were formally betrothed and on the next married — in circumstances of great scandal to the orthodox because the King, in fussing over the final perfection of his own and his bride's regalia, held up the ceremony beyond the canonical hour.

It was the last joyous week in the long Valois history — the last coronation, the final wedding. And, with the most exquisite suitability, brilliance, farce, and death elbowed each other for room in its crowded pageantry. As the glittering procession left the church door, retainers of two noble houses got into a dispute over some matter of precedence and two corpses lay bleeding on the pavement before Rheims Cathedral — a small matter, two fellows of no account. During the festivities that followed, Henry, who was in the high spirits proper to a bridegroom, looked across the table at the Duke of Luxembourg and had an inspiration: the Duke had until recently been a suitor of Louise... he himself had an old flame, Renée de Châteauneuf, whom he had been trying in vain to marry off for years and who had been pestering him ever since his return from Poland. He raised his glass to the Duke, saying, 'I have now married your mistress — it is only fair that you should marry mine!' The poor man gibbered... one did not lightly ignore such a hint from the King... asked for a day to think it over, which Henry laughingly granted... and in the night leaped on his horse and rode like mad for Luxembourg, to the hilarity of the guests.... And almost at once rode in another horseman with the news that Claude was dying. The rejoicings ended abruptly. Henry, at his mother's request, hurried his own doctor Miron off to his sister's bedside, but it was too late, and within the fortnight the poor crippled little Duchess, at the age of twenty-seven, joined the three brothers and three sisters who had gone before her.

Crowning irony, that of all of Catherine's six children to marry she, the least in rank, should be the only one to leave a legitimate son... to inherit the petty Duchy of Lorraine when Francis, Charles, Henry, Margot, failed to take their chance to fill the throne of France and Elizabeth hers to establish the seed of the Valois upon the throne of Spain. An irony that was to have grave consequences when Catherine had no more to hope from her idol....

A year passed, and another, and a third, and still Louise bore Henry neither son nor daughter. More and more frequently they trudged barefoot the long road to Chartres to kneel before Our Lady of the Conception. They brought her silver vessels for her underground shrine, left their sleeping garments exposed to her gracious infection. Exhausted, with feet cut and bleeding, they trudged home again bringing with them the holy water to sprinkle on the nuptial couch. Throughout France their subjects marched in procession and burned candles to sustain their prayers... for a time. Upon Louise there descended a stream of advice from her mother-in-law, but that experienced matron's methods had passed out of date. The black arts were not what they had been thirty years before; not only were they being widely damned as sacrilegious, but many people were beginning to despise them as unscientific.

By the second year evil whispers, unfounded or inconsistent as popular rumours usually are, swelled into an ominous buzz that Heaven had placed its supreme curse upon the House of Valois. That the King was diseased, impotent — the Queen confessedly sterile — that he was on the point of divorcing her. The slanders touching himself Henry disdained to refute, but when he heard the rumour of the divorce he flew across country from Poitiers to Chenonceaux where Louise was staying. She had heard the rumour, too, but sadly said nothing, only waited. He took her in his arms, comforted her with the promise that nothing should ever part them. She loved him already; for that she worshipped him all her life, to the end of a seven years' widowhood.

If only she could have evoked an answering love in him to save him... but that was impossible and she knew it. All that remained for her was to stand by him with placid loyalty while the morbid domination of her dead rival over his spirit completed its dissolution. And that she did, like the thoroughbred she was, in the very abyss of ignominy.

In the second year of his reign Henry seemed about to settle down after the wild oscillations of the first. The bewildering succession of sartorial fantasies gave way to a plain black or grey tunic buttoned up the front and surmounted by a simple collar of white linen turned down in the Italian style. He and Louise together roamed Paris in search of the fluffy little white dogs of which she was as fond as he; went off to Dieppe in June of 1576 for a cure of sea-bathing, bringing back a collection of parrots, monkeys, and more little dogs; he bought a country house for her at near-by Olinville in July and they set about furnishing it with all of a newly married couple's enthusiasm. A few days later, Paris stood still, gaped and sniffed: through the streets strolled at their ease a group of young men made up to the eyes, their hair long and artificially curled under velvet bonnets 'like those worn by the whores of the brothel quarter,' dressed all alike in coats of many colours and linen shirts with horizontal frills so starched and so wide 'that their heads sticking out above looked like Saint John's on his platter,' and trailing behind a delicate odour of violets as they passed. It was the King's first public appearance with his *mignons*.[1]

[1] The word had previously been used, in a not insulting sense, of royal favourites of low birth, usually in its feminine gender.

The Elegant Misfit 191

The equation of character stood resolved down to its last factor. A man overstrung, oversubtle, overindulged, with the outward physical delicacy and the obscure inner sensibilities of a woman: there was not a great way for such a man to travel between flagellation of the body to ease a malady of the spirit and commuting thwarted desire into desire's perversion.

Maugiron, Caylus, and Saint-Mégrim, D'O, Saint-Luc, and Livarrot, Mauléon, D'Arques, and La Valette — syllables for a troubadour's song woven into the obscene doggerel of the Paris gutters. Rowdy paladins, mincing *condottieri* of the swift dagger and the leering codpiece, the brotherhood of Alcibiades flaunting their Renaissance prostitution. One reason their own age hated them so was because they held up a too perfect mirror in which it might gaze upon its own gaudy decay, its creaking classical postures, its senseless violence, its reeking unchastity. Every man's hand against them and theirs joyously against every man... cynical of all things, afraid of nothing; sentimentally, passionately loyal to their King and to one another. Ridiculous and somewhat repulsive, the years would have made them too unspeakably horrible had they not had the grace to die young: their royal master would have raised them to destinies too high for their worth, so they outwitted him by laying down their lives vindicating his honour against insults too trivial for his notice.

'They sprang up in three nights like mushrooms...' and they vanished almost as quickly. Their ears eternally cocked to detect some slight to the King from Alençon's or Guise's men, they never had any trouble in the whispering-gallery of the court finding good grounds for a fight. One went and another, then they departed wholesale. On April the twenty-sixth, 1578, during a party in the Louvre, Caylus came to words with one of Guise's followers; Maugiron and Livarrot stepped to his side and three met three the next morning at five o'clock in the Horse Market hard-by the Bastille. Maugiron was killed outright; Livarrot recovered from his wounds after six weeks; Caylus, with nineteen sword-thrusts in his body, lingered for over a month between life and death, Henry daily at his bedside, offering him a hundred thousand crowns as an incentive to recover and the surgeons a hundred thousand francs to pull him through. But his injuries were beyond the healing power of money — he died murmuring 'My King, my King,' thereby scandalizing those who observed that 'he failed to mention either God or His Mother.'

Two of Guise's men also fell and neither party waited long for its revenge. Saint-Mégrim, a rip-roaring Gascon blade with the face of an Adonis, made the first move by seducing the Duchess of Guise. From a *mignon* this was adding insupportable insult to what would otherwise have been regarded as friendly injury, so Guise's brother, Charles, Duke of Mayenne, with twenty masked followers, waylaid Saint-Mégrim as he was leaving the Louvre late at night and left him for dead on the pavement riddled with sword and shot. Nevertheless, he managed to hang on till next day, just long enough to pronounce a last will and testament of the most breath-taking obscenity and expire with a grin at his own joke.

In barely three years over half the original band lay in the church of Saint-Pol — 'the Seraglio of the Mignons' — and they had no successors. Only D'Arques and La Valette rose to the responsibilities Henry had intended for them all, the former, as Duke of Joyeuse, marrying Louise's sister and dying gallantly in command of a royal army during the last civil war; the other, as Duke of Épernon, becoming one of the chief men of the kingdom — and returning, after Henry had been made to cast him off, to stand by him in his darkest hour when all advantage lay the other way.

Nothing could have been more fitting than that 'the court of blood and silk' should have gone up finally in an explosion of violet-scented powder.... Paris, at sight of the *mignons*, went into a paroxysm from which nothing could thereafter induce her to recover: the pulpits shrieked reminiscences of Sodom and Gomorrah, the printing presses belched and the walls perspired wittily epigrammatic filth in French and Latin upon the King and his bevy of peacocks — abuse of a kind and quantity beyond any that had yet fouled the name of a ruler of France, possibly any ruler anywhere. But what charged that mine of feeling was less perversion than politics: one per cent of outraged morality and ninety-nine of partisan malice. It was not the King's vice that the good people of the capital objected to — any contempt they felt on that score was the contempt of excessive familiarity — so much as whom he selected to practise it with. A harem of pretty boys would have mattered little to anyone in an age too used to fads to waste indignation over them, but the *mignons* mattered a great deal to everyone for the use Henry frankly intended to put them to in the government of his realm.

The finest political brain of the time, then at Henry's court inside the head of Francis Bacon, wrote with approval, 'It is counted by some a weakness to have favourites, but it is of all others the best remedy against ambitious great ones; for when the way of pleasure and displeasure lieth by the favourites, it is impossible that any other should be over-great.' That was precisely Henry's idea; but as always with him the sober thought of his brain came forth in a frivolous, posturing, chromatic shape of fantasy. The *mignons* were the weird but logical extension of the dream he had first embodied in the reform of the ceremonial and the petitions: his 'sons' whom he would establish in life, as he often affirmed, and then settle down to administer his estate with their help. All of them came from good, none from exalted families. They were bound to him uniquely by ties of gratitude and deep personal affection; he alone could raise them, they had no interest in serving any cause but his. Given time and experience they would, he reckoned, provide him exactly with the instruments he needed to supersede the unruly lords whom his father had had to bribe and his mother vainly tried to balance into keeping the peace. To Catherine, who of course loathed the *mignons*, seeing in them possible rivals, he declared, 'I shall raise them so high that after my death no one will be able to pull them down again.'

But to carry through such a revolution wanted an iron hand, a dissimulating tongue, and a mind ruthless in the conviction that its way was the only way ... the qualities of a Richelieu and a Louis XIV which Henry so painfully lacked. He could catch a secret fire from the glowing patriotism of Tacitus and Machiavelli, to apply their maxims of craft and force was utterly beyond him. To build the great new thing he planned he had first to destroy, and before all to destroy the enemies whose lewd abuse of his favourites had no other motive than to discredit him for their own protection. He knew, no man better, that if they were allowed to go on supplying their 'wood, straw, and sulphur to the braziers of rebellion,' not only he but his whole people must pay for their calumnies. The axiom that the King can do no wrong rose out of no idle flattery, but the hard experience of the human race in pursuit of safety through ordered institutions.

His advisers, the wisest and most upright of them, implored him to lay hold of his traducers and silence their tongues. The very people who slandered him worst would have respected him most for taking a line of kingly firmness. He would not, he could not. There was that in him which compelled him to admit in his heart whatever there was of right on the other side: a patience to understand the grievances of those who maligned him, an unwillingness to punish where he could not convince. What his people had welcomed on his return from Poland was the hero of Jarnac and Moncontour, the man of blood and steel — and in his place there ruled the poet gone astray.

The Elegant Misfit

A preacher named Rose attacked him virulently for leading the *mignons* through the streets during the usual riotous festivities of Lent. Henry sent for the man, who expected nothing less than sewing in a sack and a plunge into the river: there were few who in their hearts would not have approved. Rose came, Henry reprimanded him for his *lèse-majesté*, the man humbly answered. The King thought over the answer a moment and, though seeing no great harm in the mere act of making merry like everybody else, added thoughtfully on the implied larger criticism, 'But I shan't do it again, it is time I showed some sense.' Next day the preacher received a gift of four hundred crowns with a note instructing him 'to buy sugar and honey to help you pass Lent pleasantly and sweeten your tart tongue.' A monk who held him up to the most shocking ridicule he ordered to his abbey outside Paris (sending him there in one of the royal coaches) and released after a few days as an innocent tool of the Guises with the observation that 'the fellow has too much knowledge and too little judgment.' Man after man against whom the magistrates laid complaint he refused to prosecute; one he allowed to be hanged, but only after vainly pleading with him to save himself by a public apology.

'I know very well, it seems to me, what I ought to do,' wrote Henry in 1584, at the turning-point of his reign, to his secretary and intimate servant Villeroy, 'but I am like a man who feels he is drowning and from an instinct of surrender is content to do so rather than save himself. And then, nobody else would agree with me and I may possibly be wrong.' There is a haunting familiarity about this nerveless confession — perhaps because it is the theme of a nearly contemporary play that has since become the most famous in the world:

> The time is out of joint: O cursed spite,
> That ever I was born to set it right!

The hero of that play is, like Henry, a prince of affable and generous but highly elusive and complicated character. He, too, is summoned to a duty which he can neither evade nor satisfactorily perform, for though he sees clearly what he ought to do, his will is paralyzed by the perception that he may possibly be wrong. He, too, is content to drift rather than save himself by acting, until driven by external forces to do so: with the result that he destroys not only the enemy designated by duty, but himself and many innocent people as well.

> ... Now, whether it be
> Bestial oblivion, or some craven scruple
> Of thinking too precisely on the event, —
> A thought which, quarter'd, hath but one part wisdom
> And ever three parts coward, — I do not know
> Why yet I live to say, 'This thing's to do,'
> Sith I have cause and will and strength and means
> To do't.... Rightly to be great
> Is not to stir without great argument,
> But greatly to find quarrel in a straw
> When honour's at the stake....

It was no more for the living Hamlet to remove what was rotten in the state of France than for the fictitious one, but for the greater Fortinbras at hand strong and ready to perform that splendid operation....

Chapter XV

ONE BROTHER TOO MANY

Meantime, the younger members of the House went merrily on to pull it down round their own ears.

Imperceptibly, almost mechanically, the power had lapsed from the King who could not make up his mind to use it to the mother who could not live without it. But the old thrill had gone from it. Ruling had become less a business of outwitting those she distrusted than of thwarting those she loved. Guise and Condé and Coligny were gone, leaving heirs too immature at Henry's accession yet to count greatly, but in place of those fictitious cousins had risen her own flesh and blood to plague her. And with so few children left, it was becoming increasingly painful to refuse any of them anything that would make them happy.

Catherine managed to keep the peace for twelve months — or just so long as she kept a vigilant eye upon her three nurslings of trouble. Particularly on Alençon, the ugly duckling fretful to try on his swan's wings and fly away. During that year he walked amongst invisible mirrors, his every coming and going noted, compelled to account for his every movement. If he so much as stayed out too late at night, he caught a severe scolding from his worried mother for the hours he kept. The King's gentlemen, amused by the disparity between his infantile treatment and his grandiose ambitions, teased him unmercifully. 'I, the second person in the realm,' wailed the unhappy young man, 'am the most wretched person in it,' but the more eager he was to be off, the closer naturally Catherine watched him — and the more closely she restrained him, the more he burned to be free.

She kept the same rein on his ally of Navarre, though in his case the precautions seemed to be superfluous. Her son-in-law had apparently, since the collapse of the La Mole plot, resigned ambition definitely and without regret. Even the indignity of being forced to attend Mass drew from the hope of the Huguenots no stronger protest than a screwing of his mouth into such an expression of wry distaste when swallowing the wafer as to wring from his mother-in-law a loud guffaw. People laughed in his face for his wife's infidelities and he laughed back as if he had no idea that the joke was on him. Nothing seemed to offend or disturb him, no story to be too tall for his gullibility or friend too low for his company. It was as if the clown in Antoine de Bourbon, having reproduced himself, had contrived to shuffle off all the rest of his heredity, his sire's pride and his mother's dauntless spirit.

Unforgiving, secret, dangerous, Margot waited her chance to strike once more at the brother she hated through the brother she loved. Though the sight of Alençon's humiliation sometimes carried her quite outside caution and the filial awe that had as much power as ever to make her tremble. 'Pardon me, Madame,' she struck in once when the exasperated Catherine threatened the miserable little king-in-embryo with a whipping for having stayed out all night without explanation, 'there are others who better deserve a whipping. [She had Henry's gentlemen in mind — perhaps Henry himself!] If you keep on nagging him like this, you will *force* him to run away.' Instead of resenting her daughter's interference, Catherine sighed helplessly.

THE DUKE OF ALENÇON, IN 1570

Plainly what Alençon needed, mused his sister, was another, if possible larger La Mole: a man to guide, strengthen, and, pending larger arrangements, stand up for him against Henry's favourites. (Not *mignons* — their era began only the next year.) She looked around, tested one possibility and another, until finally she found exactly what she wanted in the ranks of those favourites themselves, the most stalwart by far of the lot.

It would scarcely have been possible to invent a more suitable adjutant than Bussy d'Amboise to direct the insane adventure that Alençon called his career. If La Mole attracted trouble, trouble magnetically attracted Bussy: when it failed to turn up, he at once went out to look for it. No civil disorder, no street brawl was complete without him, the number of his duels lay buried in the hazy annals of his twenty-six years. His exploits on Saint Bartholomew's Day, when he hacked his way to an inheritance, would alone have made him legendary. No other century would have stood for him and he could have stood for no other, since handsome swashbucklers commanded a premium and for picturesque excellence in the profession Bussy towered above all rivals. 'I was born an ordinary gentleman,' he affirmed, 'but there is an Emperor in my belly.' When Amyot's new translation of Plutarch came into his hands, Bussy (who wrote verses on the classic model in his spare time) perused the exploits of its heroes and declared with simple conviction, 'There's nothing here I couldn't have done myself.' One would have said that he was born to be the hero of a Dumas novel had not Dumas perceived the fact first.[1]

Half in hot blood, half in cold, Margot detached this paragon from Henry and appropriated him to herself. In that time of acute partisan feeling the *liaison de convenance* enjoyed as recognized a standing as the *mariage de convenance* at any time: and Margot herself could not have said how much she

[1] Bussy is the hero of Dumas's *The Lady of Monsoreau.*

desired the man's talents for Alençon's sake and how much his superb vitality for her own. As for Bussy, how could a man with the spirit of a worm, let alone of an Emperor, in his belly hesitate between the respectable security of the King's service (before the *mignons* entered it, at least) and the exciting uncertainties of his brother's, with the favours of the beautiful Queen of Navarre thrown in? Over he came, heart, sword, and (for what they were worth) convictions.

Du Guast, the unsleeping watch-dog of the Navarre-Alençon menace, knew the thing almost before it happened. He told Henry and Henry told Catherine, but the matriarch, more and more depressed by the bickering amongst her children, assured him that there was nothing in it: 'My daughter is born in an unhappy time; in my time girls mingled freely with men without getting themselves so unjustly gossiped about.' This harking back to her youth may have been the first sign that Catherine was getting old — old enough, at any rate, for her vigilance to have slipped. Or perhaps she preferred not to know.... She mentioned the matter in passing to Margot, who chalked up one more, almost her last, count against Du Guast.

That gentleman, finding his warning unheeded, took matters into his own hands. Collecting the toughest of the regiment of guards which he commanded, he went after Bussy one night in the streets of Paris with the intention of exterminating him and a score of other of Alençon's men in his company. But Bussy, though outnumbered and with one arm in a sling as the result of a recent duel, beat off his aggressors and turned up next morning at the Louvre 'as joyous as if he had just come from a tourney of pleasure.' Catherine, fearful of reprisals, begged Alençon to send him away for a time. Alençon at first swore to take vengeance on Du Guast with his own hands — Margot had to hold him tight to prevent him — then suddenly capitulated: and Bussy, from outside Paris, aided by Margot within, cunningly arranged his master's escape while the ducal coach waited innocently outside a brothel.

Alençon fled south, intending to raise an army for Flanders, and, under the title of Protector of the Liberties of France for the King, invited the dissatisfied to join him. Huguenots and Catholic malcontents flocked from all parts of the country; the dreaded Reiters, enlisted by Condé, hurled themselves joyously across the frontier to fight for the God of Luther and whatever more tangible rewards might come their way. A chance like this, to force concessions from the Crown and pick up stray loot under the covering authority of the heir to the throne, had not occurred for a hundred years and might not occur again.

In a panic Henry sent Catherine to fetch her youngest son home. Alençon ran away from her. She followed. Pursuing one or another of her troublesome family across country was to remain the principal occupation of her old age — fat, gouty, but indomitable despite occasional damp cells for bedrooms; always with the flying squadron, sometimes with half the Council or more, a perambulating government; often successful in conciliating, often snubbed for her pains. When finally she caught up with him, she could do nothing. Every card was in his hand and he knew it: he would not return home until they acknowledged his right to be a king. The King's position was impossible. He dared not crush his brother, the last barrier between the House and extinction, yet if he went on he would partition the country or if he slipped off to Flanders bring Spain down on its back. On Alençon marched from town to town, throwing out royal governors and putting his own in... his mother trudging breathless after him.

With her protégé making Henry's life as miserable as she could desire, Margot took advantage of the general distraction to square her account with Du Guast. The agent she employed was the Baron de Viteaux, one of Alençon's men, in whom rankled a suspicion that her enemy had seduced his wife; the method adopted the same as Du Guast's against Bussy, a night attack in the Rue Saint-Honoré, but carried out with greater thoroughness.

Viteaux's turn came next, and then Du Guast's avengers', by mechanical rotation 'in the Italian manner.' A once orderly nation looked on with dismay as feud-law ruled... the Valois lost more of the life-blood of their prestige on the Paris pavements than on all the battle-fields of France.

Then came Margot's turn for a shock. At the very height of the confusion, in February of 1576, her husband disappeared. For twenty-four hours no one took much notice of his absence. It was the season of the riotous Lenten street fair, he had gone out to look for amusement, no doubt he had found it.... But when he failed to turn up the second evening, the King sent a search party out to hunt for him. A joke was a joke, but not if it ended in turning the second Prince of the Blood loose on the country as well as the first. The following morning, while the court was at Mass in the Sainte Chapelle, in he slouched, booted and spurred, with a loud 'Ha! ha! You thought I'd given you the slip, didn't you?' at sight of their startled faces. A little defensively he added, 'You see it wouldn't be hard — I hope you won't ever suspect me of such a thing again.'

The court smiled; it was impossible not to. With a sheepish grin he asked if he might go stag-hunting in the forest of Senlis to the north. The King hesitated. Navarre turned to the Duke of Guise, the best possible guarantor of his not getting away, and invited him to come along. The Duke, fancying that he saw a Huguenot dagger wrapped in the invitation, declined, but it served to allay the King's doubts. A little later Henry of Navarre rode out of Paris with his fellow huntsmen — and that was the last Paris saw of its favourite clown until he rode in again nineteen years later as Conqueror and Pacifier.

He went to Senlis and shot his stags till word came that his followers had mustered on the other side of the Seine... till a messenger rode out from the capital to say that the King was growing suspicious.... 'Then we'd better go,' he said, and rode away to the south. About the time he was expected back at the Louvre, he drew rein on the far bank of the river, turned and chuckled, 'I've left two things behind, the Mass and my wife; the Mass I can manage to do without, my wife I'd rather like to see again.' He was far from being finished with either.

He left behind him something else, the foolish motley that Nature had lent him as a mask for Destiny's service. Clearly Destiny is not so strait-laced as to forbid her favourites to offer lip-service to other mistresses until she is ready for them; what she principally asks in the meantime is that they stay alive for her. Shortly before Navarre's flight a friend came into his room to find him dropping tears upon the lines from the eighty-eighth psalm:

> Thou hast laid me in the lowest pit, in darkness, in the deeps.
> Thy wrath lieth hard upon me, and thou hast afflicted me with all thy waves.   Selah.
> Thou hast put away mine acquaintance far from me; thou hast made me an abomination unto them: I am shut up, and I cannot come forth.
> Mine eye mourneth by reason of affliction: LORD, I have called daily upon thee, I have stretched out my hands unto thee.

'Sire,' exclaimed the friend, 'it is true! The spirit of God still lives and works in you.' Had it been an enemy with an understanding eye who intruded upon that secret, Coligny would never have left a successor nor France found in Henry of Bourbon her saviour.

He ran away to fight the war, but failed because it collapsed on his appearance. A second Liberator of the Oppressed struck Alençon as redundant, so to avoid sharing later he decided to take what he could get now. It worked out at a great deal, nevertheless. Henry, the hero of Jarnac, the man of Saint Bartholomew's, had become intolerably sensitive to the shedding of his subjects' blood, and instructed Catherine to get rid of the mercenaries without quibbling over terms; while she, with her unerring instinct for balance to prompt her that it would do no harm to stand in well with her younger son if she ever fell out with the elder, carried out her instructions well beyond the letter. Alençon obtained for himself Henry's old dukedom of Anjou, together with other estates and privileges that made him almost an independent prince: to the Huguenots were granted far more than ever before — complete equality for their religion, the restitution of confiscated property that had long been sold, the payment of all their expenses including the huge sum promised to the Germans, a formal apology to the ashes of Coligny, La Mole, and those who had perished with them.

Gaily, with the whole flying squadron about her to add cheer to the occasion, Catherine signed at Easter of 1576 the death-warrant of the House of Valois. For that was what the Peace of Monsieur [1] amounted to. The dynasty was old in France, but the Catholic religion a thousand years older and of considerably greater importance than the aggrandizement of the troublesome little heir presumptive. Though it was less upon him than upon Catherine that the orthodox poured out their grief. To have spent so much blood in putting down heresy only to find heresy enthroned, so much treasure to pay rebels for bringing in the foreign butchers....

The town of Péronne, given in pledge to the victors for the enforcement of the treaty, refused to receive the Huguenot

[1] The title of Monsieur was for centuries traditionally worn by the eldest brother of the Kings of France. Though Alençon henceforth called himself Duke of Anjou, the older designation will be used to avoid confusion.

garrison and formed a secret society to throw it out. The idea spread like wildfire; within a few months the extremer Catholic leaders met to lay the foundation of a similar alliance on national lines which they called the Holy League. The articles of association made no mention of deposing the family — yet; on the contrary, they vowed to support Henry and his Most Christian successors in all their rights and splendours... provided he restored France to the state of religious purity it had enjoyed in the time of King Clovis. A party had at last arisen prepared to withdraw its obedience unless the Crown governed according to its will — the immemorial prelude to revolution.

As by natural right the leadership fell to the twenty-four-year-old Duke of Guise. An alarming choice. A wound upon the cheek received during a skirmish with the Reiters — 'which embellished his reputation,' remarked Navarre, 'more than his face' — recalled to the Paris mob the scar of honour worn by the late Duke and transferred once for all to the son the combustible worship once given the father. In addition to which he had inherited that hypothetical claim upon the throne through his descent from Charlemagne: a most useful hypothesis in the case that France should ever clamour for the succession of a *truly* Catholic king....

The League's agents, unsuspected friars and commercial travellers, seeped through the country inciting people not to pay their taxes, to secrete arms. From mysterious cellars the League's muffled presses spouted forth pamphlets, signed often with Huguenot names, accusing the King of buggery and buffoonery, his mother of the wholesale rape of heiresses to bestow upon her Italian extortioners, the sale of the Faith to appease the vanity of her youngest... all the crimes in the calendar, personal and political, which could be decked out with a touch of plausibility. A secret war, the most dangerous sort, which no authority could suffer and survive.

Henry awoke from his trance and issued writs for the election of an Estates-General. It was a daring but risky move to bring his enemies into the open, make them declare themselves. He hoped to induce the country to accept the treaty until a better religious settlement could be found by peaceful means, to obtain the money he needed to liquidate the last war and for urgent current expenses. If he succeeded, he would be able to confront the League with such evidence of popular support as would cut away the whole reason for its being. If he failed — but his position seemed so right that he did not think he could fail.

The Estates met at the end of the year in the great pillared hall at Blois. He opened the sessions with a speech that revealed the Henry that men had been prepared to die for: a creature of fire, courage, and superb eloquence. In a touching reference to Catherine, weeping with pride amongst the high dignitaries sitting on the platform behind him, he damned those that dared pour their scurrilities upon 'the mother of this realm' after her long years of devoted service to it. He candidly notified Guise's followers that his first duty was not to appease their bigotries and greed, but to protect the common man in his right to work and enjoy the fruits of his labour in quiet. Their state within his state he would not tolerate, but if they had grievances he was ready to listen and redress according to the ancient usages of the kingdom.

He had guessed wrong: the penalty of judging brutal facts from the ivory tower of the mind. The treaty had thrown the country into such a mood that the Huguenots had not even thought it worth while to put up candidates, and the League, with a strong nucleus of the three hundred and sixty-two delegates in its pocket (obtained by an appeal to terror judiciously mixed with terrorism), turned up at Blois with strange new ideas in its mind of a sort rarely spoken of in France before except by cranks. They advised the King to pay his bills by cutting down his expenditures on his favourites;[1] if he wanted anything further let him repudiate his treaty and make war on the heretics until there were none of them left. Henry inquired how they expected him to make war without money: '*Pace non trovo*,' he quoted ironically from Petrarch, '*e non ho da fare guerra*.' By seizure and confiscation of Huguenot property, they suggested. The funds to start the campaign they would provide, but on condition that he did not have the handling of them.

Step by step the full thought of the League comes out. To substitute the will of the Estates (now that they controlled it) for that of the sovereign as the fundamental law of the land, take from him the administration of his finances... the programme to be fulfilled only by the Revolution of two hundred years hence. The spokesmen for the League added the sinister but unofficial hint that if he were reluctant to defend the Faith, another defender might have to be found.

Furiously Henry denied the whole proposition. The principle that 'there can be only one religion in my realm' he freely acknowledged, but he would not be dictated to as to how it should be procured. Anything here decided must 'be commanded by His Majesty after having heard the Estates' remonstrances,' never 'in execution of the resolution taken by these Estates.' He would not be browbeaten into persecution of his subjects, however deluded their beliefs. Rather than that he would sell his own lands, if the assembly

[1] Lest it seem confusing that Henry should be able to squander money on his favourites and yet be so deeply in want, it should be explained that he did his spending soon after the revenues came in and the rest of the time did without. Also what the favourites received consisted less of cash than estates that fell to the Crown. This was as much policy as extravagance, his method of building up his new men to the detriment of the old nobility, who naturally bewailed the loss of their ancient perquisites.

Nevertheless, when all is said, Henry's generosity was reckless even for a Valois. On his arrival in Poland he was presented with a bowl of gold-pieces to give away. The delay in the act of distribution, occasioned by the formal speech of presentation to the King, so worked on him that he broke into a profuse sweat as he let his fingers play with the largesse, so that he had to leave the ceremony immediately afterward and change his shirt. The Poles also gave him some lands, which he promptly distributed, saying it was more kingly to give than to receive.

would assist him in clearing the mortgages — which, after all, had been incurred for the needs of the State. They retorted that the lands were not his to sell, merely a property of which he happened to be user for life. It was the crowning insult. What became of the royal grandeur, and the lofty hopes he had founded upon it, if he had to beg, hat in hand, for the right to deal with his own inheritance?

But on what was the royal grandeur to sustain itself when his pages had to pawn their embroidered cloaks to pay for their food — when, indeed, 'the only topic at court at this moment is that there is nothing for the King's dinner'? He resisted a little while longer, but in the end had to climb down and agree to make war on the Huguenots if the Estates would relieve his immediate necessities. With tears of impotent rage, vowing that he would master them yet.

Behind him on the platform, drinking in his humiliation, sits the original agent of it — Margot, dressed in a fantasy of orange and black on which glitter tiny steel-cut ornaments like ten thousand mocking eyes.

The Huguenots obligingly relieved the situation with an assault upon the town of La Charité by way of protest at the turn of affairs at Blois. There could be no doubt as to who was at fault this time. Henry sent Alençon at the head of the royal army to put down his former allies on money voted without protest by the Estates, who were then dissolved. The League, frightened of its own strength — for there still existed a majesty in a king that made it dangerous to press him too far — thought it prudent to retreat for a term to its various lairs; and Henry took advantage of the reflux of Catholic loyalty to declare himself its *ex officio* head. An adroit manoeuvre but a grave mistake, since he thereby acknowledged its right to live: 'Un roi ne devait jamais endurer,' a wise contemporary remarked, 'autre parti que le sien, parce que c'est le plus beau parti du monde d'être roi.' But Guise also made a mistake, not to have perceived that he was dealing with a pride that might turn ferocious if driven into a corner....

Alençon returned victorious, Henry patched up a new peace — '*My* peace' — which both sects, miraculously, observed more or less for eight years. A precarious reprieve which Catherine celebrated with a Babylonian banquet at which her ladies waited on table with their hair down their backs and their bodies naked to the waist.

Again the second person in the realm was left with nothing to do but eat his heart out for what he could not have. The kingdom of his own, no nearer for all the honours and titles he had won — those bagatelles, his own by right, for which he had fought only to compel the respect due his rank and help him on to the greater thing. Often in the night he woke in his own cold sweat and coughed up little drops of blood. And then he shivered and cried out that he would die before he had had his chance to do that for which he had been born. He was only twenty-two, but time had a way of flying fast for a Valois....

Only one person understood. His mother and brother repeated painstakingly over and over that the peace was too new to be put in jeopardy; but he could read in their eyes their doubt of his ability to stand up against the Spanish commanders in the Netherlands. Most of the world, led by the *mignons*, openly jeered at him. Two victorious wars in eighteen months might make him the most eminent general in France, but nothing could make him look the part. Only Margot, his guardian spirit, 'the Dido to his Aeneas,' saw him as he saw himself, nor rested till she had set him on his way.

The consequences to the House she did not even stop to think about. 'The heart, though the clearest, is not the most constant instructor of the head; the heart, unlike the often obtuser head, works for itself and not for the commonwealth.'

There lay the catastrophe of the House, that those who loved it were driven by irresistible impulse to destroy it. Their loves and hates and desires — the need, in short, to live their own lives — were stronger than they, and so they rushed on, all the time knowing that if they destroyed it they surely destroyed themselves.

A stubborn attack of erysipelas on her arm extracted for Margot Henry's permission to try the healing properties of Spa. The waters saw little of her, the Flemish noblemen a great deal. Looking at her beauty, listening to her wit, observing her cool courage when the bullets began to fly against a castle in which they entertained her, they recalled with homesickness that they too had once been French and urged her to send her brother along. Just as the ladies of the English court imagined the unseen Alençon to be a royal La Mole, so the gentlemen of Flanders prefigured him as a masculine Margot. She concluded her visit with a call on the Spanish viceroy, the young Don John of Austria, who remarked thoughtfully, 'Although this Queen's beauty is more divine than human, she is formed rather to damn men's souls than to save them.'

She returned at the end of 1577 to find Alençon nearly off his head from the *mignons*' mockery. They found him absurd, bumptious, and a nuisance, and told him so in words that failed to make up in wit what they lacked in amiability. Bussy was doing what he could to redress the balance, but he was one against many and his methods tended rather to incite than to mollify. Into a ballroom where the *mignons* strutted in their peacock finery, Bussy led a troupe of his companions dressed like a lot of undertakers' mutes. The *mignons* saw the point only too well: they challenged Bussy to fight it out, as many on each side as he pleased, but the King forbade the duel. Caylus and some friends then went after Bussy in the streets, but the brawl resulted in a draw and Henry in annoyance ordered both his own and his brother's champion out of Paris — to Alençon's clamorous indignation and even greater fright at being left without his right arm.

A few days later came the breaking point. The occasion was the marriage of the *mignon* Saint-Luc (February 9-12, 1578), a festivity in which Henry, incomparably the most inspired Master of the Revels in Europe, surpassed himself for originality and splendour. Alençon begged to be excused, but his brother, furious at the thought of the irritating little 'maggot' (his own private nickname for him) putting a slight on one of his 'three eldest sons,' sharply commanded him to be present. The Duke, wandering about forlorn and disconsolate, strayed into the supper-room, where a cluster of his tormentors at once began to laugh and exchange audible quips on his appearance. It was the last straw. Forgetting his habitual caution he dashed upstairs to his room, exclaiming, 'I can't bear this any longer! I'm going away.'

The threat drifted through the festival-lit salons of the Louvre until it reached Henry treading a care-free measure in the ballroom. With a blasphemous oath worthy of Charles he commanded Souvray to be sent for. Was the maggot forever to wreck his peace, make him go on eating dirt before his subjects? When Souvray appeared, he directed him to have Alençon's followers rounded up into the Bastille and to return immediately he had given the order. 'We are going to do a strange thing,' he muttered as they started up the winding private staircase of the Louvre together by the light of Souvray's single candle. 'Better not do it by halves, Sire,' nodded the other.

Meantime someone informs Catherine of what is afoot. She flings a robe over her nightgown and flies to Alençon's room. Wakes him — for he has already fallen asleep, the tear stains fresh on his cheeks — and tells him that his designs are discovered. That the King is coming to take his life... he must think quickly, have a story ready. Before she finishes or he is fully awake, Henry is standing by her side.

He orders his brother to get up. Alençon falls on his knees and blurts out, not a story, but the truth. About the insults heaped on him, the misconstruction put on his actions. He can bear it no longer... He means no harm to anyone, he swears it... wants nothing but to slip over the border with a few horsemen. He curses, rants, blubbers, all at the same time. It is his destiny, without which he cannot live. France's destiny, too, after all.... Flanders is French by right.... Charles saw it, so did Coligny....

Henry's fury evaporates. The lad looks so ill, so pathetic in the candle-light — and, yes, so exalted that it sends a pang of self-reproach to the elder brother's heart. That this ugly little man should be ready to sacrifice his everything for that glowing dream, while he, the King, 'the blessed of Heaven's gifts,' reclines in indolence and turns his thoughts from great actions because he does not dare their consequences. Henry muses a while in silence, trying to defend himself. It cannot be good that this uncouth boy should tear the realm in pieces once more or even live to succeed to it. He himself is young yet, only twenty-seven, Our Lady of the Conception may still be moved to graciousness. Yet his own brother, the last of his line...

Grimly Henry reminds him that the last two times he cherished the project of going into Flanders it had led him into a plot on the throne and a civil war. Turning on his heel he directs Souvray to post a guard outside the Duke's room and hold him there *incommunicando* until he can examine those of his followers already in the Bastille and find out what lies behind the whole thing. Catherine vigorously nods approval and heaves an inward sigh of relief.

She does not want Alençon dead or in the Bastille; almost less does she want him loose on the country or provoking Spain to war. In her perplexity she sends for Margot, trying to probe into the lad's mind through the one that knows it best. Margot looks surprised, doubtful — she is sure that

Alençon would never have planned to run away without telling her and he has not breathed a word on the subject. He must have spoken on an impulse — she asks to see him and make sure. Catherine arranges it. Margot returns with a smile to report that his temper has blown over: she is willing to go bail with her life that he will not leave without permission. 'Think well what you say,' cautions Catherine sternly. Margot repeats her offer. Her mother's eyes bore into her — but Catherine finally accepts the perjury because it is more convenient to do so.

First thing in the morning she hurries to Henry with the tidings that Alençon is all contrition, a reformed character: 'Never have I seen such a beautiful repentance nor a sinner give so great a hope of conversion.' Henry, never dreaming that she had feigned to agree with him the night before in order to be in a better position to speak for Alençon later, is staggered by *her* conversion and impressed. He promises to defer drastic action for the present and meantime relax his brother's arrest.

That evening the guards outside the palace notice a blaze coming from the Queen of Navarre's chimney and in fear of fire rush to her room. Her maids open the door and tell them to go away again, that nothing is wrong. Had they insisted on admittance they would have found a thick rope burning in her fireplace, a rope smuggled in by her lute-player in his music-case and employed a few minutes before to assist Alençon into an unwatched moat below. At the moment the guards rapped on the door he was leaving Paris through a hole knocked in one of its walls from the outside, near the church of Sainte-Geneviève, by his friend Bussy.

This was Bussy's last service to either his master or mistress. Next year, while Alençon was in England courting Elizabeth and Margot in the south reunited to her husband, he took up with the Lady of Monsoreau, whose husband was of the King's party. The lady, at her lord's direction, made an assignation with Bussy in a lonely lodge: where the husband appeared at midnight with a dozen men. Bussy had naturally come alone to the rendezvous, but it took the dozen's best efforts to account for him. His sword broken to the hilt after he had stretched prone four of his opponents, he then defended himself with chairs and tables and nearly got away through the window when someone managed to stab him in the back. The night that the news of his death reached Paris, crosses appeared on various Huguenot doors, and the whole of the Reformed population in the capital locked and barred their houses with special care that night in the belief that Bussy's spirit was returning to conduct single-handed a new Saint Bartholomew's.

Shortly after his escape, in July, 1578, Alençon crossed the border and stepped into the midst of the great European conflagration from which France had so far been screened by luck and Catherine's shrewdness. His intention was to free Catholic Flanders, which had lately joined Protestant Holland in the revolt against Spain. The title of Defender of Belgian Liberties had been officially awarded him, but he found four other Defenders already on the spot and himself, with no particular backing, taken rather less notice of than any of the rest. To remedy his lack he went to England, but Elizabeth, though enchanted (she said) at the sight of him, willing to kiss him and give him money out of which to buy jewels for his courtship, explained regretfully that she could not possibly marry him so long as he remained his brother's outlaw. He must go home and get himself made France's accredited general for the Netherlands.

Back he went to Paris, bursting in on Henry at five in the morning, aglow to repeat Elizabeth's promises, describe her caresses, flash her jewels. If only Henry would help him now ... in a few months he would be King of the Netherlands, King-Consort of England, and France the undisputed mistress of Europe. Henry looked at the flushed, sallow countenance of his brother and reflected that his good sister of England must have a queer taste in men: but he put his arms round the boy's frail shoulders and tried to explain to him gently what Elizabeth was up to. How she was trying to make him her catspaw, and France through him, to pull her own chestnuts out of the Spanish fire. And how Philip, meantime, though unable to punish France for his trespass by arms, was feeding the Guises with money so as to prepare his revenge on their common House at another day....

To all of which Alençon scarcely listened in his chagrin. For four years he made the rounds of Flanders, England, Paris... until in the end patience won, and the united Netherlands, almost at their last gasp, offered him their sovereignty in the desperate hope of dragging Henry in on their side. They were shrewd bargainers, they gave little till they were sure of what they were getting. So that Alençon, a king without money, without power, without even greater respect as first person in his own realm than as second in his brother's, presently turned on their cities in the effort to wrest from them by force what they would not grant freely. They drove him out: he fled to the seclusion of his estate at Château-Thierry, where, his spirit broken by disappointment and grief, he passively succumbed after a few months to a galloping consumption.

He died on June 10, 1584, his last regret that he would never rule in the palace at Brussels so that he might leave it to the King. 'I carry to my grave,' added the will over which he laboured in his last hours of pain, 'the substance and tears of many people, without being able to discharge myself of them to God or man.... If only I could, by what I have to bequeath him, repay my brother for all the sorrow I have brought on him.' One final wish he expressed, to be buried under his sovereign title of Duke of Brabant; but to have allowed him that symbolic remnant of his glory even in death would have increased the already formidable ire of Spain, so they laid him in Saint-Denis plain Duke of Alençon, just as he had begun.

Chapter XVI

DÉBÂCLE

All the trouble that Alençon had caused in his life was as nothing compared with the fearful dilemma he raised by his dying. The next of blood was Henry of Bourbon, a heretic — a thing inconceivable, against nature. How could a heretic swear the solemn coronation oath to uphold the One Holy Church, defend it as its Eldest Son, receive the sacrament and the holy oil on his investiture? The divine law forbade it, the people would not suffer it. Yet how could the lawful successor designated of God be set aside without plunging the State into anarchy?

Henry, Duke of Guise, had ready the answer. For him had arrived the opportunity for which his House had waited during nearly three generations. He revived his League, sleek and fattened from the long nourishment surreptitiously administered to it by the King of Spain for Alençon's offences — those hundreds of thousands who would have no king but a Catholic, ready for faith's sake to dedicate themselves to him who would have no king but a Guise. With their help he reckoned to bring his sovereign to heel, to trample the House of Valois into the earth before the end of its mortal term, so as to be in a position to arrange the future according to his desire.

Henry of Valois vowed that it should not be so: the Faith that he loved should not serve the turn of an adventurer's bloody pretensions upon the land that he loved. For himself personally there remained nothing to strive for, no son nor near of kin — nothing but to discharge the duty of his House to God and to France so that it might at least go out in peace and dignity. He sent the Duke of Épernon, his 'eldest son' and stout right arm, to press upon Navarre the danger of losing his rights unless he turned Catholic and to offer him full recognition as heir, with all honours and appurtenances, if he would do so. Meantime he passed a series of vigorous edicts to reform justice and transfer the burden of taxation from poor to rich. Simultaneously he outlawed the League in a proclamation which skilfully pointed out to its less educated adherents its essentially treasonable nature and the private designs upon the public order behind their leader's pious professions.

It was too late, the country too torn by passion to wait for palliatives or listen to reason. Only force unshrinkingly applied could by now have restored the royal authority: and force signified either suppressing the League with the help of the heretics or suppressing the heretics with the help of the League. Henry recoiled from either solution, with the result that both sides, knowing it, dared the consequences of disobeying him. Navarre declined his offers and dismissed Épernon after Margot had done her enthusiastic best to make the visit of her brother's chief *mignon* as miserable as possible. The Guises, with almost contemptuous protestations of loyalty, continued to augment their strength.

Their propaganda became ferocious. One of the attacks began, 'Henry, by the grace of his mother doubtful King of France and imaginary King of Poland, janitor of the Louvre, bell-ringer of Saint-Germain l'Auxerrois [Guise had his nerve to bring this one up] and all the Paris churches... his wife's lady's-maid and hairdresser, hosier to the palace, inspector of the brothels, patron of the mendicant orders and conscript father of flagellation....' They clamoured for the repeal of all taxes added since the time of Louis XII, an effective demagogic appeal which artfully placed the rise in the cost of living since Louis XII's time on Henry's gifts to his *mignons*. The Paris cemeteries blossomed forth with gruesome posters depicting the Catholics tortured and burned in England by Elizabeth as a warning of what would happen if the Huguenots got the upper hand in France. As fast as Henry tore them down, they reappeared.

The propaganda and the alluring element of secrecy in the League's make-up (like that of the Carbonari or the Ku Klux Klan) swept the tepid with the fanatical. A broad belt of towns down the eastern half of France in swift succession declared for its obscurantist programme and threw out their royal governors. Within a few months it had swelled into a quasi-sovereign power with its own laws and officials: and its own foreign treaties, of which by far the most important was one with Philip II, whereby the Guises virtually sold him their country's independence in return for his help in conquering it. They then turned round and served notice on Henry that he must either finish with Navarre once and for all or stand aside and let them do it for him. A first step on the road to reducing him to a puppet king.

Henry sent Catherine to Lorraine as his plenipotentiary to negotiate him out of his predicament. She was the best card he had to play — and the worst. Her experience, her age, had settled upon her a vast mysterious prestige tinged with something not unlike superstition. The Guises, in genuine fear of her, extremely eager to win her to their side, made a tremendous fuss over her, admitted her into their confidence or affected to, boasted of their strength... apparently with complete success.

For strange fantasies, new and intricate combinations, had begun in these latter years to take shape in Catherine's mind.

She accepted it as a fact now that Henry would die childless ... even perhaps go mad and be deposed. She harboured with growing confidence a weird notion, 'that she herself will never die.' She wanted the House of Lorraine to succeed to the throne rather than the son-in-law she had never liked — but not in the person of the Duke of Guise. That was the trick she was holding up her sleeve. There existed an elder branch with prior rights stemming from Charlemagne, and the twigs of that branch were her own grandchildren by Claude, the young Marquis of Pont-à-Mousson and the little Christine whom she adored more than any living creature except Henry. Once she had thought of marrying Christine to Alençon. Now she brooded over the possibility of divorcing Margot from Navarre and joining her with her twenty-year-old nephew. Of finding for Christine — but there her thoughts still remained nebulous. In any event, of going on and on as eternal Regent for whomever Fate and herself might wangle onto the throne if anything happened to Henry. What good was immortality without power? or power without immortality?

Everything that the Guises dared yet to ask as the price of their submission she agreed to — the wholesale banishment of the Huguenots, the forfeiture of Navarre's rights. Henry, stunned at the treaty she put before him, refused to sign. Navarre tried to stiffen his resistance by an offer to come to his aid with an army. So did Elizabeth of England, terrified by the threat to her throne in the alliance of Guise and Spain: for it was a major part of their joint design to supplant her with her prisoner Mary Stuart. Venice, too, promised help in money and the Dutch hurried commissioners to arrange a common action with the harassed King of France. For one dizzy moment Henry's imagination winged toward Coligny's dream. The Spanish ambassador Mendoza, recently expelled from England, rushed to him in a panic with a protest against his receiving the Dutch emissaries or giving refuge to the

Flemings driven by the Spanish Viceroy over his borders. Henry refused both requests point-blank, with the haughty rejoinder that 'My realm of France has never refused hospitality to the oppressed.'

But Catherine was back at his side, to work upon his fears as she had once worked upon Charles's. She painted the League's resources in numbers that would have astonished no one more than its leaders. She implored him not to divert the terrible Armada now building, whose might nothing on earth would be able to resist, from its destination in England to the shores of France. She soothed him with her craft: let him but wait, as she had always done, dissimulate awhile, and his chance would come. Anything else was certain suicide. . . . She was sure, he was not; he trusted her, as he had always done, more than he trusted himself. Sadly he abrogated the edicts of toleration, the fruits of twenty years of civil war, sardonically he listened to the cheers of 'Vive le roi' — a sound he had not heard in many a long day — from the Paris mob: 'I fear that you will not destroy the preaching without endangering the Mass,' he acutely warned the magistrates who registered the edicts. But no one was any longer in a mood to reflect upon so reasonable a proposition.

'The King is on foot, the League on horseback,' commented a sympathetic witness of his humiliation. Dreary and dispirited Henry began to gather an army to fight his own subjects at his subjects' dictation — a depth to which it would have seemed so short a while ago inconceivable that any King of France should sink. One clause of the treaty, however, he flatly refused to ratify. If he must use force he must, but if the use of force resulted in the lawful heir's conversion, the way to the throne should still lie open to him. Even if he had to die fighting to keep it so. He sent Catherine to make one last appeal to his brother-in-law while he wrestled with the League's impatience to begin hostilities.

The Guises, frightened lest the manœuvre succeed — for if

it did the effect on the people would be annihilation to their cause — tried to forestall it by having Navarre excommunicated before Catherine left. The matter proved exceedingly difficult to arrange. The new pope, Sixtus V, had no love for rebels and said so frankly. But Philip insisted, and with Europe so tensely divided into black and white, Sixtus could not hold off with one hand the mighty ally whom he was helping with the other to finance the Armada.

He published the Bull — and the Guises discovered that they had gone too fast. Even the majority of Frenchmen to whom Navarre's name was anathema would not tolerate the intrusion of foreigners into their national affairs. The Paris mob itself hooted with glee as the papal messenger knelt in apology on the cobbles for bringing the offensive document and the magistrates ceremoniously destroyed it in a public bonfire. The Guises recoiled in dismay; Catherine, racked with gout and rheumatism, bounced painfully over the endless familiar road to the south on the most momentous of her life's many errands.

On the lips of one man hung peace or war. He was not anxious to pronounce the word. For two months he contrived to avoid the interview with his mother-in-law. From place to place he flitted seeing to his slender resources for the struggle to come, the while she trudged after him with dogged patience. At length he allowed her to catch up with him and the final colloquy took place between the woman for whom life was a transaction and her son-in-law for whom it was an adventure. Worry and responsibility had whitened his hair (the other two Henrys bore the same trace of premature age, though none of the three was over thirty-five), but otherwise had left him unchanged from the huge jolly boy, the lover of good eating and pretty women, who had fled from Paris a decade before. 'As you knew this prince, Sire,' reported the Duke of Nevers, 'so he is today. The years neither alter nor embarrass him.'

Catherine opened with a characteristic gambit: why should he not divorce Margot (she herself would see to the papal decree) and marry Christine, thus double-crossing the League and settling the question of faith and the succession at a single happy stroke. He burst into peals of laughter. She amused him with her schemes and her marriages, and he told her so. With an inward sigh of regret that he was not more like his father, she read him a lecture on what he must do if he ever hoped to assert the prerogative of his birth. He reminded her that whatever trouble existed on that score was not his fault — it was not he who had repealed the edicts of toleration and encouraged the League. Ignoring the thrust she threw herself on his pity: 'Must I always be in this turmoil, I who desire only repose?'

He grinned. 'This turmoil, as you call it, is your breath of life, Madame. If you had to live in peace and quiet, you wouldn't know what to do with yourself.'

With another sigh because he was so like his mother, she asked him why he doubted her good-will toward him. Ungallantly he replied, 'Oh, it's not your good-will I doubt, but your age, which seems to have so impaired your memory that it causes you to forget your promises to me.' So that was that — Saint Bartholomew's had spoken his answer. If, relying on her promises, he abandoned his Huguenot friends, what assurance had he that she would not toss him to the Guises, as she had tossed his master Coligny, when the occasion and her power seemed to demand it?

She did not see Margot because Margot was not there to see. She had fled to serve her first lover the Duke of Guise.

After Alençon's departure for Flanders she had been allowed to join her husband in Béarn. Under her magic touch Jeanne d'Albret's stuffy little Protestant court became a circle of sparkle, wit, and gaiety over which La Reine Margot happily reigned for two years to the delight of its gallants and the rhapsodies of its poets. Then came trouble. She haughtily declined to serve as a rag for the reputation of one of her husband's mistresses — an insolent chit whom she had generously befriended. Hard on top of that, the flocking of the local Catholics to her private chapel started a fracas which forced Navarre, in the interest of peace, to forbid her the practice of her religion. Her Valois pride joined with her imperious need for equality to reject living with any man on such terms: she left him and returned to Paris. There, with nothing to do (for Alençon was at the crisis of his Flanders adventure), she took up with the worst company in the capital, became involved in a dozen scandals in less than a year and in a running guerrilla war of words with the *mignons*. Finally, to annoy Joyeuse, she had his courier rifled of important despatches for Rome — and Henry, bursting into a crowded ballroom over which she was presiding in the absence of Queen Louise, furiously flung into her face the whole catalogue of her misdemeanours (amongst them an aborted child by Alençon's squire, Harley de Chanvallon), and ordered her to get out: 'Go back to your husband; you are doing no earthly good here.'

She left that same night. Next day Henry, informed that she had stolen some important papers, rode after her with an escort of guards and put her and her retinue through a humiliating search. Nothing was found and she was allowed to proceed: the final parting of the brother and sister who had once loved each other so dearly.

But after her public disgrace her husband declined to take her back unless her brother first made a complete retraction. It was a good deal to ask of a king. Henry wriggled and tried to explain to Navarre how easy it was to be misled by gossip: 'Remember how your own mother was calumniated,' he wrote. Navarre slapped his thigh and roared, 'First he tells me I'm *cocu*, and now he implies that I am the son of a bitch.' Catherine wrote him a long letter on the proper deportment of a husband, in which she held up her own and Henry II's discretion in these matters as a model for his guidance — the only time in her life that she ever referred openly to her husband's affair with Diane de Poitiers. Navarre, untouched by this fragment of autobiography, held out for a year before accepting satisfaction, Margot meantime wandering homeless.

The vagrant life seemed to have had some compensations. At any rate she returned restless to be off again. Navarre was no longer her underdog to protect, but a hard-working commander of men who kept his own counsel and smoothly contrived to keep her hands out of his affairs. Two years later, in 1585, she ran away to Agen, a city that formed part of her dowry, raised a company of soldiers, threw out her brother's garrison, and declared for the League. The populace, exasperated by the misconduct of her men, in turn threw her out; she mounted a horse behind one of her gentlemen and fled to the fortified town of Carlat. Her brother sent a strong detachment to take her, who, to avoid bloodshed, simply bought her from the townspeople. They removed her to the impregnable castle at Usson in charge of the Marquis of Canillac, the governor of Auvergne, whom she proceeded to seduce without delay. Her gaoler thus lulled to sleep, she adroitly concocted a revolt against him and drove him out. After that she was left alone. For fourteen years she ruled the castle as its mistress, a prisoner to the outside world.

She grew fat and went in for good works. She collected a drove of lovers from amongst her own squires and a herd of camels and rode them both over the countryside in search of picturesque spots for *fêtes champêtres*. In time she patched up a form of truce with her brother and wrote him for permission to import wine without duty. At first he refused, saying she would get drunk and break her neck by falling off her camels; then relented, in the possible hope that she would do so. In the shadow of extinction the family had characteristically managed to disperse itself into its ultimate antipathetic particles.

Catherine returned with her message of failure. The League, in arms, peremptorily called upon Henry to fight. Elizabeth of England powerfully reinforced their ultimatum by making an end of Mary Stuart. A spasm of hatred for all Protestantism shook Catholic France, accompanied by a great wave of sympathy for the Guises in the tragic death of their niece, once France's Queen. Henry, who had worked day and night to save her, was forced to bow before the clamour. The Reiters hurried things on by pouring in hordes over the Rhine to Navarre's assistance.

Henry girded on the armour discarded nineteen years before after Moncontour, surveyed the situation and coolly decided '*de meis inimicis vindicabo inimicos meos*' — 'through my enemies I will revenge myself upon my enemies.' To Guise he assigned the task of stopping the Reiters in the hope that the Reiters would prove the end of him; to his *mignon* the Duke of Joyeuse he entrusted the defeat of Navarre and his Huguenots for the glory it would bring to the Crown. He himself took up his station at Gien between the two armies.

His calculations went completely awry. Guise's zealots shattered the lukewarm mercenaries, better always in a raid than in a full-dress war. Joyeuse ran into zealots too. On the eve of battle Navarre confessed openly to his followers that he had seduced a girl and was absolved with pious acclaim. His army marched into action behind their preachers' banners singing the One Hundred and Eighteenth Psalm: 'This is the day which the Lord hath made; we will be glad and rejoice in it.' And so it turned out. The dashing young blades who had followed Joyeuse from court broke the Huguenot line with their impetuosity, but Navarre rallied his men and in the streets of Coutras cut down the royal army in hand-to-hand fighting. Joyeuse the debonaire, the mirror of his King, seeing that all was lost, turned to his fellow *mignon* Saint-Luc and inquired, 'What do we do next?' 'Die at the cannon's mouth,' answered the other, 'a general has no other retreat.' Joyeuse thought the advice good and took it. It was the first Huguenot victory in seven civil wars. Navarre, having got out of the Lord what he wanted for that day, went off to spend the night with his mistress, to the horror of his battalion of preachers, who certified that he would come to no good end.

Henry gathered the remnants of the shattered army and hurried east to stop Guise's sickening slaughter of the fugitive Germans. It was a humane move, but an injudicious one. Paris, convinced that he had let off Navarre and called off Guise out of secret favour to the Huguenots, for the first time openly muttered the word abdication. When he returned with the victor for the triumphant *Te Deum* in Notre-Dame, the populace outside sang, like some revolutionary anthem, 'Saul hath slain his thousands, and David his ten thousands.' Unable to get at poor Joyeuse, the League had pamphlets cried in the streets on 'The Exploits of the Duke of Épernon in the War,' which when opened contained on every page the single word 'Nothing.'

The Guisards (as the League was now called) gave the screw another turn. They demanded that the King enter the Catholic coalition with the Pope and Spain and restore the Inquisition.

They wanted to move the clock back twenty years, a hundred and twenty. The poet in Henry kindled into passionate life. 'I will not do it,' he answered:

> The wheel and the rack, the thumbscrews and the cord, the underground cell and the yellow robe painted with devils and — last act of this pitiful tragedy — the fire, have rendered the Inquisition, which may be necessary in Spain, so horrible to the French that they would suffer a thousand times more than the Flemings have endured rather than submit to it. To estab-

lish it amongst these light-hearted French, suppress the curiosity of mind that is as natural to us as the air we breathe — there would not be enough forests in France to burn my subjects. I won't do it. I prefer a sick body to a dead one, a heretic to a corpse. I won't have religion become a butchery or the altar of God's sacrifice a shambles. No, the King of France no longer desires to kill in order to compel belief. He will never undertake to force souls so long as the bodies render him true obedience. It is for God to accord false beliefs with those which are in harmony with His service.... I have given them all they have asked for, till every nerve in this body politic aches and every member languishes. They have constrained me to hazard my Estate on the chances of war. I have lost half, let them give me leave to retire on the other half and live in peace.

The words were beautiful, the conclusion gave away the uncertainty that bedevilled him every time. The Guises pressed implacably on. They designated their henchman the Cardinal of Bourbon, oldest surviving Prince of the Blood after Navarre, as heir to the throne — a sly, stupid old man with the popular nickname of the Red Ass. He was sixty-eight, and, though he talked largely of defrocking himself and marrying, unlikely to fulfil his own ambition of producing a son. Henry was to be interned in a monastery, the Cardinal to rule as Mayor of the Palace under the thumb of the League, the office and the succession both to pass to Guise when he died.[1] The method Pepin the Short had taken to be rid of Childeric, the last Merovingian, the scheme the old Duke of Guise had been brewing before the death of Francis II. The young Duke's sister, the Duchess of Montpensier, 'Queen of the League,' a rich widow with a pretty face and a pro-

---

[1] The claim of the Cardinal of Bourbon, as urged by the League, rested on the fact that Antoine of Navarre had not been heir when he died, therefore had no rights to leave his son — a feeble hypothesis which, if admitted, gave the Cardinal priority over his nephew as first Prince of the Blood. The Guises made little secret of their ultimate intention. They subsidized books setting forth their genealogical tree and their consequent claim as heirs of a House, the Carolingians, antedating not only the Valois, but all the Capetians.

nounced limp, who hated Henry because he had rejected her advances, went ostentatiously about Paris with golden scissors at her girdle which she boasted was to provide 'Brother Henry' with his third crown — the tonsure of a monk.

The gods themselves stepped in to assist in the destruction they had decreed. Never since the Middle Ages had France been visited by such a sequence of floods, droughts, earthquakes, famine, pestilence, and portentous lights in the heavens as in the two years preceding 1588 — the *Annus Mirabilis* predicted by the astrologers since the beginning of the century. The League's preachers had more than ample material with which to embroider their texts upon the divine wrath overhanging the realm for the sins of its ruling House. The starving peasantry streamed into the capital by the thousands to swell the volume of sedition. The atmosphere grew sultrier a dozen times than on the days preceding Saint Bartholomew's. It became unsafe for Henry to appear in the streets — his advisers daily pressed him to leave for one of his fortresses in the Loire. But he would not, because he loved Paris more than had any other of his line; whichever way his eye turned, it fell upon some work of use or beauty with which his fondness had embellished it. And, like all the Valois, he disdained fear. Round him stood a picked bodyguard, the Forty-Five, ready to die in his defence; he entrusted his life to their devotion and stayed to face out the storm.

It broke with violent suddenness. Early in May the leaders of the League met at Soissons to concert plans for taking over the government. While they debated came word from Madame de Montpensier, a lady with more nerve than all her male colleagues together, of a plan hatched between her and the League's secret revolutionary organization in Paris (known as 'The Sixteen') to kill Épernon, kidnap Henry, and bring him to Soissons to sign his act of virtual abdication. Her brother, frightened at her temerity, hesitated: it was still an act of unheard-of sacrilege to lay forcible hands on the person of a king. Henry's spy Poulain meanwhile brought him word of what was afoot. He acted with vigour. Four thousand troops were moved to the outskirts of the city, and the police ordered to begin a house-to-house search for the League's agents. Épernon was sent to Normandy to oversee its defences against the dreaded Armada, the Louvre fortified, and the peremptory command sent to Guise to stay away from the capital.

The supreme test had come. The adherents of the League in Paris sent a panicky message to Guise that unless he hurried to their aid they would all be exterminated. Again he hesitated: if he refused, the League was crushed and his own prestige gone forever — if he accepted, he entered the lion's mouth self-convicted of high treason. Another order arrived from the King, similar to the first, but couched in even stronger language. Another hysterical appeal from his followers. On the evening of May 8 he left Soissons with nine men saying, 'I'll see the Louvre or die on the way,' and at noon of the next day rode through the Porte Saint-Martin.

He muffled his features in his cloak, since he wanted to be in a position to claim that he had tried to avoid recognition and had only come to plead with the King for a redress of grievances, but his friends in Paris saw to it that he had a proper reception, like his father's when he drove Catherine and her children before him to Fontainebleau twenty years earlier. A group of young girls strewed flowers in his path. One of them reached up and tugged the cloak from his face, saying it was time he made himself known. The people poured out of houses and shops to shriek, 'Vive Guise... now we shall be saved,' and kiss his garments, his very stirrups. 'They adored him like a saint,' held up their chaplets as he went past, touched them to their foreheads. With a mob he was to the manner born: 'caressing it with eye and voice he made even Huguenots Leaguers when they looked at him.'

HENRI DE LORRAINE, DUKE OF GUISE

He went straight to Catherine, who for the past few years had been living in a converted convent in the centre of the city known as 'The House of Repentant Girls.' She was rather a repentant girl herself at the moment he burst in on her. Terrified of Henry provoking the League to extremities, she had to the last moment worked in surreptitious opposition to him. Through Bellièvre, the very official through whom Henry had transmitted his instructions to Guise to keep out of Paris, she had sent the Duke another letter all honey and appeasement; and Guise, relying on the Queen Mother, took the chance that the King's anger was not so intense as he represented it to be. 'Offend no one, risk nothing, the remedies are often worse than the evils,' was the motto she had adopted for herself during the recent troubles, and fastened like a ball and chain to Henry. Her policy of caution had miscarried, everything began to move too fast for her — 'Glad as I am to see you,' she blurted at sight of Guise, 'I would more gladly have seen you at another time.'

He broke into a series of protestations that he had only come because he knew that his enemies were slandering him and begged her to arrange an interview with the King. She called her litter and, with Guise on foot beside her and an enormous throng following, had herself carried to the Louvre. Meantime the Secretary of State Villeroy had received the news of the Duke's arrival and hurried with it to the King. Henry, frothing with rage, exclaimed, 'Then he's come after all. God's death, he shall die for it!' He flung open the window giving onto the garden, listened for a moment to the noise of the mob, then gave orders for the Duke to be received in his wife's apartment while he retired to his cabinet for an emergency council.

His principal ministers join him there and the captains of the Forty-Five. One of the latter, Alphonso Ornano, a Corsican, says briskly, 'Sire, there is only one question: do you hold Monsieur de Guise to be your friend or enemy?' Henry's expression is sufficient answer. 'Then, Sire,' pleads the Corsican eagerly, 'that being so, if you will deign to honour me with this charge, I will lay his head today at your feet without giving you or any other man in the world further trouble.' Henry thanks him with a glance, but still says nothing. The ministers are aghast; the avalanche had been released too rapidly for their sober wits. Bellièvre, Cheverney the Chancellor, and others — Catherine's men chiefly — urge that it is too dangerous, that it would be more prudent to bring the Duke to trial for high treason. The bolder spirits ridicule the idea. The thing is impossible: the mob would get its idol out if it had to tear the Louvre down stone from stone... a servant interrupts the colloquy with the news that the Duke has arrived.

Louise is ill and Catherine carries on an uneasy conversation at the side of her bed while waiting for her son to appear. The Duke of Guise, fidgeting restlessly, exchanges a few desultory words by the window with Christine, Claude's daughter, his eyes fixed on the door. All turn their heads abruptly at a sound like the clicking of a lock. The King enters by a small secret door to which he alone holds the key, the glint of many cuirasses visible before he closes it. Guise makes a deep reverence. The King strides slowly toward him, halts, and asks quietly, 'What are you doing here? I warned you not to come.' Explanations pour from Guise's lips, profuse and ready. 'I have come to put myself in Your Majesty's hands to ask justice for my enemies' slanders. Nevertheless, I should never have come had I received any explicit injunction against it from you.' He fails to mention that he was forewarned of Bellièvre's second letter and rode out of Soissons by a side road in order to avoid meeting the courier.

The King turns to Bellièvre and asks him if he failed to carry out his instructions. Bellièvre gives vent to a stream of explanations as voluble as the Duke's. Yes, he had sent both letters... expressed the King's will to the best of his ability

... the second he had forwarded by the regular courier, not thinking it justified the expense of an express... he had said so and so... The King cuts him short with 'I told you to say a good deal more than that.' His tone is menacing, but his brow begins to knit in perplexity.

Catherine, alarmed not only for the Duke, but for herself if he finds out too much, hurries to his side and in a hoarse whisper beseeches him to sleep on his anger... to think of the mob seething against the palace walls. Some of its members climb up and hurl threats through the closed window while she speaks. Henry scarcely hears what she or they say. Several times he glances over his shoulder at the closed door, as if about to raise his voice in summons to Ornano waiting behind it with his men. The word remains unuttered. He ponders the Duke's defence — a plausible, an excellent defence: the more he considers it the more the rights and wrongs, as always, seem to strike an even balance. If he were his father, even his easy-going grandfather, Guise would not have a ghost of a chance of leaving this room alive. But Henry's own nature, at war with both his judgment and impulse, intercedes for his enemy at the threshold of death.... And so he is lost, and his kingdom with him — all to procure Guise a paltry seven months of grace...

His eye on the King's face, the Duke warily backs toward the room's principal door. The dinner bell — grotesque anticlimax — interrupts Catherine's monologue and Henry's reflections. The little company stirs and begins to draw normal breath again. Guise takes advantage of the relaxed atmosphere to bow himself out... Henry saying, as Charles had said to him in the adjoining cabinet many years before, that he would know where to find him if he wanted him.

Little good the knowledge did him. Pale and trembling from the narrowness of his escape, Guise hurried back to the Hôtel de Lorraine and converted the house into a miniature fortress. Scarcely was he gone when Henry repented of his weakness and determined to finish with him next morning when he came to the *lever*. But it was too late: he arrived accompanied by four hundred retainers who had trickled into the city from Soissons one by one during the previous eighteen hours. And meantime Paris crackled on the verge of explosion.

Henry pressed the search for the League's hidden agents. The populace began to murder his police. Wild rumours flew about the city that he planned to arrest every high magistrate and hang the lot as ringleaders... to call in the Huguenot armies and deliver the city over to their mercies.... The shops closed, that night no glimmer of light showed from any house. In the morning the King sent Villequier through the city to order the shops to open: no sooner had he ridden on than they shut again. The rioting continued, grew... Henry brought the troops into the city to restore order and enable the police to get on with their quest. It was the final spark. Paris had never yet tamely submitted to a garrison. The explosion takes place.

Barricades spring up in the streets, manned by artisans, merchants, students, nearly every class of the population but the prosperous. It is no fortuitous mob demonstration. The Sixteen, working under orders from the Hôtel de Lorraine, have brought out the terrible denizens of the quarters, the veterans of Saint Bartholomew's Day and their sons, in a state of formidable discipline. Whichever way the troops advance to their positions, they run into a hail of paving-blocks and showers of boiling oil poured by the women from the housetops. In order to avoid bloodshed in his capital, Henry ordered them — a ghastly mistake — not to fire on pain of death. The mob halts them, pushes the barricades relentlessly forward toward the huddled companies 'standing round like statues.' Their nerve breaks; they are not used to this kind of war. They fling down their arms, kneel in the streets and beg mercy of the 'gentle citizens.'

News of their plight reaches Henry in the Louvre. A frantic

council takes place. The King agrees to give the order for the troops to fire: Paris must be mastered now or never. Some advise an assault in force on the Hôtel de Lorraine. Catherine and Louise, weeping frantically, beg him to change his mind: not to provoke the capital to a last murderous desperation. Henry heeds them. The word goes out to withdraw the troops. But it is easier said than done. Once they turn their backs on the mob, it will rend them to the last man. To save them the King must now abase himself into the dust. An emissary runs from the Louvre to the Hôtel de Lorraine under a white flag to offer Monsieur de Guise a full pardon for rebellion against his King and to beg that he will permit His Majesty's soldiers to depart unharmed.

Guise goes into the streets dressed in white from head to foot and armed with nothing but a small ornamental staff. Paris is his, utterly. People lift him on their shoulders with the cry of 'To Rheims! Let us carry Monsieur to Rheims!' — the historic site of coronation. He has only to hold the troops imprisoned, walk to the Louvre, and dictate his own terms to a captive sovereign. But somehow that interview with Henry intimidates him; the man awes him, he has more than once admitted it frankly. He says to the shrieking folk round him, as if displeased at their suggestion, 'Friends, that's enough. It's too much. *Vive le roi!*' He wants now to pass as the serious man, the statesman of moderation. At his word his followers open their ranks and allow the troops to depart — harquebuses pointed to the ground, matchlocks extinguished, flags furled, drums on their backs, out by the Saint-Honoré Gate... It is the mistake of his life, the mistake that will soon cost him his life... 'He who desires to drink the wine of the gods must forget that he is mortal.'

That night, Thursday the twelfth, no one in Paris slept. Messengers picked their way between the palace and the Hôtel de Lorraine carrying offers of parley through the torchlit darkness. The mob paraded the streets in arms, rushed hither and thither in panic as rumours flew that the Montmorencys were coming with fresh troops — actually one of them appeared during the night with twelve hundred men, but was refused admission by the League watchmen at the gate — and feverishly built more barricades closer and closer to the Louvre. On the morning of Friday the thirteenth the tumult swelled again: the voices of the students chanting, 'Let's go get Brother Henry — let's drag the bugger out!' could be heard within the palace itself. The King sent Catherine to conclude what terms she could with Guise.

It was a short journey, but the most fearful of her life. The rioters snarled at her, hurled threats of physical violence, refused to let her through. Finally by orders from above they opened a passage and hauled her litter over the barricades, she sobbing heart-broken within. The conditions Guise laid down proved to be nothing short of a conqueror's. The Lieutenant-Generalship of the realm for himself, the banishment of Épernon and all the King's friends, the exclusion of Navarre, the dispersal of the Forty-Five, every office in the government for his own party — the whole to be confirmed by an Estates-General held under his auspices in Paris. Catherine gasped and could scarcely answer. It was ruin, absolute ruin, far beyond anything she had visualized in her worst nightmares. She asked and received permission to send one of the royal secretaries, Pinart, to consult with the King.

Pinart found Henry strolling moodily in the garden, staff in hand, waiting... Without comment he listened to the secretary's report, then called Du Halde to him and ordered him to draw on his boots. The valet's hands trembled so from excitement that he put on a spur backward. With an apology he fumbled to correct the error. The King smiled and said: 'It doesn't matter. I'm not going to see my mistress. We've a longer road to take.' Unhurried, though the mob was barking almost at his heels, he strolled to the stables in the

Tuileries, mounted and rode out through his private gate, the only one in the city still open to him.

On the bridge over the Seine he paused for one last look back at his capital, and his lips quivered. He saw the spire of the Sainte-Chapelle which he had just endowed with its exquisite altar screen... the graceful Pont-Neuf recently finished after his design... the embankments he had raised against the spring's calamitous floods. 'Ungrateful city,' he murmured, 'I loved you more than my own wife.' Then, followed by a motley array in robe and armour, soldiers and councillors, on foot and on horseback, he rode away to the west — a king without a capital and a doubtful quantity of kingdom.

Chapter XVII

PASSING OF THE FAMILY

Paris tumbled from its elation, Guise fell into black dismay. The King free in the country was a menace they had not counted upon. Rural France, not easily moved to excess and with no great fondness for sedition, might line up behind him... and they, the traitors, be drowned in a loyalist reaction. At all costs he must be made to return and legalize what they had done. Guise hurried a message to Chartres, where the court had taken up temporary residence, to explain that somehow, despite the benevolence that had brought him to Paris, 'God had inscrutably stirred up the whole populace to arms.' He pressed Catherine — than whom no one knew better how easily these unfortunate 'accidents' could happen — into service as a not too reluctant decoy, and even bamboozled the most devoted amongst the royal magistrates into becoming his ambassadors.

'Humph,' said Henry on receipt of the Duke's message, 'maybe he only came to Paris to order his spring outfit.' When the League got out, he told the delegates from the capital, he would consider coming back: it was not for a king to treat from a level of inferiority with his own subjects. Particularly a king who had been wronged.... 'Never since I came to this throne by my brother's death have I used severity toward anyone. You know it and can bear witness to it.... Do you think that if I intended any evil toward you I could not easily have executed it before the Barricades? What kept me from it, had I desired it? No, I love the Parisians better than they deserve.... Go back to your duties and show yourself as gentle subjects as I have shown myself a king.'

From the country round common folk and small gentry flocked to pay their homage, queer processions of monks to pray and flog themselves for his welfare. He astonished them with his imperturbable, almost amused, acceptance of misfortune, drew them to him by his easy graciousness. But they were only the few.... To the great multitude with whom he could only speak by proclamation he had shrunk to the most pitiful of objects, the king who has run away. The League could issue proclamations, too, whose subtle taunts were more capable — the eternal advantage of fanaticism over moderation — of provoking scorn for his conduct than the perfectly valid reasons for it of compelling respect for himself. He had quitted his capital to save his realm, and within two months he had almost no realm left to save except the soil on which he stood and a small strip to the north in Normandy.

On the east the League began cautiously to close in, on the south the Huguenots to thrust forward in answer. He lay between the hammer and the anvil, like his predecessor Charles VII when Joan of Arc rode to near-by Chinon to save him. In worse plight even, for at the Maid's coming the foreign invader had nearly shot his bolt, while for Henry the potential invader was only on the way — well on the way now, skimming the ocean to the west of him, the hundred and forty sail of the Invincible Armada. The day that it dropped anchor on the coast of Flanders would mark the end for him as surely as for his well-wisher Elizabeth of England.

It never would, but that he could not know.... His friend Épernon begged permission to sound out the price of an alliance with the Huguenots, his mother was entreating daily to let her make terms for him with the League. The gamble on the heretics he dared not risk: it would cost him the last shred of Catholic loyalty without bringing him anything like enough strength to stand off both Spain and the Guises. Catherine assured him that his enemies were eager to be reconciled... it might be so, since they could no more do without him as yet than he could do without them. In any event, she was his last hope... an adroit and resourceful negotiator whom he might at least count upon to exploit to their utmost whatever assets he had left. He empowered her to treat in his name.

And Catherine betrayed him. Not consciously, as she had once deceived Charles, yet just as thoroughly. She wanted him back in Paris reinvested with the outward insignia of splendour, she wanted the Guises contented with her that they might be the more easily duped when the day came for rebuilding the dynasty upon her grandson under her direction; and for the accomplishment of these desires, the one so insubstantial, the other so chimerical, she stood ready to give away almost anything that would pacify them for the time being. The information she transmitted to Henry (who perforce relied on her entirely for what was in his enemies' minds) consisted, not exactly of lies, but of figments of her own panic and of her ambitious fantasies. The man she entrusted to carry and interpret it was one she knew to be no longer entirely loyal, the secretary Villeroy, who nursed a bitter grudge against Épernon for thwarting a rich marriage he had projected for his son. Even the gentle Louise stood up to her husband's adversary with more spirit: 'Since you won't accept the King's offers, do you want to fight him?' she demanded in a temper, and when her cousin of Guise tried to evade the embarrassing question, persisted, 'I ask, do you *want* to fight him?' Catherine knew as well as Louise that the Duke was riding on the crest of a wave which had swept

Passing of the Family 241

him off his feet more than half unwilling, nevertheless he had but to ask for the distracted old woman to recommend her son to grant....

Floundering in the dark, almost alone, he let himself be persuaded by her for the last time. The Treaty of Reunion, signed as the Armada turned the corner of Brittany into the English Channel, recognized the League as the supreme effective authority in the State. Henry had to confer upon Guise the sole command of the army and the right of appointment to civil offices, lend his name to a war of extermination against the Huguenots without retaining any control of its direction, banish Épernon, his 'eldest son' and last living symbol of the great kingly dream he had brought with him to the throne. The enforcement was as harsh as the terms. Épernon fled south and held a city for the King in his own domain. Catherine and Villeroy, who hated him equally, intrigued to expel him: the burghers, puzzled, sent to ask Henry whether it was really his will that they should take arms against him, and Henry was given no option but to turn against the oldest and staunchest of his friends. For Épernon, fugitive and wanderer, there still remained the privilege of fighting; for his master, only the name of King with the cloister and the tonsure in the offing.

Very few saw the tears that he shed as he put his signature to the document. When Catherine, Guise, and the Cardinal of Bourbon, with a brilliant retinue all dressed in cramoisy velvet studded with gold, travelled to Chartres on August first, he greeted them with such light-hearted gaiety as to set them all marvelling. Had misfortune really succeeded, puzzled Catherine dolefully, in driving him off his head? Or, wondered the Duke with a touch of contempt, was he perhaps glad to be relieved at last of a burden of sovereignty plainly too great for his strength? Though some of the shrewder of the Duke's colleagues looked at the King, uncomfortably... as if they suspected him of chuckling over some newly discovered secret, dissimulating some diabolic scheme for their confusion. The answer was not to be read in his face or manner; he had subtly changed, that was all anyone could say with certainty.

If they could but get him back to Paris... but to Paris he would not go. He agreed to their demand for an Estates-General, but only on condition that it be held at Blois. They turned to Catherine: she took him aside and pled with him to return, now that everything was happily settled, so that his presence might disperse distrust by showing that he bore no resentment. He looked at her quizzically and shook his head. The ready tears started to her eyes. 'How, my son, what will people say of me?' she sobbed. 'What respect will they pay me when they see that I, the mother who bore you, has so little credit with you? Is it possible that you can have suddenly altered your whole character — you who were always so quick to forgive?'

'It's true what you say, Madame, but what do you want me to do?...' Dumbfounded she beheld in his eyes the mocking imp which she, perhaps alone of all who knew him, had never seen in them before. He burst out laughing. 'It must be your friend, that wicked Épernon, who has spoiled me and quite perverted my good character.' She dared not broach the subject again.

Next day he gave a banquet of reconciliation at which he asked the Guise to drink with him. 'To whom would you like to drink?' he asked with a smile. 'It is for Your Majesty to command,' replied the Duke, as was his place. 'Good!' said the King, 'then I propose our friends the Huguenots.' Guise, to show he could take a joke as well as anyone, smiled in return: 'Very well, Sire,' and raised his glass to those the Treaty had sentenced to death... 'and,' continued Henry, 'to our good barricaders of Paris: let's not forget them.' He laughed and tossed off his glass. The Duke and his friends looked at one another uneasily. What did he mean? That he still regarded them as rebels equally with the heretics? Apparently he was not altogether tamed yet... With a forced grin the Duke drank down his glass too.

A month later they found out the secret he had discovered, the scheme he had been meditating under that feline submissiveness. Drake and his fellows fired the Armada out of Calais roads and dispersed it all over the northern seas. The Great Design had unravelled; it would be a long while before the Guises' paymaster would be able to help them again. Then Henry remarked, 'It is now time I ceased to be valet and became king,' and without warning dismissed Cheverney, Bellièvre, Villeroy, the whole parcel of Catherine's men from the offices they had held ever since he came to the throne. In their place he appointed a new lot from the middle classes, including a loyal and able Paris magistrate whom he did not know even by sight to direct his affairs as Chancellor. No more yielding, not another inch of compromise — *Il faut monter à cheval, baton porte la paix*,' was the motto on which he launched his lightning palace revolution, and he never again looked back.

Catherine, 'completely beside herself,' hurried to protest. One glance told her that it was useless: he knew everything, had evidently known for a long while and had bided his time as she would have done in his place. Her power was ended so long as he lived. Stricken, she retired to bed and poured out to Bellièvre her woe at the 'wrong done me in teaching the King that it is right to love his mother as God has ordained, yet not give her enough authority and influence to make them stop doing what they want. It is all a plot to poison his mind against me....' She maundered on, praying, as she had so often prayed before at the death of her husband and each of her children, that God would let her die. This time she meant it... nor did her prayer go long unanswered.

The Estates met on October sixteenth. Henry opened it with a speech that for beauty and eloquence surpassed, by his enemies' confession, every previous effort of his life. He paid a glowing tribute to Catherine sitting broken beside him: 'for the ungrudging pains she has taken to meet the evils which afflict the State. I think it just to give her public thanks before this illustrious assembly, in my own name and the kingdom's. Whatever good there may be in me, I owe it all to her.' In biting, unminced phrase he cited the Guises, glowering amongst their cohorts, before the bar of public opinion for incitement to bloodshed and the deliberate sacrifice of religious peace to their unbridled ambition, giving chapter and verse for what he alleged. 'I admit my own faults and promise to mend them.... Let us close the past and join together in rebuilding this stricken realm. I take my sacred oath to hold inviolate all acts passed in concert with these Estates to that end.... I warn the three Orders that they will stand responsible to God and man if they do not loyally second my design.'

He might as well have saved his breath. The League had taken no chances (one of the counts in Henry's indictment) with 'true liberty of election': the hall was jammed with its partisans, whom it elected to fill the offices and managing committees of all three Orders. It demanded that the King's reference to the Guises be expunged from the record. In a dramatic session, during which a storm of thunder and hail so darkened the room that candles had to be brought in, Henry fought to have his words published. He was overruled. Someone called out as the vote was recorded that this was the testament of the King of France and that the candles had been lit to enable them to see him breathe his last. His olive skin flushed, his lids drooped over his dark eyes. He looked much younger than for a long time past, and yet, in his sober costume, his face lined and his hair grizzled, far older than his thirty-seven years.

They defied him, they flouted him. No plea, no argument, had the least chance of being listened to, since everything was decided beforehand in committee and instructions passed on to the delegates. Guise and his colleagues circulated amongst them behind closed doors, cajoling, threatening. In their eagerness to degrade the King, they forgot that they were architects of the future of France, remembered only that they were the League's instruments for usurping control of it. Until at length the Duke (after consulting with his astrologers) thought the time ripe for his supreme stroke, the manœuvre that would mount him *via* the shoulders of the aged Cardinal of Bourbon to the throne. His lieutenants brought forward a resolution to exclude Navarre from the succession by formal and irrevocable act of the Estates.

The King refused to receive it. 'They have degraded me enough — they shall not degrade my House to the remotest generations.' Nor did he propose, foreseeing their next step, to open the way for them to declare him incompetent and appoint his heir to be his guardian. The delegates refused to go on unless he put the resolution. He struggled for delay, offered to send for Navarre. Was it fair that a man should be condemned unheard? Would it not be better that the lawful heir should succeed with adequate guaranties for the safety of religion than that anarchy be unloosed — better for religion even? Navarre himself, in a broadcast appeal, put the question even more simply after his own downright fashion: 'Is it likely that a handful of my folk will be able to constrain a great majority of Catholics to what they have never been able to constrain us? — there's no sense in it.' But the Estates had not come to Blois to have heresy (or what amounted to the same thing, toleration) preached at them. Guise, from his place at the King's feet on the Grand Master's violet stool embroidered with the fleur-de-lys, flashed a signal to his fellows. In a trice the assembly had threatened to break up and leave the King to stew in his own juice unless he allowed the matter to go to a vote.

Absolute deadlock. If the League gave ground now, the retreat might become a rout: for it would have to re-form its line of battle on the shifting sands of public opinion, amidst endless indiscipline and confusion. The King, with his back to the wall, could not retreat a step without being crushed irretrievably. From the diplomats' gallery a fascinated spectator wrote, 'The day of the dagger will soon be here.' It came sooner than he anticipated.... Henry, still urbane, but with a deadly rage boiling inside of him, asked time to consider. A short adjournment followed for the marriage of Christine, whom her grandmother had betrothed to the Grand Duke of Tuscany — a Medici of the younger branch, in the absence of anything better. It was Catherine's last appearance in a ballroom. She became overheated, fell ill of pleurisy.... Meantime Henry called together his confidential advisers to consult them on the most suitable means of ridding himself of the Duke of Guise.

They scarcely believed that he was in earnest. After the fiasco in the Louvre... with the Duke since become master of over half the country. It was impossible, urged some, four hundred men followed him wherever he went. 'Let anyone start that sort of thing with me,' he had recently said with justifiable assurance, 'and I will end it more violently than I did in Paris.' As Grand Master of the Household, with the keys of the castle in his keeping, the guards could not be posted except by his choice — and he had openly boasted of the number who took his bribes. Arrest and try him, suggested the timid again... what would the Pope say to an assassination? The more ardent cut in with rebuttals from Cato and Machiavelli — 'A traitor should be executed first and judged afterward... The safety of the commonwealth is the supreme law.' The old Henry would have let himself drown in this morass of opinion, the new Henry merely answered, 'I have not asked you whether I may but how I can.' On that Larchant and Ornano, together with two other leaders of the Forty-Five, Crillon and Loignac, undertook to prepare a feasible plan.

After several shifts of date the attempt was set for the morning of Friday, December twenty-third.

Rumours began to circulate. At dinner on the twenty-second, the Duke received a warning wrapped in a napkin. 'Bah! he wouldn't dare,' he ejaculated, and flung the note under the table. He did not yet recognize the new Henry to whom he had been midwife. Plots were so common, warnings of them a hundred times commoner. He had received nine himself, he laughed, all based on the almanac in the past nine days. In any event, he could scarcely throw away a winning hand by running away now. Later in the day, Larchant came to him to say that a council meeting had been called for the following morning at seven, since the King was leaving shortly afterward for the monastery where he planned to spend Christmas, and to ask for the keys that he might assemble the guards, who had a petition to offer with regard to their pay, before the Duke arrived. Unsuspecting, the Duke handed over the keys and went off to spend the night with the hardy perennial Madame de Sauve.

He left her at three and was called a little before seven. Dressed in a new suit of grey, he strolled across the courtyard of Blois Castle, winter's blackness overhead and thick snow underfoot, to the glorious porch and staircase built by Francis I, where the guards presented their request, which he accepted with a brief acknowledgement. In the act one of them trod on his foot, perhaps to warn him, but he paid no heed. The staircase gave immediately into the Council Chamber on the first floor: as he mounted, the thought occurred to him that there was an unusual number of guards standing about, but he vaguely concluded that the ceremony of the petition had brought them out. His own guards had difficulty in following him because of the press. He entered the building and Crillon silently locked the door behind him.

The other Councillors were already there, but not the King. The Duke, who was suffering from cold and his late night, went over to the blazing log fire, where his brother, the Cardinal of Guise, foxiest and most unscrupulous of the League's politicians, joined him while he warmed his hands. The heat nauseated him slightly and he sent a boy to fetch him some Burgundy plums. The lad returned with the fruit in a silver comfit-box, which the Duke was munching as Revol, one of the new secretaries, came in to say that the King wished to see him in his cabinet.

Henry had been up since four, seeing to the last dispositions. His bedroom, a long apartment, adjoined the Council Chamber. At one end it led into the 'new' cabinet, his study which gave onto the garden, at the other the 'old' cabinet, which faced the town. In the first and on the private inner staircase near it, leading down to Catherine's room directly underneath, Loignac stationed his assassins; Henry took up his post of observation in the old cabinet. At six he sent one of his officers to his chaplain with a request 'to say Mass that God might give the King grace to carry through an enterprise which he hoped to conclude within the hour and on which depended the salvation of France.' The chaplain did so.

Guise entered the bedroom and crossed it in the direction of the new cabinet, where he expected to find the King. As he raised the tapestry portière one of the Forty-Five seized his right arm and plunged a dagger into his breast. Others followed suit. The Duke began to cry, 'God have pity on me! Mercy...' Several held his arms to prevent his drawing his sword. So powerful was he that he dragged the lot across the room, breaking the nose of one with the silver comfit-box, before he finally fell and expired at the foot of the King's bed.

Meditatively, with no sign of emotion, Henry came and stood over his dead enemy, murmuring, 'We are no longer two — now I am King.' He turned the body over with his foot — as this same Guise had once done to a far greater than he — and said, after a pause, 'How large he is'; adding as a whimsical thought crossed his mind, 'Perhaps larger in death than in life.'

Meantime in the Council Chamber the Duke's friends, hearing his cries and the clank of steel, rushed hither and thither, to save the Duke, to find a way out, or merely to tear their hair and shriek, 'Treachery!' and 'France is lost!' — until the King's officers entered to notify them that they were under arrest. Other detachments left the palace to round up the trouble-makers in the Estates. None suffered worse harm than a few months of prison except the Cardinal of Guise, who was stabbed to death the next day. That their bones might not be preserved as relics, the bodies of both brothers were buried in quicklime.

In the room below her son's, Catherine, ill with pleurisy, quaked as the scuffling feet overhead notified her that some fearful act of terror was taking place. Presently Henry pushed open the small door leading from the private staircase and stood before her. With a great gasp of relief she asked what had happened. 'This morning I have made myself King of France again,' he replied, so evenly that the doctor in the room could scarcely believe that he heard aright; 'I have just had the King of Paris killed.' She stared at the ceiling, as if intent on a private vision of the future. 'God grant,' she moaned, 'that it will not end in your being King of nothing.' A long time ago she had read in her Machiavelli, 'If you must sin, sin boldly'; but perhaps by now she had forgotten it.

She was not so old, not yet seventy, but she was very tired and her power of resistance to shocks almost ended. On New Year's Day of 1589 she dragged herself from her bed, against her doctor's orders, to the room in which the Cardinal of Bourbon was confined, to bring him good wishes and try to make peace between him and her son. Before she could open her mouth to speak, he drove her out with savage curses, calling her the female Judas who had lured him to prison and his friends to death. She tottered back to the bed and never rose from it again. Fever set in, she babbled of Florence and of her childhood with the kind sisters in the convent of the Murate. It was more than a nostalgia born of delirium: 'Ah, how lucky you are,' she wailed to her adored Christine, now Duchess of Florence and of Tuscany, 'to be going to a realm at peace and not to see the ruin of my poor kingdom.' Always *my* kingdom — to the end she signed herself Regent, though the office had lapsed on Henry's return from Poland.

She died confessed and without pain in the early afternoon of January fifth. Strange irony of the gods that she, for thirty years the principal actor in the vast tragedy now nearing its bloody climax, should alone of its personages have been selected to die in her bed of old age, gout, and pleurisy. Though none of these nor all of them together could have beaten her (according to the official *post mortem*) had not heart-break for her loss of power ended her will to live.

Long ago she had ordered a splendid tomb in Saint-Denis from the great sculptor Germain Pilon, in which she and her husband might lie side by side after her death. But Saint-Denis was in the hands of her son's enemies and the time too turbulent to allow her even a suitable funeral. They put her temporarily into a little church at Blois and there she remained for many years, until in a quieter age Henry II's illegitimate daughter Diane, Duchess of Montmorency, piously brought her ashes to the marble sarcophagus she had designed to receive them.

Her last prayer for her son, that he might not end as King of nothing, came as near as possible to being denied in the weeks that followed. On the news of Guise's assassination, Paris rose and shrieked for his murderer's blood. Little children marched in procession with candles they beat out against the pavement to the chant of 'So God extinguish the House of Valois'; priests desecrated their altars performing rites of black magic upon wax effigies to hasten his death in torment. The people, with the approval of the divine will as ascertained by the theologians of the Sorbonne, repudiated their allegiance to 'Mr. Valois' and transferred it to Guise's posthumous son, baptized François-Paris.[1] A new government was set up under the late idol's eldest brother, Charles, Duke of Mayenne, into whose hands the capital poured its treasure for the payment of armies to track down the deposed King.

Henry lay trapped on the Loire — even Chartres had become too hot to hold him. The end seemed very near now, the scaffold more imminent than the cloister. Yet the blacker grew the outlook, the gayer waxed his humour: as if this life of desperate, hunted action was precisely what he had needed to bring him back to himself. One morning, while he was still in bed, he heard that an itinerant merchant had arrived at Blois with recent news from Paris and ordered him to be brought in. The man made his reverence.

'So you recognize me?' said Henry.

'Yes, Sire, you are my King.'

'And this lady lying here beside me, who do you think she may be?'

'The Queen, Sire...'

'Yes, my friend. And what do they call me in Paris?'

The man hesitated. Henry pressed him — 'Mr. Valois, don't they?'

'Yes, Sire.'

'Then, my friend, you will take back to Paris the tidings that you have seen Mr. Valois in bed with the Queen. You won't fail, will you?'

Then Épernon appeared, the friend he had been forced to

---

[1] By Guise's second wife, who had left Blois to be confined in Paris just before the murder.

discard. He had seen Navarre, who was willing to be reconciled on reasonable terms. He would not insist on imposing his religion, he was even prepared to hand over some of the pledge towns the King had not been able to take from him, to make the King's task easier. The matter of a permanent accord could be settled later, when the League had been driven out. The Huguenots, though stout to maintain their beliefs, 'desired to be of no party but the King's.'

Henry empowered Épernon to continue negotiations. On April thirtieth, in a garden at Plessis-les-Tours, the scene of the fatal misunderstanding with Margot, the two brothers-in-law met after a lapse of thirteen years. The throng was so great that the soldiers had to force a way through for their respective masters, amidst exultant cries of 'Long live the King! Long live Navarre!' — in tones that one of them had not heard since the day he entered his realm from Poland. They embraced, and Navarre, with brimming eyes, declared, 'I shall die content from today, whatever death befalls me, since God has given me grace to look upon my King's face again.'

That night they slept on opposite sides of the river Loire. Early next day Navarre announced to his gentlemen that he was going across unaccompanied to 'say good-morning to the King.' They tried to dissuade him... the accord was not yet certain... the King might change his mind and offer his new ally's head as the price of conciliation with the League. Navarre laughed their caution aside: in any event, he assured them, 'no power on earth could now prevent me from attaining my destiny, since God guides and walks with me.' Arrived at his brother-in-law's quarters, he greeted him with a cheery 'Courage, Sire, two Henrys are worth more than a Charles.' Even two Charleses, Bourbon and Mayenne. And so it proved.

An extraordinary, an almost miraculous wave of emotion swept the country overnight. Partly it arose from sheer reaction — the people's weariness of excitement and longing for order, their resentment of the uncontrolled brigands who largely made up the League's widespread armies. Even Paris was growing sick of what it had started. Taxes had risen instead of fallen, morals grown worse rather than better, since the exiled 'tyrant' had given place to the Sixteen 'little tyrants.' But far above these commonplaces a gleaming fact beckoned aloft the imagination. The people at last saw one simple issue and saw it clear. Politics, whether secular or religious, were complicated, unfathomable affairs, but the King and his heir, the Lord's anointed and the Lord's appointed, stood side by side — and together they stood for France.

Recruits poured in to Tours. On every front the League's triumphant armies began to give way. At Senlis, the Duke of Longueville, heir to Joan of Arc's Bastard of Orléans, shattered Paris's own troops under the Duke of Aumale, Mayenne's brother. 'After that no one in Paris was seen to smile.' Madame de Montpensier wrote a furious letter to Mayenne accusing their younger brother of flagrant incompetence. Navarre's men intercepted the letter, which he forwarded to Aumale with a polite note offering to be his second if he cared to call out his sister for the insult. South of the Loire Mayenne himself made a determined effort to capture Henry, and would have succeeded had not Navarre's Huguenots in their white scarves come *ventres à terre* to the King's rescue. 'Go back, White Scarves!' cried the Leaguers. 'Go back, Châtillon, it's not you we're after, but your father's murderer!'

'You are all my father's murderers,' retorted Châtillon as he drove them in rout before him, 'and traitors to your country as well. When I entered my Prince's service, I trampled all private vengeance and interest underfoot.' From the mouth of Coligny's son Henry had received on the field of battle all the absolution he could hope for on this earth for his part in Saint Bartholomew's.

On August first, three months after his meeting with Navarre, Henry beheld his capital from the heights of Saint-Cloud to its west. Round him lay encamped his victorious army, near-by at Meudon Navarre's. Of his enemies' nothing remained but Mayenne's dispirited rabble hundreds of miles away; and Paris, torn with dissensions, had no stomach for a fight. The assault was ordered for the morrow: it could not fail. Soberly the King thought of the future, the wounds to be healed after twenty-seven years of civil war, the passions that would be so appallingly difficult to restrain in the hour of triumph. A fearful task altogether, a high work of dedication.... From the group behind him — men who had paid for their fidelity in the slaughter of their kin and the loss of their goods — he overheard a graphic forecast of what would happen to the Leaguers when the city was taken. He cut short the general approval to say, 'They will do their duty as children hereafter if I do mine as father. They are Frenchmen — merely led astray.'

At about the same hour a meagre little man in monk's robe issued from the Dominican Monastery in the Rue Saint-Jacques and trudged westward across Paris. In his broad sleeve he carried (like all monks on their travels) his eating-knife, in his shaven head a vision he had received several nights before. An angel had appeared to him and said: 'Brother Jacques, I am the messenger of Almighty God, come to forewarn you that by your hand will the tyrant of France be put to death. Prepare yourself, then, for your martyr's crown awaits you.' His prior, an ardent Guisard, had approved his vision. So had Madame de Montpensier, gleefully, and tried to advise him on how he might make good his escape after he had carried out the heavenly instruction. But he wanted none of her advice, lest it jeopardize his promised crown. He had a short black beard and large, far-away eyes; his name was Jacques Clément.

At Saint-Cloud the sentries stopped him. He explained

Passing of the Family

that he bore a private message for the King from an aristocratic loyalist imprisoned by the League in Paris and exhibited a passport forged with the signature of another. The soldiers told him to come back another time. Just then a law-officer of the Crown, La Guesle, came by, who, after examining the passport, took the monk to his quarters for further interrogation. Clément satisfied him with a detailed and on the whole truthful account of the state of affairs in Paris, but refused to divulge his private message to anybody but the King. Since it was already late, La Guesle kept him in his home overnight.

Early next morning, while Henry was still at his toilette, La Guesle brought him word of the odd visitor who desired an interview with him. Several of those in the room protested that the King ought not to receive him, but Henry, who was fond of holy men, would not give Paris cause to say that he declined to receive one. Clément was shown in, Henry asked him several questions about his friends in Paris. 'And what is your private message for me, father?' he inquired presently. The monk cast a shy glance at the gentlemen round the King's chair; Henry ordered them to retire a few paces and beckoned the monk forward. Clément whispered a few words in his ear, then swiftly drew the knife from his sleeve and plunged it into the King's intestines.

Henry slumped over, both hands clutched to his abdomen, gasping, 'Wretched monk, you have killed me!... Why... what have I ever done to you?' La Guesle fell on his knees clamouring to be put to death since the fault was his for introducing the miscreant. Clément flung himself down between the room's two beds, whence the rest, shrieking, dragged him out.... 'Don't kill him,' whispered the King, 'before we find out who sent him ——' But a dozen swords had already run him through, a dozen arms lifted his corpse and threw it out of the window.

Henry was carried to bed, where the doctor who examined his wound at first pronounced it to be slight, not enough to keep him out of the saddle for ten days. He thought so himself; when Charles's little bastard, the Count of Auvergne, came running into the room and burst into tears at the bedside, Henry, who had brought him up as his own son, stroked the boy's head, saying, 'Don't upset yourself, my son; these rogues wanted to kill me, but God has spared me from their malice. It's nothing.' To Navarre, who galloped over from Meudon, he gave the same message and sent him out to reassure the army.

But at eleven that night he was suddenly attacked with violent pains. The doctors tried to relieve him by washing out the intestines, a treatment which only intensified the agony. 'Lord God,' he prayed, 'if You know that my life is of use to my people and the State you have placed in my charge, save me and prolong my days; if not, dispose of this body as it pleases You and receive my soul into Paradise.' He fell unconscious for a few moments; when he awoke it was to learn that he would not live till morning. He asked that his chaplain be sent for and an altar set up by his bed.

Navarre came in again to assure him that he would be up and about in no time at all. Henry smiled at him affectionately with a faint shake of the head; the other knelt and kissed his hand. 'My brother,' whispered the King, 'see how your enemies and mine deal with me; you must take care they don't do the same to you.' Strangely, they did.... He begged his followers to acknowledge Navarre as his successor, but to Navarre he said, 'You will never be accepted as King in France if you do not turn Catholic and make your peace with the Church.' Nor was he.... The dying man had seen farther into his people's hearts than he had ever, unluckily, allowed them to see into his. But then his had never been simple, like theirs.

He worried greatly over the murder of the Cardinal of Guise — not of his brother, for in that he felt fully justified — since the Pope had threatened to lay an interdict upon him and he did not know whether he might properly receive the communion. 'If you desire God to forgive your sins you must first forgive your enemies,' said one of those present. 'I do, I forgive them with all my heart,' returned the dying man. 'Even those, Sire, who brought about your death?' 'Yes, even them.... I pray God He may pardon them their sins as I hope He will pardon mine.'

His voice faltered. Perhaps from mere exhaustion and pain — perhaps because a face interposed itself between him and his forgiveness. Margot's, mocking it. He did not speak of her... had not since he commanded his mother, as her last act almost, to delete her daughter's name from her will. He did not speak of Catherine either: what he felt toward her was his heart's last unresolved perplexity. Nor even of the third woman in his life, the laughing Marie who might have so completely transformed it.... Now and then fragments of sentences revealed to those listening that his thoughts had strayed outside himself, into a past beyond memories.... Presently he called for light, saying he could not see. More candles were brought in — by the bed the priest prayed on in an undertone.... Evoked by the dying man's murmured syllables the great ghosts began to people the room for his listeners... Medici and Valois assembling for the finale of their mortal pageant. Cosimo and Piero and Lorenzo the Magnificent... Philip, founder of the House and John with whom it had all but collapsed on the field of Poitiers; Charles who was Wise and Charles who was Mad and Charles the Lucky to whom God had sent a saint for its deliverance; Louis who had restored it and Charles who had caused it to prosper; Louis again, the Twelfth, who yearned to bequeath it Italy, and Francis, who, in losing Italy, yet made it beautiful with a sunset glory....

At four he asked for the last sacraments to be administered. Afterward he started to repeat the *Miserere*, but as he reached the line beginning,

Redde mihi laetitiam salutis tui,

his voice failed. With a flutter of his long delicate hands he tried to make the sign of the cross, then died. With a little sigh that seemed to be one of happiness, according to the witnesses who attested the scene in a paper signed with their blood — as if, perhaps, he had found assurance at the end that the Giver of Redemption might see him a little as he had seen himself.

The royal army disregarded the dead King's request and melted away. On the hill of Saint-Cloud, Henry IV drew rein for a moment to let his eye travel up the green waters of the Seine winding away toward the distant towers of Notre-Dame, round the dark grey battlements of the city that had once laughed at and now mortally feared him. Calm and grave he lifted his gaze beyond it, beyond his immediate disappointment, into the future he had been elected by Destiny to build upon the past, more glorious even than the past. Then, at the head of his Huguenots, he rode off again to the west, away from the capital that would never be his until he had agreed to say a Mass for it.

In the fortress of Usson, Margot, last on earth of all who ever bore the name of Valois, sang her little songs, sewed on her embroideries, slept with her squires. She was Queen of France now, an odd business: with no other duty toward the State than to keep Henry IV from making a fool of himself by marrying beneath him. In the end she let him off — to marry a Medici! And meantime she grew enormous, lavished her allowance equally on the needy and those whom she loved, and in her spare time composed the charming bit of fiction she had come to believe was the true history of her family.

FINIS

Bibliography

ALBERI, *Relazioni degli Ambasciatori Veniti*. Florence, 1860.

ALBERI, *Vita di Caterina di Medici*. Florence, 1838.

ANGOULÊME, DUC D', *Mémoires*. Included with VILLEROY.

ANONYMOUS, *Elogio della Gran Caterina de Medici*. Paris, 1568.

BRANTÔME, PIERRE DE BOURDEILLE, SEIGNEUR DE, *Oeuvres complètes*. Paris, 1864-82. 11 vols.

Bulletin de la Société de L'Histoire de France, t. II, no. 5, pp. 163-76, May, 1835. (For Jeanne d'Albret's letters to her son Henry of Navarre in 1572.)

Calendar of State Papers, Foreign Series. London. Various years covering in consecutive volumes the period 1558-88.

Calendar of State Papers. VENICE. Vol. VII, 1558-80. London, 1880.

CATHÉRINE DE MÉDICIS, *Lettres*. Comte Hector de la Ferrière et Comte Bagenault de la Puchesse. Paris, 1880-1907, 10 vols. (The incomparable, monumental work.)

CASTELNAU, *Mémoires de*. Brussels, 1721. 3 vols. fol., ed. le Laboureur.

CHARLES IX, *Letters à M. de Fourquevaux, 1565-72*. Ed. by the Abbé C. Douais, Montpellier, 1897. (Fourquevaux was Charles's ambassador to Spain.)

CONDÉ, *Mémoire du Prince de*. Paris, 1746. 6 vols. Ed. de la Haye.

DAVILA, H. C., *The Historie of the Civill Warres in France*. Translated by William Aylesbury. London, 1647.

DESTIGNY, J. F., *Histoire Mystérieuse*. Incomplete. Paris, 1847.

Dictionnaire de la Noblesse. De la Chenaye-Desbois et Badieu. 3 vols. Paris, 1873.

DIGGES, DUDLEY. *The Compleat Ambassador*. 1655.

ESTIENNE, PIERRE (attributed to), *Discours Merveilleux de la Vie, Actions et Deportemens de Cathérine de Médicis, Roigne Mere*, s.l. 1575.

ESTOILE, PIERRE DE L', *Journeaux*. Paris, 1885–96. Vols. I–III. (Best of all diarists for the reign of Henry III; his journals continue to the reign of Louis XIII.)

FÉNELON, BERTRAND DE SALIGNAC DE LA MOTHE, *Dépêches et Correspondance Diplomatique, 1568–75*. Ed. 1838–40.

FERRIÈRE, COMTE HECTOR DE LA, *Le XVIme Siècle et les Valois*. Paris, 1879.

FORCE, JACQUES DE NOMPAR CAUMONT, DUC DE LA, Marshal of France, *Mémoires*. Paris 1843, 4 vols.

HENRI III, *Lettres*. MSS. in Nouvelles Acquisitions Françaises. B.N. from Saint Petersburg MSS.

LE CLERC, JEAN, *La Vie des Graves et Illustres Personnages qui ont diversement excellés sous les Régnes de Louis XII–Henri IV*. Rouen, 1609. (A useful table of genealogies and office-holders.)

MARGUERITE DE VALOIS, *Mémoires et Lettres*. Ed. M. F. Guessard.

MARTIN, HENRI. *Histoire de France*. Vols. VIII–X. Paris, 1857. 4th ed.

MATTHIEU, PIERRE, *Histoire de France sous les Régnes de Françis I–Louis XIII*. Paris, 1631. (Official historiographer to Henry IV.)

MICHELET, JULES. *Histoire de France*. Paris, 1856. Vols. VIII–IX.

MONLUC, BLAISE DE, *Commentaires et Lettres*. Ed. by Alphonse de Ruble. Paris, 1866–72. Vols. II–V. (Monluc was a Marshal of France under Charles IX.)

MONOD, HENRI, *La Sainte Barthélemy, Version du Duc d'Anjou, Vera et Brevis Descriptio*, in Bull. Soc. Prot. LVI, p. 499.

Bibliography

Nevers, M. le Duc de, *Mémoires*. Paris, 1665. Ed. Gomberville. (Borrows heavily from Matthieu, Margot, *et al.*)

Nostredamus, Michel, *La Vie et le Testament de*. Paris, 1784.

Nouaillac, J., *Sieur de Villeroy, Secrétaire d'État et Ministre*. Paris, 1909.

Reumont, A. de, *La Jeunesse de Cathérine de Médicis*. Ed. Armand Baschet, Paris, 1866.

Roth, Cecil. *The Last Florentine Republic*. London, 1925.

Tavannes, Gaspard de Saulx, Seigneur de, *Mémoires*. In Petitot's *Collection Complète des Mémoires*. Paris, 1822. Vols. xxiii–xxv.

Van Dyke, Paul, *Catherine de Medicis*. London, 1923, 2 vols.

Villeroy, Sieur de. *Mémoires d'État*. In Petitot's *Collection Complète des Mémoires*... Paris, 1824.

Index

Alba, Duke of, 60, 66, 67, 91, 100–01
Albret, d', Jeanne, 24, 104–09
Alençon, Francis, Duke of, *see* Hercules
Angoulême, Duke of, 30
Antoine, King of Navarre, interview of, with Catherine, 23–25; as protector of Huguenots, 27; Catherine accused by, 33; son of, 36; defeat of, by Catherine, 37; affair of, with Triumvirate, 46–49, 52; death of, 56
Aumale, Duke of, 253
Auvergne, Charles, Count of (son of Charles IX), 156, 256

Bacon, Francis, 193
Bellièvre, 161, 162, 163, 166, 232–33, 243
Bérenger, de, Louis (Sieur du Guast), 88, 90,
Biragues, de, René, 121
Blanche of Castile, 35, 41
Boland, *see* Bondol
Bondol (Boland), 120, 127
Borgia, Lucretia, 19
Bourbon, Charles, Cardinal of, 23, 113–14, 228, 241, 245, 249–50
Bourbons, desire of, for power, 15; Guises enemies of, 20, 29; Catherine's interview with, 21–25; squabble of, with Guises at Henry II's funeral, 26; resignation of, to Catherine, 52
Bussy d'Amboise, 199–201, 210, 213–14

Canillac, Marquis of, 225
Capet, Hugh, 4, 22
Carlos, Don, 10, 47, 64, 65, 70
Catherine de Medici, marriage of, and death of husband, 4; children of, 5–10; relation of, to her court and to France, 10–16; with the Guises, 17–21; with the Bourbons, 21–25; during Great Conspiracy, 30; procures appointment of L'Hôpital, 30–31; accused by Antoine of Navarre, 33; visit of, to the astrologer Nostradamus, 35–36; letter of, to Elizabeth, 37–38; quotation of, about herself, 41; her Edict of January, 1562, 44; love of, for ruling, 45–46; trouble of, with Guises, 46–53, 68–73; retinue and ladies of, 54–59; hobbies of, 63; with Elizabeth and Philip II of Spain, 64–68; watch of, over her children, 78; delight of, in hoping for marriage of Henry and Elizabeth of England, 96–97; alarm of, at influence of Coligny over Charles IX, 98–99; attempt of, to murder Coligny, 99–100; interview of, with Jeanne d'Albret, 106–09; conference of, with Charles IX and his ministers on eve of St. Bartholomew's, 121–30; letter of, to Philip II of Spain, 136–37; efforts of, to make Henry King of Poland, 144–46; discovery by, of attempt to bar Henry from French throne, 152–55; letter of, to Henry, 156–57; goes to meet Henry, 172–73; interview of, with Navarre, 223; advice of, to Henry III to yield to League, 240–41; death of, 250
Catherine of Aragon, 4
Catherine of Navarre, 30
Caylus, 161, 165–66, 210
Chanvallon, de, Harley, 224
Charlemagne, 17
Charles IX, as a child, 7, 61; seen by Catherine in mage's mirror, 36; proclaimed king, 37, 57; Catherine seeks a wife for, 64; jealousy for Henry of Anjou, 79–80; nature of, 80–81; Margot punished by, 89; marriage of, 90; adoration of, for Coligny 92–95, 98, 101; at Council on eve of St. Barthol-

Index

omew's, 121–28; as friend of Rochefoucauld, 131; during massacre of St. Bartholomew's, 132–33; death of, 138–39; crown of, resigned to Henry, 156; children of, 156
Châteauneuf, de, Renée, 188
Châtillon, de, Gaspard (Lord of Coligny), character and political position of, 92–95; desire of, to be rid of Henry of Anjou, 98; Catherine's hatred of, 99, 103
Châtillon, the brothers, 23
Christine, 220, 232, 246, 250
Claude, Duchess of Lorraine, 9, 59, 89–90, 188, 220
Clement VII, 3, 11, 15
Clément, Jacques, 254–55
Coligny, Lord of, meeting of, with Catherine, 23; as a prominent Huguenot, 27, 28; watched by Guises, 34; trouble of, with Guises, 57; attempt of Catherine to kidnap, 69; Catherine's effigy of, 71–72; quoted, 114; shot, 115–16; death of, 133–34
Condé, Henry, Prince of, his wife, 145, 151
Condé, Louis, Prince of, meeting of, with Catherine, 23; as Huguenot leader, 27–29, 32–34; as adjutant to Catherine, 56–57; wife of, 58; Paris besieged by, 69; Catherine's statue of, 71
Condé, Princess of (Marie de Clèves), 145, 151, 161, 183–84
Correr, Giovanni, 169
Cosimo I, Duke, 48, 63
Cosimo the Elder, 15
Cossé, Marshal, 153
Crillon, 247
Curtin, Madame, 88

Damville, Duke of, 150, 154
Dandelot, François de Coligny, 66, 71
Dauphin, the (Francis), 12
Du Ferrier, 167–68
Du Guast, 88, 90, 153, 200, 201–02
Du Halde, 161, 166, 236

Edward III, 22
Elizabeth of Austria, 136

Elizabeth of England, aids Scottish Reformers, 29; religious difficulties of, 44–45; plan of Triumvirate to depose, 46, 47; plan for marriage of Henry III to, 96–99; plan for marriage of Duke of Alençon to, 149, 151; offer of, to aid Henry III, 220; Mary Stuart executed by, 226
Elizabeth of Spain, marriage of, 9; letter to, from Catherine, 37–38; Catherine's pride of, 49–51; still-born twins of, 60; pleading of Catherine with, 66; farewell of, to Catherine, 67; report to, from Catherine, concerning state of France, 68; death of, 70
Entremonts, Lady of, 94
Épernon, Duke of, as a messenger of Henry III, 218; death of, plotted by Holy League, 229; sent to Normandy, 230; Villeroy an enemy to, 240; Henry III forced to desert, 241; return of, to Henry III as negotiator from Henry of Navarre, 251–52
Ernest, Archduke of Austria, 144–45 167
Este, d', Anne, 19, 29

Ferrara, Duke of, 170
Fleming, Lady, 12
France, de, Diane, 153
Francis I, marriage arranged by, 3, 11, 15; quoted, 13; prediction of, concerning Guises, 18; stand of, on Huguenot question, 26; selling of offices by, 42; secret of control of France by, 175
Francis II, as a boy king, 5–6, 29; illness and death of, 34–37
Francis (Dauphin), 12

Genlis, Captain, 100–01
Guise, Charles of, Cardinal of Lorraine, 18–19, 28, 31, 86, 88, 186–87
Guise, Francis, Duke of, 18, 56, 57
Guise, Henry, Duke of, Cardinal of Lorraine's plan for marriage of, 86–90; superintends murder of Coligny, 134; leader of Holy League, 205; Holy League revived by, 217; Marguerite returns to, 223; war of, with Henry III, 230–49

Index

Guise, Louis, Cardinal of, 249, 256
Guises, desire of, for power, 15; Catherine's interview with, 17-22; squabble of, with Bourbons at Henry II's funeral, 26; as supporters of Huguenots, 27-34; suppression of, by Catherine, 37, 52; conspiracies of, against Catherine, 46; reconciliation of, with Coligny, 68; war of, against Henry III, 218-22, 226-49
Guitry, Captain, 151-52

Henry II, marriage and death of, 3-5; mistress of, 11-12; later life of, with Catherine, 14; relations of, with Guises, 18; feeling of, concerning Huguenots, 26; selling of offices by, 42; Constable a beneficiary of, 46
Henry III, nature of, as a child, 8, 62; seen by Catherine in mage's mirror, 36; a wife sought for, by Catherine, 64, 67; made Lieutenant-General of the Realm, 69; Charles IX jealous of, 79-80; characteristics of, as a young man, 81-83; Catherine's desire for marriage of Elizabeth of England to, 96-99; account of conference on eve of St. Bartholomew's by, 128; made King of Poland, 144-46; Marguerite's attempts to keep French throne from, 150-55; letter to, from Catherine, 156-57; nephew of, 156; becomes King of France, 159-61; flight of, from Poland, 162-67; welcome to, in Vienna and Venice, 167-72; conduct of, as King of France, 175-96; dealing of, with the Holy League, 205-09; hears of Alençon's plot to escape to Flanders, 211-15; war of, with Guises, 218-49; assassination and death of, 255-58
Henry IV, 44, 47
Henry VIII, 4
Henry of Navarre, as a child, 30; seen by Catherine in mage's mirror, 36; Charles's scheme of marriage for, 91; marriage of, 110-15; heir to throne after Alençon, 150; part of, in plan against Henry III, 151-55; member of Henry III's flagellant order, 186; disappearance of, 202-03; claimant to throne of France, 217; advised by Henry III to turn Catholic, 218; interview of, with Catherine, 222-23; crowned Henry IV, 258
Hercules (Francis), Duke of Alençon, as a child, 7-8; as suitor of Elizabeth of England, 100; enemy of brother Henry, 145; description and nature of, 148-50; attempt of Marguerite to gain throne for, 150-55; Catherine's watch over, 197-98; flights of, into Flanders, 201, 211-15; death of, 215-16

John of Austria, Don, 99, 210
Joyeuse (Anne d'Arques), Duke of, 224, 226, 227

La Guesle, 255
La Mole, 150-55
La Noue, 150, 151, 154
Larchant, 161, 163-66, 246-47
La Renaudie, 28, 57
L'Hôpital, Michel, 30, 33, 44, 71
Limeuil, de, Isabel, 58, 59
Lippomano, the Podestà, 170
Loignac, 247, 248
Longueville, Duke of, 253
Lorenzo, the younger, 10
Lorenzo the Magnificent, 10
Lothair, 17
Louis IX (Saint Louis), 22, 35, 41, 150, 175
Louis XII, 19, 42
Louis of Nassau, 95, 100, 150, 151
Luxembourg, Duke of, 188

Machiavelli, Niccolo, 25, 249
Margot, *see* Marguerite of Navarre
Marguerite of Navarre, nature of, as a child, 7, 50, 61, 62; attempt of Catherine to marry Don Carlos to, 51, 64; Catherine's desire to marry Philip II to, 70; nature of, as a young woman, 83-85; misunderstanding of, with Henry, 85-86; suitors of, 86-90; Charles's scheme of marriage for, 91, 101; Jeanne d' Albret's opinion of, 107; relations of, and marriage with

Index

Henry of Navarre, 112–14; during massacre of St. Bartholomew's, 135; parting of, from Henry, 146; relation of, to brother Hercules, 149–50; attempts of, to place Hercules on throne, 150–55, 198–201; attendance of, at Henry III's philosophical séances, 180; disappearance of husband of, 202–03; Alençon aided by, in his flight to Flanders, 209–13; returns to Duke of Guise, 223; trouble of, with Henry and consequent wanderings, 223–26; as queen of France, 258
Marie-Isobel, daughter of Charles IX, 156
Marot, Clement, 43
Mary I ('Bloody Mary'), 9
Mary Stuart, 6, 15, 46, 47, 52, 226
Matthias, Archduke of Austria, 167
Maurevert, 99, 127, 154
Maximilian, 167
Mayenne, Charles, Duke of, 251, 253, 254
Medici, de, Gian Angelo, 48
Méré, de, Poltrot, 57
Mignons, the, 190–94
Miron, 164–66, 188
Mocenigo, the Doge, 170, 171
Monsoreau, Lady of, 213
Montgomery, Count of, 35, 137, 139, 150, 151
Montmorency, de, Anne, with Francis II, 6; dismissal of, 20, 21; nephew of, 23; visit to, by Catherine and Francis II, 26; summoning of, by Catherine, 37; as one of Triumvirate, 46; as adjutant of Catherine, 56–57; death of, 69
Montmorency, Diane, Duchess of, 250
Montmorency, Duke of, 150, 153–54
Montmorencys, 20, 25, 52, 147, 151
Montpensier, Duchess of, 228–29, 253, 254

Nassau, Louis of, 95, 100, 150, 151
Nevers, Duchess of, 180
Nevers, Duke of, 121–22, 128, 169, 180, 222
Nostradamus, Michael, 16, 35–36, 60

Ornano, Alphonso, 231–32, 246–47

Paré, Ambrose, 117, 119
Pepin the Short, 33
Philip II of Spain, husband of Elizabeth, 9, 10; offers to, for invasion of Navarre, 32; place of, in Great Design, 47; refusal of, to meet Catherine, 60; Catherine's attempt to control, 64–68; belief of Catherine that Elizabeth was poisoned by, 70–71; marriage of, 90; letter to, from Catherine, 136–37
Philip of Valois, 22
Pibrac, 161, 164, 165–66
Pius IV, 48
Poitiers, de, Diane, 11–12, 18, 20
Pont-à-Mousson, Marquis of, 220

Raleigh, Sir Walter, 95
Retz, de, Count (Albert de Gondi), 89, 101, 121, 124–25, 128, 133
Retz, de, Madame, 89
Robert of Clermont, 22
Rochefoucauld, 129, 131, 135–36
Rouet, de, Mademoiselle, 49, 56, 58
Ruggieri, Cosimo, 154–55

Saint-André, Marshal, 46, 56
Saint Louis, see Louis IX
Sauve, de, Charlotte, 153, 247
Savoy, Duke of, 172
Sebastian of Portugal, 86, 90
Sixtus V, 222
Souvray, 161, 163–66, 180, 185
Strozzi, Filippo, 96

Tavannes, 69, 82, 97, 121, 128
Teligny, 116, 117
Tenczynski, Count, 163, 164, 165–67
Touchet, Marie, 156
Tuscany, Grand Duke of, 246

Vaudemont, de, Louise, 187–88, 189–90, 232, 240
Villequier, 161, 164, 165–66
Villeroy, 240, 241, 243
Viteaux, de, Baron, 202

MAR 18 1999

MAY 1 2 2001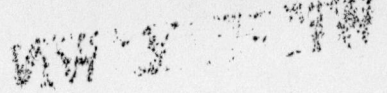

MAY 1 0 2006